SAP and BW
Data Warehousing

SAP and BW
Data Warehousing

How to plan and implement

Arshad Khan

Khan Consulting and Publishing, LLC.

SAP and BW Data Warehousing
How to plan and implement

Copyright © 2005 by Arshad Khan

Khan Consulting and Publishing, LLC.
PO Box 700012
San Jose, CA 95170
khan725@aol.com

ISBN: 0-595-34079-2

Printed in the United States of America

CONTENTS

INTRODUCTION

SAP and BW Data Warehousing: How to Plan and Implement is an introductory book for professionals and end-users associated with SAP and BW data warehousing. It addresses their need to obtain an overview of SAP and BW features and functionality as well as project planning and implementation. *SAP and BW Data Warehousing: How to Plan and Implement* will be beneficial to a broad audience including those planning an SAP or BW project, senior executives, directors, functional managers and analysts, power users, end-users, project managers and project implementation team members (including technical staff, configurators, developers, and trainers). *SAP and BW Data Warehousing: How to Plan and Implement* can also be used as a supplemental text in IT courses that cover the subjects of ERP and data warehousing.

SAP and BW Data Warehousing: How to Plan and Implement is divided into two parts:

❑ Part A, which covers SAP
❑ Part B, which covers BW

Part A covers a wide range of topics including the need for ERP software, SAP characteristics and functionality, and implementation methodologies. It extensively covers the five ASAP implementation methodology phases: Project Preparation, Business Blueprint, Realization, Final Preparation, and Go-Live & Support.

Part A also discusses common problems, issues, and risks faced by SAP projects, which are unique despite some common characteristics. Besides providing guidelines and tips, that can help avoid common mistakes, Part A also identifies trends that are expected to impact future ERP growth.

Part B starts off by introducing data warehousing fundamental concepts before addressing BW data warehousing specifics. It reviews data warehousing evolution and growth drivers, process and architecture, data warehouse characteristics and design, data marts, multi-dimensionality, and OLAP. Part B also shows how to plan a BW project as well as build and operate a data warehouse.

Part B contains step-by-step procedures for creating an InfoCube (Data Mart) and a BW query (using the Business Explorer). The objective is to show the relative ease with which they can be created—not teach how to become proficient in creating cubes or queries (both of which require comprehensive hands-on training). Part B also covers, in depth, common failure causes and mistakes that characterize data warehouse projects. Finally, it provides useful guidelines and tips for avoiding common mistakes.

You should keep in mind that *SAP and BW: How to Plan and Implement* is only an introduction to SAP and BW, which are complex software that require in-depth study and practice before they can be mastered. Therefore, I encourage you to read other books to enlarge your knowledge of any topics touched on here.

I would like to take this opportunity to thank Matt Christensen, Sonya Bennett, Ram Ramamoorthy, Christian Jensen, Farida Ansari, and Gautam Ghosh. The contribution of these individuals, who reviewed the manuscript or provided valuable input, helped in making this book a reality and a quality publication.

TERMINOLOGY

❏ Aggregated data: Data obtained by combining data elements into a summarized format.
❏ Attribute: A data item containing information about a variable.
❏ Clickstream data: Data captured during the web browsing process.
❏ DSS (Decision Support System): A system, based on information systems and software, designed to support decision-making.
❏ Data element: The fundamental data structure or most elementary unit of data in a data processing system.
❏ Data mapping: The process of matching (assigning) a source data element to a target data element.
❏ ERD: Entity Relationship Diagram, which illustrates the logical structure of a database.
❏ Hierarchy: A structure, in a parent-child relationship, that provides an alternative view of data for the purpose of reporting and analysis.
❏ Metadata: Data about data such as data element or data type descriptions.
❏ Data mart: Small data warehouse that focuses on departmental needs, rather than the enterprise, and is typically limited to one or more specific subject areas.
❏ Drilldown: Method of analyzing detailed data that was used to create a summary level of data.
❏ Fact: Quantitative or factual data about a business.
❏ Measure: Numeric value stored in a fact table and in an OLAP cube, such as sales, cost, price, and profit.
❏ Query: Data evaluation, based on the selection of variables (characteristics and key figures) that is used to analyze data.
❏ Workbook: BW report, with integrated queries, which is based on an MS-Excel format.
❏ Redundancy: Storing multiple copies of the same data.
❏ Replication: Process of copying data from one environment to another while keeping data copies in sync with the source.
❏ Scalability: Ability to support larger data volumes and/or users.
❏ Scrubbing: Process for filtering, merging, decoding, and translating source data that ensures validated data populates the data warehouse.

❑ Slice and dice: A data analysis navigation technique; calls for interactive page displays by specifying slices, or subsets of multidimensional arrays, via rotations and drill down/up.

❑ Transaction code: Shortcut, typically a four-letter code, that can be used to execute an SAP transaction instead of using a menu path

NOTES

❑ Some terms have been used interchangeably. These include:
- BW and data warehousing
- InfoCube and data mart
- Cube and InfoCube

❑ The acronyms ERP and SAP have been used interchangeably

❑ SAP BW uses the term characteristic instead of dimension (the term used in conventional data warehousing). SAP uses the term dimension to refer to a collection of characteristics

PART A
SAP

CHAPTER A1
NEED FOR ENTERPRISE RESOURCE PLANNING SOFTWARE

UNDERSTANDING ERP SYSTEMS

What an ERP system aims to do

An enterprise resource planning (ERP) system is a sophisticated software package that aims to run an organization's core business and major business processes. Typically, such a system supports and automates a company's business processes and functions such as sales and distribution, procurement, finance, manufacturing, warehousing, shipping, human resources, etc.

An ERP system implies the use of an integrated and packaged, rather than customized, software developed for customers who can use it for most of their business needs. By providing integrated software, an ERP system eliminates complex and expensive links between different applications/systems that were never designed to talk to each other. While most ERP packages are developed for sale to customers, companies can also develop such functionality in-house. However, in such cases, the cost can be prohibitive besides being risky.

ERP objectives

There are many benefits associated with the implementation of an ERP system though, typically, the primary reasons for implementing it:

❑ Enterprise-wide integration: primarily integrate financial information or customer order information
❑ Standardize and speed up manufacturing processes
❑ Decrease inventory

3

❑ Standardize HR information
❑ Fix broken processes
❑ Integrate vendors and customers
❑ Increase efficiency
❑ Gain competitive edge

ERP evolution

In the 1960's, most manufacturing systems focused on inventory control. In the 1970's, the focus shifted to materials requirement planning (MRP), which took into consideration master scheduling, raw materials planning and procurement. In the 1980's, this evolved into manufacturing resources planning (MRP II), which incorporated additional activities such as shop floor and distribution.

In the 1990's, more functionality continued to be incorporated including finance, human resources, project management, and engineering. The inclusion of these areas, which encompass the majority of the activities within a typical enterprise, led to the coining of the term enterprise resource planning (ERP).

Components

The different parts of an ERP system are referred to as modules—such as Finance, Project System, and Materials Management. These modules can be customized and configured to reflect each company's unique business. Depending on the type of business, the ERP modules selected for implementation by different companies varies significantly. Finance (FI) is a universally implemented module, while Materials Management (MM) and Human Resources (HR) modules are also widely used.

Is it all or none

An ERP system can operate independently without interfaces to an organization's own, or external, applications. However, in practice, most ERP systems require interfaces, which enable data and information integration across the organization. Interfaces, which require varying degrees of effort, can be built using an ERP vendor's proprietary tools or standard programming languages.

Main players

SAP's biggest ERP competitors are Oracle, PeopleSoft, and Microsoft. Some of the smaller competitors include Best Software (previously known as Sage Software), SSA Global, Lawson Software, and Epicor Software. According to a Gartner report issued in June 2003[1], for 2002, the top five worldwide ERP software application new license revenue market share estimate is as follows:

SAP: 25.1%
Oracle: 7%
PeopleSoft: 6.5%
SAGE (Best): 5.4%
Microsoft: 4.9%
Others: 51.1%

According to SAP[2], it is the enterprise-apps market leader with 54% of the licensing revenue, which compares favorably against its main competitors: Oracle (13%), PeopleSoft (12%), Microsoft (11%) and Siebel Systems (10%).

WHY COMPANIES IMPLEMENT ERP SYSTEMS

Overcoming existing limitations

Since the early 1990's, American companies have been competing in an intensely competitive environment—both at home and abroad. The drive to cut costs, improve productivity, and stay ahead of the competition has been relentless. Every tool available to meet these objectives has been evaluated and, when appropriate, used.

Not surprisingly, information systems have always been identified among the most valuable tools that can help management achieve their performance improvement objectives. The reason is that corporate information systems provide the information that help businesses run efficiently and achieve their objectives. However, in the past, when management attempted to utilize legacy non-ERP systems for this purpose, they experienced many limitations such as:

1: www4.gartner.com
2: Informationweek, June 14, 2004, pg 24

- ❏ Lack of integration (as data was scattered across many legacy systems)
- ❏ Incompatibility between systems
- ❏ Inconsistent and/or redundant data
- ❏ Inability to provide real-time enterprise-wide information
- ❏ Inability to support easy consolidation of groups
- ❏ Limited scalability and upgrade limitations of existing systems (hardware, software and functionality)
- ❏ Integration problems for enterprise-wide upgrades
- ❏ Need to deal with multiple vendors
- ❏ High maintenance cost due to disparate and obsolete systems

According to the 2004 ITtoolbox ERP Implementation Survey, the following were the main motivations for adding a new ERP package or replacing an existing package:

- ❏ Improved functionality: 33.1%
- ❏ Ease of integration and implementation: 18.9%
- ❏ Existing system is no longer being supported: 11.4%
- ❏ Better service: 10.6%
- ❏ Lower maintenance costs: 9.45
- ❏ More flexibility: 5.1%
- ❏ Other: 11.4%

Benefits of an ERP system

The limitations of legacy systems in meeting an organization's needs led to the search for a solution that would bypass their shortcomings. The aim was to provide a system capable of meeting a company's many divergent requirements through the use of a single program. The result of the search was the development of various integrated ERP systems, whose typical benefits span many areas and are listed below.

Business

- ❏ Supports companies with global operations
- ❏ Accommodates rapidly changing business conditions
- ❏ Enables companies to better understand their business
- ❏ Meets customer demands involving multiple locations and interrelated items

Internal integration

- Integrates company-wide data and information
- Enables easy consolidation of groups due to availability of centralized data in a single system
- Combines the functions of many applications, that an organization needs to operate, and integrates them

Process

- Creates more efficient processes that serve customers better and maximizes profits
- Enables enterprises to standardize business processes and easily implement best business practices
- Provides access to best business practices, which are built-in

Flexibility

- Permits addition or upgrade of other system components or functionality due to open system architecture
- Any change can be implemented for all locations/groups through a configuration change at one central point
- Flexibility for changes for both business users and IT

Continuous improvement

- Supports the entire life cycle—not just the initial implementation
- Additional business processes can be implemented
- Can be used to optimize existing business processes

Reporting and information access

- Availability and easy access to transaction flows and document history
- Standard reports are available but customized reports can also be developed
- Provides drill-down capability, i.e., access to detailed data

Controls

- Minimizes errors across various functions due to validity checks facilitated by an integrated system
- Provides an excellent audit trail
- Controls security through authorizations that can be maintained at different levels
- Enables easy corporate control and analysis

Costs

❑ Cost savings are realized (though few companies implement ERP for this reason)
❑ Easier and cheaper to maintain a single enterprise-wide system than a multitude of disparate, incompatible, and obsolete applications/systems

Performance

❑ Creates a responsive and agile organization
❑ Enables the performance of different groups to be compared easily due to a common standard format

Technical

❑ Provides real-time information
❑ Portable across operating systems, databases, and presentation formats
❑ Provides high reliability

Other

❑ Supports extended supply chain management
❑ Improves return on information and return on investment (ROI)
❑ Facilitates efficient resource planning in a dynamic environment characterized by rapid changes in resource availability, plant capacity, etc.
❑ Reduces tedious jobs like matching purchase orders to invoices, month-end closing, etc.
❑ Provides user-friendly interface

ERP PROBLEMS AND CHALLENGES

All across the world, businesses have been implementing ERP systems as a cost efficient alternative to their disparate and incompatible systems that were put together over a number of years—some over decades. While replacement ERP systems provide many benefits, as listed earlier, they also face challenges and shortcomings. These limitations can become barriers to their selection and implementation, especially for small and mid-sized companies. Some of the major shortcomings are described in the following sections.

Implementation cost

The implementation cost of an ERP project is usually very high. Additional costs for consulting, integration and testing can be significant. Therefore, when the total implementation cost is calculated, a potential ERP investment can often be ruled out due to the huge cost involved. According to the 2004 ITtoolbox Implementation Survey, the annual ERP implementation/new deployment budget was:

- ❑ More than $2 million (18.4% respondents)
- ❑ $1-2 million (11.10%)
- ❑ Less than $100,000 (30.30%)

Hence, it becomes very important to estimate, as accurately as possible, the total implementation cost. This is a difficult task due to the large number of, and conflicting, factors that need to be considered for such an evaluation.

Factors to be evaluated

For each proposed project, the factors to be evaluated can vary considerably because enterprises are not identical, even though they may be similar. The differences can be attributed to:

- ❑ Size
- ❑ Industry
- ❑ Number of corporate divisions
- ❑ Functionality to be implemented
- ❑ Type and number of existing (legacy) information systems
- ❑ Management style
- ❑ Corporate culture
- ❑ Method of conducting business
- ❑ Processes
- ❑ Existing hardware and network infrastructure
- ❑ Number of users
- ❑ Other factors

Therefore, the scope and cost of every implementation will be different. Hence, it is usually not feasible to use other implementations as benchmarks for cost evaluation. Another problem faced by executives trying to compare a similar ERP implementation is the lack of cooperation by competitors. Most companies, especially competitors in the same type of business, will not share their cost figures for obvious reasons.

Cost estimation

A method used for cost estimation is based on estimating the total project cost as a multiple of the software cost. For example, one analyst estimates that the total cost of an ERP implementation ranges from 3-10 times the cost of the software. However, this rule-of-thumb is anything but widely accepted. A more widely used number is 3-5 times the cost of the software. Another benchmark is based on the cost per user.

In general, even though ERP projects have a higher overall cost than other software projects, they have a lower cost per user. This is due to the far larger number of users at ERP installations.

Implementation time

It used to take a very long time to implement ERP projects which seriously interfered with, and impacted, ongoing operations. A few years ago, it was not unusual for an ERP implementation to take 2-3 years. Delays were common and ERP projects got a bad name. However, in recent years, SAP projects have been implemented in a far shorter time frame, which can be attributed to the introduction of the ASAP™ methodology as well as experience gained from prior SAP implementations. While a typical ASAP™ implementation takes about a year, some projects have been completed within six months. According to the 2004 ITtoolbox Survey, the implementation time for deploying a new ERP package and/or add new modules would be:

❑ More than 24 months: 3.70%
❑ 12-24 months: 20.70%
❑ 6-12 months: 39.60%
❑ Less than 6 months: 21.10%

Customization

The need to tailor ERP software to the business requires customization. However, in some cases, it can be impractical because it might require the company to fundamentally change the way it runs its business. A common problem with customization is that it tends to be overdone because companies cannot distinguish between needs and wants. Excessive customization can be time consuming and also cause serious problems during software upgrades.

Inadequate preparation

ERP projects require extensive planning and preparation. Inadequate groundwork and preparation by the organization for migrating to the new system can cause serious problems or even lead to outright failure. It can also prevent the new software from being used to its full potential.

Fear of failure

ERP failures, when announced, become headline news. The costs involved with write-offs can be staggering. Bad news travels fast and, therefore, it is no surprise that ERP failures have been well publicized within the IT and business communities. Therefore, whenever an ERP implementation is evaluated, it causes apprehension within company management. The decision to risk the business and one's own career, knowing that failure is a possibility, is not made easily or quickly.

Upgrade cost

In the early 1990s, the average time between upgrades was about three years, which has now shrunk to 18-24 months. A major ERP upgrade will run about 18% of the original installation cost according to a 2002 AMR research survey. For companies with 500 users of ERP software, the average cost was $533,594 or about $1000 per user. For companies with 2,000 users, the cost was $1.2 million or about $595 per user. For large companies with more than 8,400 users, the total came to $2.6 million or $300 per user[3].

Capabilities are not exploited

According to a survey by IBM[4], Chief Financial Officers do not make full use of their ERP systems. Worldwide, only 19% of the 450 CFOs reported that they exploited the full capabilities of their ERP systems, which indicates that better utilization of the available assets is required in most organizations having implemented ERP systems.

3: CIO Nov 15, 2002

4: www.silicon.com, November 27, 2003

ERP challenges

According to the 2004 ITtoolbox ERP Implementation Survey, the main challenges to successful ERP implementations are inadequate definition of requirements (46.5%), resistance to change/lack of buy—in (43.9%), inadequate resources (43.10%), inadequate training and education (36.2%), lack of top management support (32.4%), unrealistic expectation of benefits and ROI (30.6%), miscalculation of time and effort (27.7%), poor communications (27.4%), incompatibility of application software with business processes (23.1%), poor project design and management (16.8%), poor ERP package selection (6.4%), and other (4%).

SELECTING AN ERP SYSTEM

Basic guidelines

Undertaking an ERP project, with its potential for big risks and rewards, can be a daunting task for even the largest companies with deep pockets. If the implementation is successful, it can provide many benefits while failure can lead to disastrous consequences. This underscores the necessity for performing a very thorough evaluation before the ERP software is selected and a decision is made to proceed with the proposed project. The following are the basic guidelines for the evaluation and selection process:

❑   Evaluation should be objective and based on facts
❑   A well proven methodology should be used

An evaluation process based on these two criteria enables a well-informed decision that can be easily justified. The following sub-sections describe additional basic guidelines that, if followed, will ensure that an appropriate ERP system will be selected.

Evaluate the business strategy

Before the ERP software is selected, the company's business strategy needs to be understood. If it is inflexible and does not permit the use of new processes, the selection choices will be reduced. Therefore, it is imperative that the business strategy be determined before embarking on a project of this nature because it is impossible to back out, after the project has started, without serious financial and political repercussions.

Study the business processes

The software needs should be defined based upon the results obtained by analyzing the existing business processes. It should not be done the other way around, i.e., by selecting the software first and then studying the business processes. The process should start by comparing the existing business processes and strategies with those supported by the new system (as-is versus to-be). This should be followed by the software selection process, which includes evaluating the functions and features. If the functions are evaluated right upfront, without examining the business background and processes, the initial progress is rapid. However, in such a case, the end result may not be what is best, or optimal, for the organization. Therefore, it is advisable to follow a selection process that starts by evaluating the organization's strategy and business processes.

Evaluate the impact of re-engineering

If a company has already made a decision to perform re-engineering, which means redesigning practically everything, it will significantly influence the software evaluation and selection process. While there are advantages to this approach, it has its drawbacks such as greater implementation risk, requiring complete business process redesign, higher implementation cost, slower deployment, and greater configuration complexity.

Favor industry-specific templates

Depending on the industry, implementation can be accelerated by the use of industry specific templates, if available and applicable. These templates contain pre-defined best business practices for specific industries. A vendor able to provide industry-specific templates will start off with an advantage in the evaluation process. SAP has created pre-configured industry-specific templates, which enable simpler and faster deployment. However, because industry-specific best business practices are incorporated in the templates, their use forces companies to make trade-offs and compromises due to reduced flexibility caused by the use of these templates.

It should be realized that templates only cut some initial work off the implementation. Even when they are used, the configuration and processes still need to be verified, at every step, for applicability to the implementation site. When required, such as a situation where a particular process is not supported by the template, appropriate changes need to be implemented.

Obtain input from business users

An ERP project is not a technology project. It should be owned and driven by the business users. Viewing an ERP system as a technology or software project is one of the surest ways to failure—as many companies have learned. The logic for this is simple. IT does not have the business expertise to evaluate the implications of various trade-offs that need to be made throughout the project—from software evaluation and selection through implementation. It also does not have the capability to evaluate decisions based on their strategic versus operational impact. Those decisions are best left to the business users and their management.

Be wary of proof-of-concept offer

It is fairly common for vendors to propose a proof-of-concept offer. In such a scenario, the vendor implements and demonstrates a working model of its software based on the potential client company's business data. These offers should be carefully evaluated before they are accepted. If an offer is accepted, the vendor should be made to demonstrate carefully scripted business scenarios developed by the client's employees.

Additional points to ponder

As part of the evaluation process, a company needs to look inwards and study its strengths and weaknesses. The result of this analysis can help in deciding whether or not to implement an ERP system. It can also help in identifying the ERP package that is more suitable for the company. The two fundamental questions that need to be answered during the evaluation process are:

❑ How should this business be run
❑ What are the business problems that the ERP package should address

Other factors to consider include assessing priorities, gaps between the existing system and the ERP package, costs and benefits, as well as proposed tasks and implementation schedule. Also to be evaluated are the implementation options possible for the ERP package being evaluated—such as availability of implementation partners versus using the company's own employees supported by consultants.

Basic selection considerations

Model of doing business

ERP packages are based on business models that may be incompatible or fundamentally different than the way the company conducts its business. To enable implementation when there is incompatibility, either the company has to change the way it runs its business or the software has to be modified. Both these choices have potentially serious implications that need to be evaluated before making any selection.

Functionality

The first step should be to identify the business problems that need to be addressed. They determine which specific functionality the software package must support. The suitability of a software package can vary considerably depending on where the functionality requirements originate from: Finance, Manufacturing, Human Resources or some other group. For example, the need to integrate financial data has different requirements than those for standardizing production systems across the enterprise.

ERP packages have different features, despite a common base and approach, and some excel in specific areas. Therefore, their suitability for a particular implementation can be dramatically different. This, to some extent, can be attributed to their different evolution paths. For example, some ERP vendors started off by developing manufacturing software while others started off down a completely different path—such as PeopleSoft, whose first module was Human Resources.

Analysis and reporting

The need for reporting varies at different organizational levels. The requirements of top management are quite different compared to a line manager's needs. Again, management style can vary across organizations. Some like to drill-down and look at the lowest level of data (transactions). Others are only interested in looking at the big picture. Therefore, the ability of the software to provide high-level reporting as well as access to granular data is a factor to consider during the selection process.

The ease of use in accessing data through standard reports can be a big plus. Also to be considered, when evaluating reporting capabilities, is the current or future availability of an integrated data warehouse that, besides providing better analytical reports, is more user-friendly.

Showstoppers

During the evaluation process, as features are evaluated in-depth, there is a fair chance that a showstopper may be discovered, which can be a business process not supported by the ERP package or it can be a critical piece of missing functionality. The following are examples of showstoppers:

❑ Does not support the needs of the company, with international operations, which requires 24x7 support and service
❑ Does not support multi-currencies or languages
❑ Critical process is unsupported
❑ Estimated implementation time is unacceptable

What to do before buying

Evaluate using cross-functional teams

An integrated ERP system must be evaluated by business experts who represent various functional areas impacted by the software, such as Finance, Manufacturing, and Sales. This ensures that functionality and processes are evaluated in all functional areas and, therefore, all bases are covered. This involvement also enables easy buy-in.

Check references and sites

It is always advisable to move beyond the evaluation phase sales pitches. One of the best ways to obtain useful information is to visit sites that have already implemented the ERP package. For example, a semiconductor company evaluating SAP should communicate with, and visit, other semiconductor companies that have already implemented SAP.

It should be realized that more than a few phone calls are required. It is far more effective to visit an operating site and talk to the personnel closely involved with the implementation and operation at that site. The intelligence gathered during such trips, along with tips and warnings, can ensure that mistakes are not repeated.

Useful information can also be obtained by attending user conferences and events such as the SAPPHIRE® conference, which is SAP's annual event where it usually announces new functionality and news. This event is attended by thousands of users and the discussions there, with other participants and SAP experts, can be very useful and informative.

Request onsite demo

The vendor should be asked to demonstrate support for the processes and functionality it seeks to replace. This demo should be based on detailed business scenarios that are created by the various functional groups. The ability to support critical processes can be the basis for allowing the vendor to proceed to the next stage in the evaluation and selection process.

Beware of consultants involved in the selection process

Integrators and consultants are often involved in the evaluation process. Their experience is valuable since they have experienced many implementations. However, at times, they can be less than objective due to a number of reasons. For example, an integrator may be biased towards a particular ERP system because it may be more experienced in that package or most of its benched consultants may be specialized in that ERP package. Therefore, the company's employees—not the consultants, should make the final decision independently.

Identify selection criteria

In order to implement an ERP package, a company will need to evaluate and select the software package, system integrator (consulting company with implementation expertise), and the hardware vendor. Every company performing an evaluation, for each of these three items, will have its own screening and selection criteria.

Typically, the variables used for evaluating an ERP software package include flexibility, information access, functionality, technical environment, cost, ease of implementation, and vendor. Depending upon each company's own criteria, additional variables can be used. The variables used can be assigned equal or unequal weights during the scoring and ranking process. In the following list, the number within each bracket indicates the weight that was assigned to the variable by a mid-cap company during its ERP selection process.

- ❏ Flexibility (20%)
- ❏ Information access (20%)
- ❏ Functionality (15%)
- ❏ Technical environment (15%)
- ❏ Cost (10%)
- ❏ Ease of implementation (10%)
- ❏ Vendor (10%)

The importance of each selection variable will vary from organization to organization. Therefore, the weight that is assigned to each variable will, typically, be different for each implementation.

Chapter A2
What is SAP

BACKGROUND

The company

SAP AG, founded by five former IBM engineers in 1972, is based in Walldorf, Germany. SAP is an acronym for Systeme, Anwendungen, Produkte in der Datenverarbeitung, which means Systems, Applications and Products in Data Processing. SAP is the world's largest enterprise software company. It is also the world's third-largest independent software company, which is publicly traded on the Frankfurt Stock Exchange and the New York Stock Exchange. In addition to developing business applications software, SAP also provides extensive training and consulting services for implementing its software.

In fiscal year 2003, SAP's revenues were EUR 7.025 billion. 38% of its software revenues were from mySAP Financials and mySAP Human Resources. In 2003, 74% of SAP's revenues were derived from its existing customers, while 24% were attributable to new customers, which is an excellent achievement considering the difficult economic environment throughout the world. At the end of 2003, SAP's worldwide market share was 59%. In the US, it became the market leader through a 14% increase in market share in 2003. In the first quarter of 2004, SAP's flagship ERP software accounted for 42% of its total software revenue.

SAP's main competitors are PeopleSoft, Oracle, Microsoft, and Siebel Systems. SAP employs over 29,600 people in more than 50 countries. It has over 12 million users, 69,700 installations in 120 countries, and 1,500 partners. It also has over 10 million licensed users worldwide and more than 22,000 customers. Half of SAP's customer installations worldwide are in organizations with revenues under $200 million.

Main product

SAP's main product is SAP™ R/3®, a highly customizable, client/server, integrated software that was introduced in 1992. It is based on the ABAP/4® programming language. SAP™ R/3® is the successor to SAP™ R/2™, which operated on mainframes.

SAP introduced a scalable and Internet-ready architecture in 1996. With its introduction, SAP took the first step to position itself for capitalizing on the growing need for customer-centric, personalized and collaborative enterprise solutions. mySAP provides the architecture that enables an organization to bring together its customers, vendors, partners and employees in a collaborative, web-based, environment.

CHARACTERISTICS OF SAP™ R/3® SOFTWARE

Basic characteristics

SAP is a powerful and versatile software with the following defining characteristics:

General

❑ Highly integrated and cross-functional software with tight integration across functions.
❑ Real time (the R in R/3 refers to real-time). Data update are done online and in real-time. For example, if a purchase order (PO) is issued (in the Materials Management module), the amount of the PO will be immediately reflected in the Finance module.

Business

❑ Comprehensive functionality is incorporated, which enables it to run complete businesses. It incorporates best industry practices and is suitable for a wide range of industries and organizations.
❑ Supports enterprise-wide business processes.

Flexibility

❑ Highly configurable. Can be customized according to a company's needs and requirements. Changes can be easy or difficult, depending on a number of factors such as the extent of customization.

❑ Can support enterprises with subsidiaries located at geographically scattered sites.
❑ Favored internationally due to its availability in many languages and ability to customize the software to currencies, tax laws, accounting procedures, import/export regulations, etc.

Technical

❑ Portable across databases, operating systems and front-ends.
❑ Characterized by minimum data redundancy, maximum data consistency, highly secure data handling and complex data structures.
❑ Complex package with technical implications that include software development, database administration, networking and production control.

Other features

❑ Same data is used across different functional modules.
❑ Single point of entry.
❑ Capitalizes on economy of scale; is very scalable.
❑ Easy-to use graphical user interface.

Best business practices

SAP includes more than 1,000 predefined processes that represent best business practices. These encompass a wide range of functional requirements. More of these are being added as part of SAP's effort to help its customers meet the demanding needs of a rapidly changing business environment in these fast-paced times.

Industry-specific solutions

A number of industries are supported by SAP through solutions and functionality that addresses their unique requirements. The industry solutions for 27 distinct industries that SAP can deliver include:

❑ Aerospace and defense
❑ Automotive
❑ Banking
❑ Chemicals
❑ Consumer products
❑ Defense and Security
❑ Engineering, construction, and operations
❑ Financial service provider

❏ Healthcare
❏ Higher education and research
❏ High technology
❏ Industrial machinery and components
❏ Insurance
❏ Media
❏ Life sciences
❏ Logistics service providers
❏ Mill products
❏ Mining
❏ Oil and gas
❏ Pharmaceuticals
❏ Postal services
❏ Professional services
❏ Public sector
❏ Retail
❏ Service providers
❏ Telecommunications
❏ Utilities

For each of these industries, SAP has created a solution that reflects their specific business process requirements including web-enabled processes. These solutions incorporate best business practices. The industry-specific solutions contain tailored versions of mySAP Business Suite solutions. The various industry solutions are grouped into six sectors: Process Industries, Discrete Industries, Consumer Industries, Services Industries, and Financial Services. Additionally, SAP partners have created many industry-specific solutions.

Solutions for small and mid-market segments

The small and mid-market segments are supported by a range of SAP business solutions, which are provided by two initiatives:

❏ mySAP All-in-One: These solutions are software applications based on mySAP Business Suite components. Worldwide, over 350 mySAP All-in-One certified solutions are available.
❏ SAP Business One: Is a business automation software solution that targets companies up to 250 employees. It supports non-industry specific business processes such as financial management, procurement, inventory management, payment and sales force automation.

Customization

Need for customization

ERP packages, and SAP in particular, are fairly complicated. This is the result of trying to achieve all-encompassing functionality capable of meeting the varied needs of tens of thousands of customers. Typically, a customer selects an ERP package that meets most of the organization's business requirements. However, in order to run all parts of the business, the generic software package needs to be tailored so that it can meet the customer's specific needs and requirements. For example, if a functionality gap is identified during analysis, software customization becomes imperative if the option of modifying the business practice is discarded.

While it is understandable that SAP needs to be modified to meet the business requirements of a company, the problem lies in over-customization. This occurs when an attempt is made to make SAP look and feel like the legacy system(s) being discarded.

How customization is done

A number of tools and utilities are available for customizing SAP according to the specific needs of the customer. Typically, the software is customized by consultants, project team members, and IT staff. The two methods that can be used to customize SAP software, so that it can provide the needed functionality, are:

❑ Configuration changes: these involve table entries which are configurable
❑ ABAP/4® programming: this involves modifying existing programs within the SAP™ R/3® software or writing completely new programs which are incorporated into the main software

Complexity of customization

Some SAP customization is relatively simple. However, it can be fairly complex even for experienced consultants, especially during the initial implementation, to tailor the software according to a customer's specific needs. While ERP vendors have made a significant effort to simplify this process, it still requires a significant amount of time and effort.

Problem in customizing

The amount, and type, of customization that can be done by a customer is extensive. It is possible to modify the SAP source code (or logic), or add tables and columns, if the functionality to be supported requires it. However, besides being expensive, extensive customization creates a problem whenever the software is upgraded. Each upgrade and new software release, which can occur a few times every year, can become a maintenance and testing nightmare if the software has been extensively customized.

SUPPORT PROVIDED BY SAP

Partnerships

SAP uses the partnership approach, which combines SAP resources, including personnel and technology, with that of its partners. These partners, who provide worldwide support for every facet of an SAP implementation, are classified into eight categories:

❑ Software partners
❑ Service partners
❑ Technology partners
❑ Support partners
❑ Hosting partners
❑ Content partners
❑ Education partners
❑ SAP xApps partners
❑ AP Business partners

The global services partners are Accenture, Atos Origin, Bearing Point, Cap Gemini, CSC, Deloitte, HP Consulting, IBM, IDS Scheer, Itelligence, LogicaCMG, and Siemens.

The partnership approach enables fast, customer-specific, and efficient implementation for SAP clients. With tens of thousands of consultants trained in SAP™ R/3® software, there is a vast pool of resources available to draw upon for any SAP implementation.

Service and support

SAP does not limit its support to evaluation and implementation of its software. Besides aiming for continuous business improvement, it also provides 24x7 service and support to its customers.

Training

SAP provides training in a number of formats including conventional, classroom-based, training and remote real-time Internet training. It offers nearly 300 courses taught by a very large pool of instructors at numerous training centers across the world. SAP also has a program that works with colleges and universities at different locations.

SAP also offers consultant education including early product training, solution awareness education, and consultant certification. It also has SAP academies, which are centers that specialize in intensive knowledge transfer that helps consultants build skills and qualifications.

SAP Developer Network

Developers and integrators have access to the SAP Developer Network, a collaborative community. Professionals working on SAP NetWeaver and xApps are able to use this network for providing content as well as for facilitating collaboration.

CHAPTER A3
FUNCTIONALITY AND ARCHITECTURE

FUNCTIONAL ARCHITECTURE

Modules

SAP™ R/3® software consists of the following functional modules:

1 Asset Management (AM)
2 Financials (FI)
3 Controlling (CO)
4 Human Resources (HR)
5 Plant Maintenance (PM)
6 Production Planning (PP)
7 Project System (PS)
8 Quality Management (QM)
9 Sales and Distribution (SD)
10 Materials Management (MM)
11 Service Management (SM)
12 Industry Specific Solutions (IS)
13 Business Workflow (WF)
14 Basis (includes ABAP/4® programming language) (BC)

Each of these modules has a number of sub-modules. For example, the Financials (FI) module contains sub-modules for Financial Accounting, Controlling, Investment Management, Treasury Cash Management, Enterprise Controlling and Real Estate.

In the past, solutions using SAP were frequently optimized along modules, which led to less than desired integration. The recent trend has been to optimize along processes such as Order-to-Cash and Purchase-to-Pay, each one of which can span multiple modules. SAP now groups its solutions by Enterprise Resource

Planning, Customer Relationship Management, Supplier Relationship Management, Product Lifecycle Management, Supply Chain Management, and Business Intelligence.

Integration between modules

The software that SAP provides to its customers includes all the modules. However, each customer retains the choice of selecting the modules that will be implemented. These modules are tightly integrated and, in many cases, specific functionality can be accessed through different modules. For example, a vendor's data can be accessed from both the Financials and Materials Management modules.

Functionality by module

The following is a list of the most important functions supported by each module:

Financial & Asset Accounting

- General ledger
- Accounts receivable
- Accounts payable
- Asset accounting
- Leased assets
- Special purpose ledger
- Legacy consolidations
- Financial accounting information system

Controlling

- Overhead cost controlling
- Product cost controlling
- Profitability analysis
- Activity based costing
- Internal orders

Investment Management

- Investment plans (budgets)
- Investments (orders and projects)
- Automatic settlement of fixed assets
- Depreciation forecast

Treasury

- ❑ Cash management
- ❑ Treasury management
- ❑ Market risk management
- ❑ Funds management

Enterprise Controlling

- ❑ Business planning and budgeting
- ❑ Consolidations
- ❑ Profit center accounting
- ❑ Intercompany transactions
- ❑ Executive information system

Real Estate

- ❑ Rental administration and settlement
- ❑ Controlling, position valuation and information management

Human Resources

- ❑ Personnel administration
  - ○ Payroll
  - ○ Benefits administration
  - ○ Recruitment
  - ○ Time management
  - ○ Travel management
  - ○ Compensation management
- ❑ Personnel planning and development
  - ○ Organization management
  - ○ Training and events management

Plant Maintenance

- ❑ Preventive maintenance
- ❑ Service management
- ❑ Maintenance projects
- ❑ Maintenance notifications
- ❑ Maintenance orders
- ❑ Equipment and technical objects
- ❑ Plant maintenance information system

Production Planning

- ❑ Sales and operations planning
- ❑ Master production scheduling
- ❑ Materials requirements planning
- ❑ Capacity requirements planning
- ❑ KANBAN
- ❑ Repetitive manufacturing
- ❑ Make-to-stock
- ❑ Production orders
- ❑ Product cost planning
- ❑ Assembly orders
- ❑ Production planning for process industries
- ❑ Shop floor control
- ❑ Work centers
- ❑ Routings
- ❑ Bill of materials
- ❑ Production planning and control information systems

Project System

- ❑ Operational structures—work breakdown structure
- ❑ Networks and resources
- ❑ Project execution and integration
- ❑ Project evaluation (project information system)
- ❑ Budget management
- ❑ Cost and revenue planning

Quality Management

- ❑ Quality planning
- ❑ Quality inspections
- ❑ Quality control
- ❑ Notifications
- ❑ Test equipment management
- ❑ Quality management information system
- ❑ Inspection processing

Sales and Distribution

- ❑ Quotations
- ❑ Sales order management

- ❑ Pricing
- ❑ Shipping
- ❑ Billing
- ❑ Foreign trade
- ❑ Sales information system
- ❑ Availability check and requirements
- ❑ Computer aided sales

Materials Management

- ❑ Procurement
- ❑ Inventory management
- ❑ Materials planning
- ❑ Vendor evaluation
- ❑ Invoice verification
- ❑ Warehouse management
- ❑ Logistics information system
- ❑ Consumption-based planning

Service Management

- ❑ Services such as warranty, maintenance and repair work
- ❑ Service agreements
- ❑ Service notifications
- ❑ Service orders

Business Processes

- ❑ Business workflow
- ❑ Office system

Basis Components

- ❑ ABAP/4® development workbench
- ❑ Computing center management system
- ❑ Multiple system utilities
- ❑ User management and authorization concept
- ❑ Transport and correction system
- ❑ Client management
- ❑ Data archiving
- ❑ Printer management and output control

PHYSICAL ARCHITECTURE

Three-tier client/server architecture

The SAP™ R/3® system is based on the distributed client/server architecture. It includes three components: database layer, application layer and presentation layer. Physically, the system consists of database servers, application servers and clients (user desktops) connected through a network. In the three-tier client/server architecture, a distinct separation exists between the different layers as described in the following sections.

Database layer

The database layer consists of a database server where the data is stored. It provides the central storage and management of the company's working data, which includes master data and transaction data. It also holds the metadata, which is maintained in the repository, that describes the database structure. Due to the central storage of data, SAP is able to maintain data consistency and seamless integration between modules. The database server software manages and controls various functions such as database management and batch processing.

SAP, designed as an open system, uses relational databases for data storage. It supports the major relational database management systems (RDBMS) from vendors including Oracle, Informix, IBM and Microsoft. SAP™ R/3® uses structured query language (SQL) for defining and manipulating data. It also supports proprietary SQL enhancements.

Application layer

The application layer consists of an application server where the business logic/rules reside and application logic is processed. The function of application servers is to prepare and process incoming data. For example, a user request to read or write data is processed by the application server before being sent to the database server. Custom ABAP™ applications are processed by the application server. SAP administrative functions are also managed at this layer.

Presentation layer

The presentation layer facilitates interaction between the user and the computer. This layer includes the graphical user interface (GUI), which displays the R/3™ window. The presentation layer typically resides on the user's desktop. The interaction process involves the GUI receiving a user request, which it passes on to the application server for further processing.

Four-tier architecture

This architecture moves the client/server architecture to an internet-based architecture. In this configuration, a web server is added to the three tiers and access is enabled through the Internet using a web browser. In this architecture, programming is separated from formatting and work is divided between software and user interface developers. Consequently, due to separation of development efforts, the development process is streamlined, development cycle time is reduced, and new features can be added quickly.

Advantages of a decentralized system

There are many advantages of using a decentralized architecture for an ERP system like SAP. These include:

❑ Scalability: SAP supports an unlimited number of users as well as database and application servers in a variety of hardware configurations. This flexibility enables a company to start on a relatively small-scale. Later on, when expansion becomes necessary, additional database or application servers can be added to the network. For example, if the number of users increases, more clients (PCs) can be added. If the quantity of data to be processed increases significantly, more database servers can be added without requiring an overall system upgrade. This scalability advantage at any level (database, application or presentation), makes SAP an attractive option for different types of organizations—both large and small.

❑ Open system: Plug and play is encouraged by this system. Hardware/peripherals from different vendors can be used, which can lead to more competition and lower costs.

❑ Workload distribution: It is easier for an administrator to distribute the load on various servers. For example, the primary users of a specific module, such as Finance, can be routed to a particular server for load balancing.

❑ Response time: It is possible to achieve near instant response times, despite simultaneous usage by hundreds of users, with a decentralized architecture.

❑ Higher availability to users: Compared to mainframes, higher system availability is possible for users because they need not logoff to run batch jobs, which can be processed in the background.

❑ Ease of use: Decentralized systems, such as SAP, support a PC-based user-friendly interface. They are easier to interact with compared to mainframe dumb terminals.

Platforms supported

SAP is based on various hardware and software architectures. It can run on many operating systems including Unix (for which it was originally designed), Windows NT, Windows 2000, AS/400 and Linux. In recent years, the deployment of SAP applications on Microsoft Windows with SQL Server as the back-end database has become very popular. According to Informationweek[5], 40,000 SAP installations are running on Windows and it is also estimated that there are over 5,000 SAP-on-Dell installations[6]. The drivers for these moves have been lower cost Intel-based servers, database and operating system licensing and administration costs, as well as savings on the acquisition and deployment of system management software.

SAP also supports a number of relational databases including Oracle, Informix, IBM DB2, Microsoft's SQL Server and SAP DB. For presentation, SAP supports Java, Web browser, MS Windows, OSF/Motif and OS/2 Presentation Manager.

NetWeaver

In a major architecture shift, SAP introduced NetWeaver, its Web services-based computing engine, and the Enterprise Services Architecture (ESA) in January 2003. NetWeaver 2004, which is a unified integration and development platform, integrates SAP's combined ABAP and Java 2 Platform Enterprise Edition Web application server, Mobile Infrastructure, Enterprise Portal, Business Intelligence, Master Data Management, Composite Application Framework, and its Exchange Infrastructure for integration.

NetWeaver's 2004 release is built on a service-oriented architecture (SOA). In SOA, all services are based on a platform-independent interface contract, which enable clients located anywhere, in any operating environment and using any language, to use the service—with web services being one way of implementing SOA. NetWeaver integrates the platform's ten components including a portal, exchange infrastructure known as XI, Web application server, composite application framework, and business intelligence software.

5: May 17, 2004, pg 98
6: Informationweek May 3, 2004, pg 30

The open architecture will inter-connected SAP with other platforms, which will enable the creation of an integrated environment (even though it is heterogeneous) and real-time collaborative process across organizational boundaries,. SAP is planning on retooling its entire software suite so that they can run on NetWeaver and ESA by 2007. It expects 1,000 customers to be using NetWeaver by the end of 2004. SAP is very serious about its commitment to this technology, upon which it wants to build the next generation of SAP applications, and for which it has spent over $1 billion in R&D costs.

Components

SAP NetWeaver components include:

❑ SAP Business Intelligence
❑ SAP Enterprise Portal
❑ SAP Exchange Infrastructure
❑ SAP Master Data Management
❑ SAP Mobile Infrastructure
❑ SAP Web Application Server

NetWeaver tools include SAP Visual Composer, SAP Composite Application Framework, SAP NetWeaver Developer Studio, and SAP Solution Manager. SAP NetWeaver Rapid Installer is a tool designed to expedite and simplify NetWeaver platform implementation and administration.

Benefits

NetWeaver is a business foundation, which has many features and benefits including the following:

❑ Flexible business strategies.
❑ Innovative business processes.
❑ Open standards-based.
❑ Improved business performance.
❑ Reduced total cost of ownership (TCO).
❑ Interoperable with Microsoft .NET and IBS WebSphere/J2EE technologies.
❑ Integration with external entities is enabled by the new business process engine in the Exchange Infrastructure (XI).
❑ Reduced costs due to integrated IT landscape; existing IT investments, SAP and non-SAP, can be leveraged.
❑ Incorporates information and applications from virtually any source.
❑ Increases flexibility while decreasing complexity.

❑ Integrates and aligns business processes and information across organizational and technological boundaries.

❑ Provides new functionality including the integration of RFID (radio frequency identification) data into SAP software.

❑ Includes Web Dynpro technology—a web transactional-application engine, based on Java standards, which enables optimized forms to be created.

❑ Easy development of best practices.

Enterprise Services Architecture

The Enterprise Services Architecture (ESA), the blueprint for services-based business solutions, attempts to provide structure and cohesion to three architectures: Mainframe, Client/Server, and the Internet. ESA can help manage various aspects of a business process, such as:

❑ People: all roles that participate in the value chain

❑ Systems: SAP and non-SAP

❑ Information: Structured and unstructured

With ESA, existing systems and applications can be used. ESA allows customers to maintain and build upon their existing solutions investments through Web services. SAP plans on developing all future applications based on the ESA, including mySAP solutions, SAP xAPPs, industry solutions, and mySAP ERP. The foundation and engine for implementing ESA, which enables web services, is NetWeaver.

SAP Web AS

The foundation and application platform for SAP's NetWeaver is the SAP Web Application Server, also known as SAP Web AS, which drives all SAP applications and tools. It incorporates state-of-the-art HTTP technology. The R/3 Enterprise release includes the SAP Web AS as well as conventional ERP components along with various SAP enhancements. The SAP Web Application Sever is a highly scalable platform, which has been designed so that it can support all SAP applications. In addition to ABAP/4, Web AS allows Java to be used as an alternate programming language for the development of web applications.

The Web AS is the result of the evolution from the Internet Transaction Server (ITS) technology initially used by SAP when it decided to web-enable its offerings and support TCP/IP and HTTP technologies. ITS served as the connection between the Internet and the SAP R/3 transaction system—converting transactions into H™P and JavaScript before passing them onto the web server. In order to overcome ITS limitations and fully integrate standard Internet technology into SAP, the SAP Web Application Server was developed. The Web AS is an open integration platform with integrated web, XML, and Java support that can link SAP and non-SAP systems. Data and functions in back end systems can be accessed using SAP proprietary technologies such as BAPI (business application programming interface) and RFC (remote function call) or Internet technologies such as SOAP (simple object access protocol) or Java.

mySAP

mySAP replaced SAP's original three-tier architecture foundation with the four-tier architecture, with the 4th component being the web server. mySAP is based on an open, flexible, and scalable Internet architecture. It is the foundation upon which SAP customers can build and execute their Internet and e-business strategies. It supports business-to-business (B2B) and business-to-consumer (B2C) applications. Companies in all types of industries, large and small, can use mySAP to:

❑ Become more responsive to their customers' needs and demands
❑ Bring together their customers, partners, and employees
❑ Facilitate inter-enterprise collaboration
❑ Gain competitive advantage

mySAP is:

❑ An e-business platform.
❑ A business process automation platform:
   • Can extend internal and external business processes
   • Create collaborative applications
❑ Java-based, as well as ABAP-based, development and deployment platform (Web AS and Web Dynpro). Able to modify, extend, and run all core mySAP modules.

The mySAP solutions include R/3 Enterprise as the core ERP component along with mySAP Financials, mySAP CRM, mySAP PLM, and mySAP SCM. mySAP's business application areas are:

❑ e-Commerce
❑ Customer relationship management
❑ Supply chain management
❑ Strategic enterprise management

- ❑ Business intelligence
- ❑ Knowledge management
- ❑ Human resources
- ❑ Logistics execution
- ❑ Manufacturing
- ❑ Product lifecycle management
- ❑ Financials

It is estimated that only about only one-third of SAP's customers have so far migrated to mySAP, with even fewer having fully adopted NetWeaver. At this time, most customers are operating on SAP R/3, which is based on the 3-tier client-server enterprise resource planning (ERP) system. SAP has indicated that it will provide maintenance and support for R/3 until 2012.

BUSINESS SOLUTIONS

mySAP Business Suite

SAP has provided a comprehensive family of adaptive business solutions, a suite of business solutions known as *mySAP Business Suite*, with the following features:

- ❑ Based on SAP NetWeaver integration and application platform
- ❑ Best of breed functionality that supports complete integration
- ❑ Industry-specific capabilities and features
- ❑ Scalability
- ❑ Collaboration

mySAP includes the following:

- ❑ mySAP Customer Relationship Management
- ❑ mySAP ERP
- ❑ mySAP Product Lifecyle Management
- ❑ mySAP Supplier Relationship Management
- ❑ mySAP Supply Chain Management

mySAP ERP

The mySAP ERP objective is to enable companies to run their core business functions including financials, operations, human resources, analytics, corporate services, and planning. Some new terms now being used such as mySAP ERP

Financials (replacing mySAP Financials) and mySAP Human Capital Management (replacing mySAP Human Resources), which are now included in mySAP ERP.

mySAP ERP, which succeeds the last release of SAP R/3 Enterprise, is based on SAP NetWeaver, which facilitates easy integration with SAP and non-SAP systems. mySAP provides many benefits including new efficiencies in integrated end-to-end processes, incremental upgrade strategy, and lower total cost of ownership. It supports the core and extended business software requirements of large and medium-sized companies..

The key functional areas of mySAP ERP include:

❑ Financials: Includes financial accounting, managerial accounting, financial supply chain management, and manager self-services
❑ Operations: Includes purchase order management, inventory management, production management, maintenance and quality, delivery management, and sales order management.
❑ Human Capital Management: Includes employee transaction management, employee life-cycle management, e-recruiting, employee relationship management, employee self services, employee interaction center, and human capital management analytics.
❑ Corporate Services: Includes real estate management, incentive and commission management, and travel management.
❑ Analytics: Includes strategic enterprise management and business analytics.

The key functions supported within the various functional areas are:

❑ mySAP ERP Human Capital Management (mySAP ERP HCM), which includes administration, payroll, benefits, legal reporting, online recruiting, blended learning, organizational management, compensation, manager self-services, employee collaboration and workforce analytics.
❑ mySAP Product Lifecycle Management (mySAP PLM), which includes life cycle data management, life cycle collaboration, program and project management, quality management, asset life cycle management and environmental health and safety.
❑ mySAP Supply Chain Management's (mySAP SCM), which includes supply chain planning, execution, collaboration and coordination, and fulfillment processes, which includes availability checks, inventory management and delivery.
❑ mySAP Supplier Relationship Management (mySAP SRM), which includes supply cycle, supplier selection optimization, collaboration, and cycle times for the purchasing cycle.

SAP xApps

What are xApps

An xApp is an SAP horizontal application that supports and automates complex business processes across heterogeneous applications. An xApp supports business processes spanning different functional areas such as finance, human resources, inventory, etc. At this time, SAP has developed 17 applications for diverse processes such as resource and program management, product definition, emission management, invoice verification, mergers and acquisitions, etc., which provide packaged functionality. SAP is also partnering with other vendors to create new applications, based on NetWeaver, in the xApps environment.

Benefits

The benefits of xApps include business improvement and innovation, collaboration (asynchronous to real-time), speed (snap-on functionality) and flexibility in improving business processes and implementing changes, integration, reduced customization, and lower cost. XApps run on the mySAP technology platform. XApps are cross-functional, which operate across multiple applications and sources and, hence, are able to drive processes across heterogeneous systems. They support workflow and business processes without being hampered by the underlying infrastructure.

UNDERSTANDING SAP's ENVIRONMENT

The following sections describe the primary architectural elements of the SAP system and its organization structure. For those who need to implement SAP, familiarity with the organizational structure is a basic requirement because it is the foundation upon which the system is ultimately configured and built.

Structural elements

Instance

A single installation of the SAP source code/modules is called an "Instance." Each version of the SAP™ R/3® software, such as 4.0 and 4.6, requires a separate system. There is no integration of data or functionality between systems as delivered.

In a typical SAP system, the various functional requirements are usually achieved by setting up the following instances:

❑ Development instance: In this box, developers and configurators perform their development work. Configuration, programs, SAP Scripts, forms, reports, etc., are developed and initially tested here. After testing has been completed, these objects are moved to a more formal testing environment— the testing instance.

❑ Testing instance: This is the quality assurance (QA) box where rigorous testing, typically based on an established methodology, is performed. After completion of QA testing, objects are moved to the production instance.

❑ Production instance: This is the production system where the company's business is run. It is the system where the users perform their day-to-day work.

❑ Training instance: In this box, users are trained to use SAP before being authorized to work in the production instance. They can also practice their newly-acquired skills in this system before starting to work in the production system.

Client

An instance can be further organized and sub-divided into different sections, called clients. For example, a typical development instance architecture will include separate clients for:

❑ Developers (Client 100)
❑ Configurators (Client 200)
❑ Data migration and load testing (Client 300)

The following is a list of some important client characteristics:

❑ A physical database, or an instance, may have multiple SAP clients
❑ Different clients have separate, unrelated, data
❑ Data of one client may not be accessed by another client
❑ Full functional and data integration occurs within a client
❑ Minimal integration exists between clients
❑ Financial consolidations across clients are possible
❑ Single logical database; in a system, all clients reside within the same database

Organizational structure

Client

A client is the basic and highest organizational unit within SAP. It represents an organization or a logical grouping of multiple companies. It is a self-contained, commercially and organizationally independent, unit. A client has its own separate data environment including customization, master data, transaction data, user master records and set of tables.

An organizational structure client, that represents a corporate hierarchy, should not be confused with the client(s) associated with an instance, which is a unit of the SAP physical architecture.

Company code

A company code, the smallest unit displaying a complete external accounting unit, is the basic organizational unit in the SAP accounting system. It is at the company code level that the profit and loss statement is generated. It is possible for a single or several company codes to exist for a single client.

What SAP DOES TO AN ORGNIZATION

Re-engineering

SAP is a re-engineering driver. It forces companies to review all their existing business processes. The result is that many of SAP's processes, which represent best business practices, are selected to replace the existing ones that, in many cases, are quite obsolete.

Impacts corporate culture

SAP can have a visible impact on corporate culture. It can open up new and better ways of doing business. For example, at one highly bureaucratic company, it led to reducing the approval hierarchy for requisitions from an average of 10 to only 4 people. It kills the philosophy that causes people to resist change by using the excuse "because we have always been doing it this way." It forces people to think out of the box.

Changes competitive landscape

With improved processes, greater agility, quicker response to customer needs, and improved vendor relationship, a company using SAP is better prepared to mount a serious challenge to its competitors or, if it is the leader, maintain its competitive lead.

Creates interdependency

The integrated nature of the software makes employees working in different functional groups more aware of how the other functional groups operate. It creates an appreciation of the problems and issues that the other functional groups are exposed to. For example, other groups quickly know it when a mistake is made in one functional area (such as finance) because it immediately impacts other areas (such as purchasing or sales) due to the integrated nature of the software. Hence, the tendency to work in functional silos decreases considerably.

Shifts balance of power

SAP empowers business users. They take over the system and IT is relegated to a secondary role. Business users can make decisions and implement changes, such as process and configuration changes, on their own without requiring IT approval or help. While IT is a partner, it is the business users who are in the driver's seat. After implementation, low level managers and employees discover that they have access to a tremendous amount of data and reports regarding the company, and its operations, that they never had previously. This makes employees feel empowered.

Simplifies platform

With the retirement of a number of legacy systems and applications, which typically operate on different types of platforms, the total number and variety of systems that an organization needs to maintain decreases dramatically. Also, the retiring outdated systems are replaced by a system that better reflects current technology and is easier to maintain.

Impacts costs/profitability

It is simpler and cheaper to maintain fewer systems and applications. Therefore, replacing a number of legacy systems with an SAP system can translate into lower costs and, consequently, profitability.

Impacts employees

Human nature is such that change causes anxiety. Therefore, it is no surprise that an SAP implementation introduces fear and stress among employees. The fear is that with the introduction of the new software, existing skill sets will become obsolete. That translates into an inability to perform one's job after the new software is implemented. Employees also fear that existing jobs may be eliminated and/or redefined. All this forces employees to deal with change. However, the net result is that employees are forced to upgrade their skills, which is positive for them in the long run.

Impacts work environment

The work environment changes in many ways. Users feel empowered because they have increased information access and the ability to make changes to a powerful system. They are able to move out of their silos and observe what happens elsewhere. For example, a buyer is able to trace the history of a transaction that he initiated, such as creating a purchase order, all the way to the end of the process through the other modules. This would include access to all intermediate transactions such as Accounts Payable and Goods Receipt. Therefore, employees end up having a better understanding of other areas outside their functional silos.

SAP supports a paperless mode operation, which changes the way users meet their reporting needs. The philosophy is that since everything is available online, many of the existing hardcopy reports should no longer be generated. Also, due to the validity checks built in, and since a single common database is used by all users, confidence in the data and results increases.

It should be no surprise that there are also some negatives. Due to easy information access, security concerns increase. For example, a lot of problems can be created if salary information is leaked or other confidential information is compromised. Also, reports available in the new SAP system may not be comparable to the customized reports previously available to the users.

Provides flexibility

Most of the required changes, over time, can be accommodated by configuration changes—rather than programming. This flexibility is a big plus. Business users can implement these changes and, consequently, their dependence on IT is decreased.

Influences development

SAP employs thousands of software developers worldwide. It periodically provides new releases and features, based on the input of thousands of its customers. Therefore, it effectively becomes the application developer for those who have implemented SAP. Consequently, organizations that use SAP can expect to have an application that will not be outdated due to lack of upgrades or functionality improvements. They will always have access to a very current system and, hence, their need for internal development will decrease significantly.

Chapter A4
Implementation Methodologies

HOW SAP PROJECTS ARE IMPLEMENTED

Basic essentials

The basic steps required to implement SAP are the following:

- ❏ Determine that the company is ready for implementation: an organization needs to be ready for change and its management has to be fully behind the project.
- ❏ Develop an implementation plan: without it, there will either be a slow and grinding project or a disaster.
- ❏ Develop the budget: this is a very critical factor that drives many elements including scope and schedule; depending on the approach (big bang versus phased implementation and type of cost structure (such as fixed cost project), the overall implementation cost and budget can vary considerably.
- ❏ Select the implementation partners: this determines the quality and level of external skills and experience that will be available for the project.

Implementation roadmap

The essential steps required to implement SAP are the following:

1 Modeling:
   This involves defining the business processes that the organization desires to be in place after implementation. These are known as the "to-be" business processes.
2 Mapping:
   This step involves comparing the business processes, identified in step 1, to the SAP processes. This mapping identifies which SAP processes and func-

tionality meet the future requirements of the company. These processes are selected for implementation.

3   Gap analysis:
    The shortcomings or gaps, between the requirements of the modeled processes and what SAP can provide, are identified.

4   Scoping:
    In this stage, after identifying what can or cannot be implemented in SAP, the project scope is finalized.

5   Customizing:
    The SAP™ R/3® software is customized so that it can meet the business and functional requirements of the company. This is done through the Implementation Guide for R/3 Customizing (IMG).

6   Testing:
    The configured system is subjected to extensive testing to ensure that the software works as required.

Big versus small approach

There are two implementation approaches that are generally followed for SAP projects. These are the big bang approach and the phased approach.

Big bang approach

In this approach, a full-blown SAP system is implemented. All the modules required by the company are configured and implemented. All legacy systems that can be replaced by SAP are targeted for retirement. All divisions and/or subsidiaries of the company are included in the single-phase project. This approach is very time consuming, heavy on resources and costs, and very risky as well.

Phased approach

In this approach, which is modest in nature, a step-by-step implementation is undertaken. The overall project is implemented in a number of phases. The objective is to avoid risk and work on smaller, and more manageable, projects. A number of options exist within the phased approach method. The following are some of the available options:

❑   Option 1:
    • Phase 1: only Finance and Logistics for all divisions
    • Phase 2: remaining modules for all divisions

❑ Option 2:
  • Phase 1: all modules for one division
  • Phase 2: all modules for remaining divisions
❑ Option 3:
  • Phase 1: only Finance and Logistics for one division
  • Phase 2: remaining modules for the first division
  • Phase 3: all modules for other divisions

METHODOLOGIES USED FOR SAP IMPLEMENTATIONS

An SAP project needs to be approached systematically and methodically. To be successful, such a project needs to be implemented using a structured methodology. An SAP project should not be implemented without a well-proven methodology. With such a tool, risk is reduced and a mechanism is provided to handle unexpected situations and problems. Without it, serious problems can occur including project derailment.

Conventional methodology

There are two methodologies used to implement SAP projects: Conventional and ASAP™. The conventional methodology, better known as the SAP Procedure Model, was initially widely used to implement SAP. In the past few years, it has been overshadowed by the rapid ASAP™ methodology. The SAP Procedure Model implementation can be divided into four major phases:

1   Organization and conceptual design
2   Detailed design and system setup
3   Go-live preparations
4   Productive operations

This methodology requires that a very detailed analysis of the existing systems, current functionality, and business processes be conducted. A significant amount of time is spent on matching "as-is" and "to-be" systems. Decision-making is very slow as it is based on consensus, which takes time to achieve.

A drawback of the Procedure Model is that even though it did not dictate it, too many implementations tried to mirror existing systems within SAP. Another negative of this methodology is that it uses a company's existing processes, instead of the SAP processes, as the starting point for the mapping process. Therefore, it has been usual for Procedure Model-based projects to have the following results:

❑ Lengthy implementation periods
❑ Scope continued to increase as analysis dragged on

ASAP™ methodology

In an effort to speed up SAP projects and keep costs under control, SAP introduced the ASAP™ methodology, which has been quite successful to-date. While a conventional project can typically take a couple of years, or even more in many cases, an ASAP™ project can be easily implemented within a year. With the ASAP™ methodology, an implementation period as short as five months has been achieved. This methodology is explained in-depth in the following sections and chapters.

Hybrid methodologies

Many companies have opted to use hybrid methodologies for implementing SAP. In such cases, some features of another methodology are incorporated into the ASAP methodology. There are two main reasons for using this type of methodology: it permits an ASAP shortcoming to be overcome and/or allows the continued partial use of a methodology that the company employees are used to.

COMPARING CONVENTIONAL AND ASAP™ METHODOLOGIES

As with any methodology, there are pros and cons associated with both the SAP methodologies. For some implementations, especially those requiring major re-engineering, the conventional methodology is the better choice. However, as the benefits listed in the following table show, the ASAP™ methodology is the clear overall winner.

		ASAP™	Conventional
		ASAP™ versus Conventional methodology	
1.	Time frame	Fast implementation	Slow implementation
2.	Approach	Rushed without in-depth analysis	Based on extensive analysis and consensus
3.	Re-engineering	More due to implementation of new SAP supported processes	Less because tendency is to mirror existing processes
4.	Features/ functionality	Vanilla	Custom
5.	Implementation	Very focused and narrow	Comprehensive
6.	Configuration	Primarily done by consultants	Significant employee participation
7.	Upgrades	Less testing required as minimal code changes are implemented	More testing required due to extensive code modifications
8.	Cost	Low	High
9.	Documentation	Minimal	Extensive
10.	ABAP™ development	Minimal due to vanilla implementation	Extensive due to excessive custom requirements
11.	Number of consultants	Relatively few are required	Large team of experts is required
12.	Employee turnover	Low due to less knowledge gained during implementation	High as extensive knowledge gained can be leveraged for a better job
13.	Knowledge transfer for employees	Low since project is rushed and consultants allocate insufficient time	High since features are configured gradually with employee participation

Chapter A5
ASAP™ Methodology

BACKGROUND AND OVERVIEW

Need for ASAP™

ERP packages, especially SAP, encompass a broad range of functionality. During a typical project, only some of this functionality can be implemented. Since the specific needs and requirements of implementing companies can vary significantly, the software needs to be customized to meet their individual requirements. Therefore, a satisfactory implementation that can address these issues, as well as others, can take a fairly long time, be costly, and fraught with risks.

With the conventional SAP implementation methodology, it was very difficult to configure flexibly and quickly. This conflicted with the requirements of mid-sized companies who demanded rapid implementation that could be measured in months instead of years. Therefore, with time being of the essence and a fast implementation being a difficult objective to achieve, it became apparent that a different implementation approach was required.

SAP's realization that it needed to be more responsive to the needs of its customers led to the introduction of the AcceleratedSAP™ (ASAP) rapid implementation methodology in 1996. ASAP™ initially targeted mid-sized customers with revenues in the $200 million to $2.5 billion range.

A point to note is that in a shift from the past, ASAP™ reflected a change from focusing on tools to an emphasis on methodology. It is a methodology that supports project management, team members, business process consultants, external consultants, as well as technical areas.

What ASAP™ can do

ASAP™ has been designed with the objective of standardizing and streamlining SAP implementation. The following are primary ASAP™ characteristics:

- Optimizes time, quality and resources
- Leverages best business practices
- Delivers a process oriented project map (ASAP™ roadmap) that provides step-by-step directions
- Determines implementation cost and schedule; cuts implementation cost and time
- Provides process, tools, training and service
- Provides detailed help through various implementation phases
- Answers questions about implementation cost and time, how to ensure quality, tools to use, and resources required
- Provides checklists, questionnaires and technical guides
- Supports continuous improvement

How ASAP™ is implemented

Organizations implementing SAP typically do not have the in-house expertise required to implement the complex software. Therefore, it is usual for such companies to partner with an external organization, such as one of the Big 5 consulting companies or a smaller integrator, to implement their SAP project.

SAP recommends that its clients team up with an ASAP™ partner when they implement an SAP project. A company obtains ASAP™ partner certification if at least 70% of its consultants have completed ASAP™ training and it has fully adopted the ASAP methodology.

In a sharp departure from the widespread practice in the past, according to the 2004 ITtoolbox ERP Implementation Survey, 56.9% of small-sized companies do not partner with for new implementations and additions of new modules. 48.2% of medium-sized companies reported no partnering compared to 36.7% for large-sized companies.

ASAP™ implementation costs

No two SAP implementations are identical because there are too many variables involved. Variables include the company size, number of divisions/subsidiaries, number of systems, overall scope, approach, company culture, experience of partners, etc. Therefore, it is difficult to generalize the cost of implementing SAP at an organization. The main cost components are:

- ❏ Consulting fees (typically the largest component):
- ❏ In-house labor
- ❏ Software license fees
- ❏ Training fees (typically the smallest component)
- ❏ Hardware costs

When ASAP™ is not an appropriate choice

The ASAP™ methodology is not appropriate for all types of SAP implementations. It is ideally suited for enterprises that do not have extensive modification requirements or require re-engineering. For such companies, other methodologies are more appropriate.

ASAP™ is the methodology of choice when rapid deployment is highly stressed. However, when there is more emphasis on process improvement than on rapid deployment, which occurs when enterprises require significant process and operational improvements or re-engineering, the conventional implementation methodology is a more appropriate choice.

Current ASAP™ status

ASAP™ is now established as the SAP standard implementation methodology. Since its introduction, ASAP™ has been used in thousands of projects worldwide. A very large pool of experts, comprising more than 28,700 SAP and partner consultants, has been trained in this methodology. Many of SAP's implementation partners are either using ASAP™ as their standard methodology or have incorporated it into their own methodologies.

ASAP™ COMPONENTS AND TOOLS

Where can they be used

SAP has provided a number of components, tools and accelerators for supporting ASAP™ implementations. ASAP™ components, which can be used in any type of

SAP project, include forms, questionnaires, and guides. Many ASAP™ partners use ASAP methodology components in conjunction with their own implementation methodologies and practices.

ASAP™ tools and accelerators, which can be used to streamline and improve implementations, are described in the following sections. While these tools were developed for ASAP™ implementations, most of them can also be used during SAP implementations based on the conventional methodology. Various ASAP™ components, functions, and organizational structures can be tailored, or deactivated, to suit individual requirements

R/3™ Reference Model

This visual tool represents the SAP™ R/3® system using graphical models. It depicts, among other aspects, business processes along with any variants, data, as well as organizational structures. The R/3™ reference model, which enables the bigger picture to be viewed, can be accessed through the Business Navigator. This tool links the process models to SAP transactions.

Toolkit

The Toolkit includes all the ASAP™ tools such as the Business Engineer, Project Estimator, and Implementation Assistant. Each of these tools serves a specific purpose. A number of the Toolkit tools are described in subsequent sections.

Business Engineer

The R/3™ Business Engineer (BE) is a set of configuration and implementation tools for modeling, configuration, implementation, continuous improvement, and documentation. ASAP™ utilizes the Business Engineer's powerful capabilities for configuring the system. The Business Engineer and the tools contained within it:

❑ Provide a toolkit of specific business processes for expediting implementation
❑ Incorporate over 1,000 business processes and more than 170 core business objects
❑ Incorporate best business practices
❑ Simplify configuration
❑ Support custom configuration
❑ Allow graphical methods for viewing, navigation and configuration

❑ Efficiently expedite R/3™ configuration
❑ Support changes and system improvements required due to business changes
❑ Enable easy modification of the corporate structure
❑ Can adapt existing configuration to new requirements/changes

Together, ASAP™ and the Business Engineer can help to:

❑ Use industry specific business processes and templates
❑ Determine which R/3™ processes are most suitable for the company
❑ Implement new processes or restructure existing ones
❑ Optimize business processes through the use of proven scenarios and processes both during, and after, implementation
❑ Provide structured planning and pre-configuration
❑ Configure according to each individual requirement
❑ Manage time, cost and quality
❑ Reduce implementation time
❑ Attain a faster return on investment

The Business Engineer can be used by a diverse audience including consultants, business professionals and experts, as well as all types of companies—large, medium, and small. It supports H™L based documentation, new platforms, as well as modeling tools and software provided by independent vendors.

Project Estimator

This is a pre-sales tool used to estimate the resources, time and cost required to implement SAP at a particular site. The Project Estimator relies on a series of pre-defined interview questions that are posed to the company's senior executives, business and technical managers, as well as project team members. The purpose is to gather information needed to assess:

❑ Expectations
❑ Company expertise: strengths and weaknesses
❑ Degree of complexity of business processes
❑ Project scope
❑ Deployment time desired
❑ SAP team expertise
❑ Risk factors

The information gathered is used to create a high level estimate. It is also used to create the scope document and project plan.

Implementation Assistant

The Implementation Assistant serves as a navigation tool for the ASAP™ Implementation Roadmap, described in a later section, which provides guidance during various implementation phases. It consists of many tools and elements, such as the:

❑ ASAP™ Roadmap: which consists of five phases
❑ Project Plan: which contains the budget, resource and work plans
❑ Knowledge Corner: which is a warehouse of information encompassing configuration, technical tools, customizing wizards, etc.

The Implementation Assistant has the following features:

❑ Covers the five ASAP™ implementation phases down to the task level
❑ Includes a description for each Roadmap task
❑ Provides guidance through every Roadmap task
❑ Indicates which tasks are to be performed, who needs to be designated to do it, and how long it should take to complete
❑ Includes a detailed "how-to" for each Roadmap task; shows how to perform specific tasks, complete checklists, check with technical guidelines, etc.
❑ Links documents accessed through the Roadmap
❑ Includes specific examples, templates, forms and checklists
❑ Provides hyperlinks from tasks to tools, templates and documents
❑ Contains extensive testing guide that can help configure associated business processes
❑ Provides capability to drill down into work packages, activities, and tasks from the Roadmap's five phases

Question and Answer Database

This is a tool that is used to gather requirements for business processes, conversions, reports, interfaces, enhancements, and authorizations. The questions and answers are stored in a database, which serves as a useful repository for this information. The business requirements generated through the Question and Answer (Q&A) database are incorporated in the Business Blueprint document.

Issues Database

This tool is used to document issues and concerns that arise during project implementation. A common and central location ensures that all identified issues receive high visibility. It also ensures easier assignment, monitoring, and updating of the recorded issues.

ASAP™ Roadmap

This ASAP™ component defines a systematic approach and methodology that incorporates a project plan for an SAP implementation. For various project activities, it describes:

❑ What is to be done
❑ Why it is needed
❑ How it is to be performed
❑ Who should implement it

The Roadmap is a step-by-step guide that is divided into five phases. These are:

❑ Phase 1: Project Preparation
❑ Phase 2: Business Blueprint
❑ Phase 3: Realization (includes Simulation and Validation)
❑ Phase 4: Final Preparation
❑ Phase 5: Go-Live and Support

The implementation time required for each phase depends on the total project implementation time that, typically, ranges between 6 and 18 months for ASAP™ projects. For example, at a mid-cap company project, for which the total implementation time was one year, the time spent on each phase was as follows:

❑ Project Preparation: 1 month
❑ Business Blueprint: 2 months
❑ Realization: 6 months: (2 months for Simulation + 4 months for Validation)
❑ Final Preparation: 3 months

In another project at a 2 billion dollar company, which lasted 18 months, the breakdown was as follows:

- ❑   Project Preparation: 1 month
- ❑   Business Blueprint: 5 months
- ❑   Realization: 9 months (4 months for Simulation + 5 months for Validation)
- ❑   Final Preparation: 3 months

Accelerators

ASAP™ uses components called accelerators that include examples, checklists, templates, etc. Depending on a project's requirements, an accelerator can be used in conjunction with other tools. Accelerators can be used in any type of implementation, even if all ASAP™ components are not used in that implementation.

An accelerator can be used, even when a different approach and methodology is being followed, to meet implementation objectives. These objectives, which are usually in sync with those of an ASAP™ project, can include speedier implementation, lower cost, efficient resource utilization, quality improvement, etc.

Project Quality Check

A project quality review is conducted during the important phases of an implementation. The objective of this review is to assess the various areas (including technical, business and management), gauge progress made, review deliverables, and assess risks.

EarlyWatch™

This is a preventive service offered by SAP. It allows SAP experts to proactively analyze the system before going live. Based on its findings, SAP makes recommendations for optimizing applications and performance so that potential production problems can be avoided. This helps ensure that when the system goes live, most parameters are well tuned and the system is optimized.

EarlyWatch™ is just one of the many services and support that SAP can provide. Others include the Online Service System (OSS), Concept Check, and Going Live check. Each of these tools is used for quality assurance.

Concept Check Tool

This tool is used to investigate the technical aspects of the project by performing quality checks. These checks are used to verify that the application has been correctly configured, provide data for the Going Live check that is performed at the end of the project, and to provide warning of potential performance issues due to data volume and configuration conflicts.

CHAPTER A6
PHASE 1—PROJECT PREPARATION

Many factors can contribute to the success or failure of ASAP™ as well as other types of software project. A critical factor, especially for SAP projects, is organizational readiness and project preparation. This includes project planning, project organization, as well as the determination of project standards. These topics are discussed in the following sections.

ORGANIZATIONAL READINESS

Getting decision makers on board

An ASAP™ project is doomed to failure if the organization considering implementation is not ready to implement SAP. Therefore, one of the first tasks should be to determine if all the key decision makers are on board for the implementation. This step should precede the mobilization of the implementation team's internal and external members.

Management tasks

Management and key decision makers, whose support is critical, should provide a firm commitment that will increase the probability of a successful implementation. They should:

❑ Provide top management commitment and support
❑ Clearly define project goals and objectives
❑ Agree on the different project steps
❑ Provide an efficient decision making process
❑ Create an environment that is ready for change
❑ Setup a team that is qualified and represents the various functional areas

Linking personal and project success

An ASAP™, or even a conventional SAP, project cannot succeed if it lacks management support. With strong backing, a project can move along smoothly and hurdles can be navigated with relative ease. Therefore, it is imperative that management, especially stakeholders, should be intimately involved with the project. They should be made to feel that their own success, or failure, is linked to the success, or failure, of the project.

PROJECT PLANNING

Identifying critical elements

There are a number of steps that need to be taken during the initial (planning) phase of the project. These are the cornerstones upon which the success of a project is built. Weakness in any of these areas can lay the seeds for problems or even outright failure. Therefore, these basic elements should be identified, understood, and implemented.

Since the needs and requirements for each project can be different, due to the uniqueness of each business, the list of critical elements can vary from implementation to implementation. The following sections list some critical elements (guiding principles and project business drivers), which were considered by one company during the planning phase of its SAP project. However, as noted earlier, most of these elements can be applied during any software implementation.

Guiding principles

These are the high-level principles that should be defined at the start of a project. They define and communicate the company's vision. The guiding principles keep the project focused and, in case of conflicts during project implementation, are the basis upon which conflicts are resolved. The following is an example of a set of guiding principles adopted by one company:

❑   Implement R/3™ standard business processes
❑   Implement SAP™ R/3® software as an interactive online system
❑   Focus on customer satisfaction and supporting SAP™ R/3® software business transactions
❑   Adhere to business basics

Strategic guiding principles

These are the business principles that address lower level strategic issues. By following a strategy that is well defined, it becomes easier for the implementation to achieve its business objectives. The following is an example of a set of strategic guiding principles:

❑ Implement an integrated enterprise system—not best of breed
❑ Strive for "out of the box" initial implementation
❑ First phase implementation:
   • need not replace all the legacy systems' functionality
   • must run the business and be built on an expandable foundation
❑ Enterprise deployment will require business process changes
❑ Buy not make, when possible
❑ Adhere to open standards
❑ Always wear the company hat first, your functional hat next
❑ Think globally—enterprise-wide and not just headquarters
❑ Core modules must be implemented within one year
❑ Tightly control changes and minimize investment to the legacy environment
❑ Have clear signoff criteria

Project business drivers

Typically, these are the business drivers for selecting the ERP software for a particular implementation. These drivers are the main contributors to the benefits expected by implementing the software. They are the basis, in many cases, for the metrics used to evaluate and compare performance (before and after implementation). The following is an example of a set of project business drivers used by one company:

❑ Increase customer loyalty
❑ Improve revenue and earnings growth
❑ Increase profitability growth
❑ Improve performance (efficiency)
❑ Avoid risk due to obsolete computer systems

Budget, standards and metrics

During this phase, a number of other tasks that are usually associated with the start of a project are initiated. For example, the project manager starts to prepare the project plan, budgets, project standards, and metrics. The use of various accelerators starts coming into play.

BUILDING THE IMPLEMENTATION TEAM

Organizational structure and project team authority

Forming the implementation team is an important task during this phase of the project. Typically, the project team consists of:

❑ Consultants drawn from external organizations
❑ Internal company employees drawn from various functional areas

The first step involves creating the project's organizational structure and setting up the project team authority, which has the following responsibilities:

❑ Propose, approve and implement process changes if:
  • required by SAP
  • they support the business objectives
❑ Define what is in/out of scope; develop and implement a formal change of scope procedure
❑ Define high and low priorities within functionality
❑ Escalate issues outside its direct authority to the Steering Committee and senior management for rapid resolution
❑ Pull in special expertise from functional organizations, when required
❑ Develop and implement documentation control procedures for the project team

Team membership

For SAP implementations, team membership is split into the following main groups:

❑ Client personnel; these include:
  • client's employees
  • client's contractors
❑ Implementation partner/integrator's personnel; these include:
  • employees of the partner company
  • employees of the partner company's sub-contractor(s)
  • independent contractors

The client's team usually consists of two types of members:

❑ Core team members: they have to dedicate 100% of their time to the project
❑ Extended team members: they have to dedicate 20-50% of their time, depending on the project phase, to the project

An assessment is required to determine the internal strength (capability), and availability, of personnel who need to be pulled into the project implementation team. Depending on this assessment, the number and type of external team members/consultants required for the project is determined.

Selecting consultants

It is important that consultants should be selected with a great deal of care. Too many issues can arise if consultants are not carefully selected or if they are not adequately monitored and controlled. Problems that can arise include, but are not limited to, the following:

❑ High turnover due to the integrator's scheduling needs
❑ Client's requirements take a back seat
❑ Assignment of consultants with inadequate experience in the functionality being implemented
❑ Knowledge transfer is negatively impacted
❑ Excessive travel expenses

How teams are organized

The project team is typically organized by modules or functions. For example, it is usual to have different teams for Finance, Logistics, Sales & Distribution, and Project System. Usually, there are additional teams such as Basis (Infrastructure and System Administration), Quality Assurance, Training, and Communications. Some teams are also organized by processes such as Purchasing-to-Payment and Order-to-Cash.

There are two common approaches for organizing the development (programming) group. In the first approach, they are grouped by functional module and, depending on the resource requirements, a couple of developers are assigned to each module. In the second approach, all developers are assigned to a single group. This enables all development requests to be routed through a single responsible person, which helps in screening and prioritizing the numerous requests that come in during the life of the project. Another benefit is that depending on the urgency and workload within the different functional modules, a developer can be quickly reassigned to work on a different module that needs additional resources.

Team characteristics

An SAP project team is a large contingent that consists of employees and consultants of varying traits and skill levels. Even though various specific and specialized skill sets are required, the team should collectively have certain characteristics such as the ability to:

- ❑ Analyze the impact of the new ERP system on business processes, old and new, across the enterprise
- ❑ Analyze functional and implementation requirements
- ❑ Design an integrated system
- ❑ Provide ongoing knowledge transfer to employees throughout the project

Team building

During the project preparation phase, team-building activities are initiated. In SAP projects, it is important to build a cohesive team whose members understand the overall picture. This task is essential because team members are drawn from diverse groups including internal company employees, integrator's employees and sub-contractors, as well as independent consultants. Additionally, many of the internal team members may never have worked together previously or been exposed to projects of this type and size, which require a unique and different approach.

There are many types of team building activities available for such teams. A popular approach is to assemble the team for an offsite meeting lasting 2-3 days. During this extended meeting, team members get to know each other. They are made aware of the unique characteristics of the SAP™ R/3® software, business and technical implications, and their interdependence on other team members during implementation. The importance of working as an integrated, mutually dependent, team is highly stressed during such meetings.

Training for team members

In order to introduce the internal team members to SAP functionality and features, they are put through Level I, or overview, training during the project preparation phase. It is recommended that this training start as early as possible.

CHAPTER A7
PHASE 2—BUSINESS BLUEPRINT

OBJECTIVE AND SCOPE

Analyzing the business

The objective Business Blueprint, the second phase of an ASAP™ project, is to understand how the company runs its existing business and determine its implementation requirements based on the organization's future needs. To achieve this objective, a comprehensive analysis of the business is undertaken. The analysis involves understanding the company's business, determining how the existing processes work, and identifying the functionality supported by the existing systems. Subsequently, a comparison is made of the existing business practices and functionality to those supported by the SAP software.

The blueprint phase analysis also encompasses the identification of existing platforms and applications, interfaces to be developed (to systems that will not be retired and replaced by SAP), requirements for any bolt-ons (other applications integrated with SAP to form a part of the core system), data migration requirements, etc. Gaps, which refer to existing functionality that an implemented SAP will not support, are also identified.

Interview objectives

During this phase, company executives, managers, and other key employees are interviewed extensively. The interviewing is done in individual as well as group sessions. The questioning is based on a series of template questions. Based on the answers provided, and the discussions that take place during this process, the consultants understand and/or define:

- ❑ Company's business
- ❑ How the enterprise operates
- ❑ Critical elements of the business
- ❑ Desired business processes
- ❑ Business and functionality requirements
- ❑ Implementation scope
- ❑ Implementation risks

Based on the knowledge gained during the interview process, the consultants start visualizing how to tailor the feature rich R/3™ software so that it can meet the company's unique requirements.

Reference scope document

At the end of the blueprint phase, a very comprehensive document, called the *Blueprint Document*, is generated and published. The signed-off blueprint document effectively becomes the scope and reference document for the project.

Blueprint document contents

The blueprint document can be described as the visual model of the enterprise after the SAP™ R/3® software has been implemented. It documents:

- ❑ Existing functionality
- ❑ Future functionality after SAP implementation
- ❑ R/3™ processes currently in operation as well as those required to run the business in the future
- ❑ Implementation scope
- ❑ Organizational structure required for implementing SAP
- ❑ Deferred functionality (to be implemented during a subsequent phase/project)
- ❑ Gaps
- ❑ Potential risks

The blueprint document, in addition to the items listed previously, also identifies:

- ❑ Master data and transaction data
- ❑ Data conversion and migration requirements
- ❑ Interfaces required to be built
- ❑ Legacy systems to be retired
- ❑ Bolt-on requirements
- ❑ Reporting requirements

Training for team members

During the blueprint phase, project team members start Level II training, which involves understanding the R/3™ business processes. During this training, they learn how to configure the SAP system.

DEFINING THE ORGNIZATIONAL STRUCTURE

During the blueprint phase, the SAP organizational structure is defined based upon the organization's business processes. This structure significantly impacts the way in which SAP is configured to meet the needs of the enterprise. For example, the definition of plants impacts customization, data entry requirements, maintenance requirements, reporting and analysis, etc.

Organizational structure characteristics

The organizational structure, as applicable to the SAP model, has the following characteristics:

❑ Is central to SAP™ R/3® software operation and control
❑ Needs to be defined before any significant configuration can be done
❑ Provides the fundamental data and functional architecture within the SAP system
❑ Enables complex structures
❑ Enables structures to be designed based on each company's business processes
❑ Is flexible, which permits changes to structures
❑ Flexibility enables separate structures and views for different functional areas such as purchasing, sales, and accounting
❑ Some changes are difficult to implement; others are not feasible even if they are easy to configure because of their significant, and unacceptable, impact on some other functional area(s)
❑ Enables inter-company processing

Impact of organizational structure

The influence of the SAP organizational structure, which is flexible and can be modified to meet the dynamic needs of business, can be far reaching. For example, it can influence how:

- ❑ SAP functionality will meet the business requirements
- ❑ Inter-company processing will take place
- ❑ Reporting and analysis is performed

The organizational structure also determines how data is defined in the system, complexity of data input, and the size of the master data files. Therefore, it is highly recommended that the organizational structure be defined as early as possible.

While flexibility permits changes to be made, any changes made after a project is in full swing can potentially be very expensive and also delay the project. Changes to the organizational structure can be made at any stage. However, any late stage changes should be limited to fine tuning only. When the project is in full swing, changes should typically be limited to two reasons only:

- ❑ Business changes have occurred since the structure was defined
- ❑ Existing structure, if implemented, will create major problems

Important elements of the organizational structure

Company code

This is the highest element in the organizational structure. The company code is a legal and organizationally independent unit. It represents an independent accounting unit that has its own financial statements. Its other characteristics are:

- ❑ Produces its own financial documents; generates balance sheet and P&L statement
- ❑ Subsidiaries are usually classified as companies
- ❑ Financial statements for all companies can be consolidated
- ❑ All financial documents are posted at the company level
- ❑ Assignments at the company level include fiscal year, chart of accounts, and accounting currency
- ❑ Limited master data is defined at the company level

Controlling area

This represents an organizational element for which the management of costs and profits can be performed. Its two main elements are:

- ❑ Cost center, which is the basic unit for collecting costs
- ❑ Profit center, which collects revenues and costs (through cost centers)

Business structure

The various functional areas, such as Logistics, Finance, and Human Resources, can define their own structures independently. The following are examples of structure elements in Logistics:

❑ Plants
❑ Sales organizations
❑ Purchasing organizations
❑ Storage locations

Chapter A8
Phase 3—Realization

During the realization phase of the ASAP™ roadmap, the Business Blueprint is converted into reality. During this phase, the system is configured, as per the Business Blueprint requirements, and tested. This is not a straightforward process. Rather, the transformation of the company's business requirements into the "to-be" business solution is iterative in nature: build, test, refine, and re-test. The following sections describe the realization sub-phases and the various tasks carried out during their implementation.

SIMULATION

Configuration

In this first configuration step, the consultants quickly configure the preliminary design. This is the baseline system that is based upon the Business Blueprint document. This configuration covers about 80% of the company's business processes and daily business transactions. Configuration typically involves modifying the SAP™ R/3® software through non-programming methods such as changes in SAP baselines settings, flipping switches, modifying table entries, etc. Most of the changes are made through the IMG within the Business Engineer.

Playbacks

After the initial configuration has been completed, the system is demonstrated to selected managers and key members of the end-user community. These playback demonstrations introduce the new software, to a few key employees, and start the process of getting the end-user community on board. It also starts the feedback and iteration process, which ultimately leads to the final configured system. Playbacks are generally performed periodically based on the consultants' preferences and style. Some like to demonstrate the configured functionality on a weekly basis. Others prefer a schedule based on the importance of the process being configured or the completion of a particular process or functionality.

Demonstration of the configured systems and processes is an important step because the end-user community representatives are required to signoff before the system can be switched on. If they are not involved with the implementation from the beginning, they can impede the signoff process due to legitimate concerns about approving something they are not familiar and comfortable with.

Other tasks

During this phase, project team members obtain in-depth Level II training. They are also initiated in the important task of knowledge transfer, which is required for ensuring that the system will be well run and maintained in the future—after the consultants are gone. This is a task which consultants should be required to perform systematically at every stage of the project, instead of at the end.

VALIDATION

Configuration

During this sub-phase, the design is refined and finalized. The project team fine-tunes the system so that all the business and process requirements are configured. During this phase, the remaining 20% of the business processes and transactions are configured. This phase covers the customization of the company's unique business processes and exceptions. At the end of this phase, a fully configured system becomes available.

Business process procedures

An important task performed during the realization phase is the creation of a business process master list. Team members start writing business process procedures (BPPs), which document the configured system. This documentation can serve three purposes. It can be used:

❑ For training (without any changes)
❑ As the template from which the final training documentation is created
❑ As reference documentation

End-user documentation

The ultimate test of an implementation is the ability of users to use the system effectively. For this, they have to be trained on how to use the SAP application. For their effective training, quality end-user training documentation is required. Typically, for this purpose, business process procedures (BPPs), which are based on individual transactions that need to be executed during operations, are leveraged. Typically, the contract for this task is awarded to the project implementation partner or companies specializing in training and documentation.

UNIT AND INTEGRATION TESTING

Need for testing

No business software can afford to be released into production without extensive testing. A rigorously tested software can be introduced with minimum pain and disruption and, not surprisingly, is usually accepted quickly. On the other hand, inadequately tested software can have serious repercussions including the ultimate penalty—being discarded.

Testing an integrated ERP software like SAP is a very challenging task. At the high level, the software's testing objective is to answer the following questions:

- ❑ Are the new processes supporting business operations?
- ❑ Is the software performing as configured and expected?
- ❑ Is SAP interacting with external systems as expected?
- ❑ Are the performance criteria being met for the various business processes?

The benefits that can be gained by testing thoroughly include:

- ❑ Confirmation that the processes work as expected
- ❑ Have a configuration that is streamlined
- ❑ Performance that can be guaranteed
- ❑ Improved integration
- ❑ Lower costs
- ❑ Reduced risks
- ❑ Screening of dirty data, which highlights inadequate data preparation and cleanup

The testing of the implemented software is done in two phases:

❑ Unit testing
❑ Integration testing

Unit testing

Every configuration change, even though it may affect only a small part of a business process, needs to be tested. During unit testing, which is the initial testing phase, the focus is on individual transactions. For example, transactions such as creating a vendor, creating a customer, modifying a purchase order, receiving a purchased item into stock, etc., are tested. For each transaction required to be executed during business operations, a script or a business process procedure (BPP) is created.

The various transactions are tested in stages/cycles within a specific functional area. With each cycle, the testing becomes more complex. For example, the following is a typical sequence of tests that are conducted in the Materials Management module:

❑ Create a purchase order for one organization
❑ Change the purchase order
❑ Receive goods against the purchase order
❑ Return partial quantity of goods that have been received
❑ Create purchase orders for all organizations

This incremental testing in stages can continue to become more complex. When the need arises to integrate other functional areas and test complete processes, the second phase of testing, known as integration testing, comes into play.

Integration testing

Business scenarios

After configuration has been completed, a number of business scenarios are developed by the project team, in conjunction with key members of the end-user community, for the purpose of integration testing. These scenarios cover all the business areas that are impacted by the SAP implementation. They also include the testing of interfaces, which are the links between the SAP™ R/3® software and other systems. These links, which can be to disparate systems such as a warehouse system, third-party tax software, bar coding system, etc., can be very complicated and require thorough testing.

Integration testing is usually performed with a process-oriented perspective. For example, a typical scenario will include all the steps required for creating a purchase order—from order entry through shipping and invoicing. After a business scenario has been developed, it is thoroughly tested. More the customization of software that is done, greater is the complexity and effort required to perform integration testing.

End-user involvement

To validate the data migrated from the legacy systems, additional resources from the various functional groups are required during the testing phase. During integration testing, the need for end-user involvement is very high. Besides being able to take some load off the core team members, end-users can be used for validation due to their intimate knowledge of the company business.

Signoff

The configured system and business scenarios need to be approved by the end-users. End-user acceptance and buy-in should be documented because it prevents complaints from coming in later—after the system becomes operational. If the end-users are involved in the testing phase, the signoff process can be quite smooth.

Testing process

There are two ways in which testing is usually performed:

1   A quality assurance (QA) team is organized and made responsible for all testing. This team typically consists of a few core team members plus a few business users drawn from the various functional groups. Each team member is assigned a few business scenarios and made responsible for testing them from end-to-end, i.e., the complete process.

2   Each functional team performs testing within its own functional area. Each tester is responsible for only a small segment of the business process. During testing, when a process moves to another functional area, such as from Purchasing to Finance, the testing responsibility is also shifted to the appropriate functional area. The next tester, from Finance in this case, continues testing from the point where the previous tester, from Purchasing, left off.

The advantage of having multiple testers is that each tester knows his own functional area very well. Therefore, such a tester can execute and test the business scenarios very quickly. However, in such a case, the cross-functional knowledge picked up by the team members is limited due to their being exposed to only a few transactions within their functional own area.

Who does the testing

The amount of testing involved during an SAP implementation can be fairly extensive because it involves executing business scenarios encompassing different functional areas. This leads to the requirement for testers to be drawn from the following groups:

❑   Full-time project core team members
❑   Part-time project core team members
❑   Business users/Subject matter experts

DATA CONVERSIONS

When the new SAP™ R/3® software is switched on, it cannot be used effectively unless the system has been previously loaded with a large amount of data. The required data includes both transaction data and master data (such as part numbers, purchase orders, sales orders, bill of materials, etc.). Due to the large data volumes typically required, and the time and cost involved in manual data entry, migrating data from legacy systems to SAP in an efficient manner becomes a necessity.

Factors to consider

The volume and type of data that needs to be migrated into SAP from the legacy systems can vary from implementation to implementation. The factors that determine this include:

❑   Business necessity
❑   Type of data (transaction or master data)
❑   Quantity of data
❑   Quality of data
❑   Amount of data cleanup effort required
❑   Time required for loading
❑   Constraints due to data loading sequence
❑   Cost involved
❑   Complexity of migrating data
❑   Complexity of business rules to be applied

❑ Standard or custom programs required
❑ Availability of ABAP™ and legacy programming resources
❑ Historical requirements
❑ Tax and legal requirements
❑ Reporting requirements
❑ Availability of end-users for validation

Data migration methods

There are two basic steps for transferring data into the SAP™ R/3® system. The first is conversion, which requires legacy data to be formatted, into a structure called a flat file, so that SAP™ R/3® can read it. In the next step, an SAP data transfer program is used to read the flat file and move it into the SAP™ R/3® system. To transfer data, the SAP standard data transfer programs use one of the following methods:

❑ Batch input: simulates data input by processing the normal screens of the corresponding online transaction
❑ Direct input: thoroughly checks the flat file before processing it; in the next step, the R/3 database is updated directly

When to start data migration

The data migration effort is often started late during many implementations, which leads to many problems. It is highly advisable that this effort be started as early as possible. Data migration, using small sample data sets, should be practiced frequently before go-live. When this effort is started early, its effectiveness is limited during the initial data loads due to the incomplete system configuration. In many cases, loads fail due to incomplete or changing configuration. However, the benefit of starting early is that it provides valuable experience to the developers. Since data migration and loading is an iterative process, running 2-3 test loads before the system goes live can ensure that the final data load runs smoothly. The test runs also help in estimating the time it will take to completely load the SAP production system in the final run.

Which data to migrate

Every enterprise operates differently, collects different data, and has different types of legacy systems. Therefore, each implementation can be expected to have a different grouping of the data that needs to be migrated. The following lists are the master data and transaction data, automated and manual, migrated during one implementation:

Automated Master Data

❑ Chart of accounts
❑ General ledger
❑ Fixed assets
❑ Material master
❑ Customer master
❑ Price conditions
❑ Service parts
❑ Sites and units
❑ Configurations
❑ Vendor master
❑ Purchase order info records
❑ Routings
❑ Bill of materials

Manual Master Data

❑ Cost centers/departments
❑ Work centers
❑ Sales pricing/discounts condition tables
❑ Customer material info records
❑ Templates for product proposals
❑ Sales employees

Automated Transaction Data

❑ General ledger balances
❑ Open accounts payable
❑ Open accounts receivable
❑ Open quotations
❑ Open sales orders
❑ Service contracts
❑ Field service reports
❑ Open service calls
❑ Inventory quantities
❑ Consumption history

Manual Transaction Data

❑ Open production orders
❑ Open quotations

Data cleanup

Why dirty data is an issue

A common problem is that the issue of dirty data is ignored or given insufficient importance. Therefore, the cost and effort required to perform this task is frequently underestimated. In many cases, data quality is given scant attention until it starts creating serious issues in the SAP production system. When that happens, it seriously impacts business and, often, requires crisis management.

What cleanup involves

Even if the legacy data is clean to start with, it may need to be modified or filtered before it is loaded into SAP. For example:

❑ There can be a mismatch in the parts numbering scheme (alpha versus numeric)
❑ The number of characters used for identifying existing parts may be in excess of what SAP permits
❑ Vendors who have been inactive for a certain period, such as 24 months, may need to be screened out

Another common problem is duplication: an existing customer may be having multiple entries, such as IBM and International Business Machines. Such entries would indicate that there are two customers instead of only one. Such issues require that the data be filtered and/or restructured—by changing field length, type, etc.—before it is moved into SAP from the legacy system.

Where is the data checked

The data that is migrated into SAP needs to be clean and validated. There are two options available for ensuring that only clean data resides in SAP when it goes live. These are:

1   Cleanup on the legacy system side before loading (at the source)
2   Cleanup on the SAP side after loading (at the target)

In the first case, most of the cleanup effort takes place on the legacy side. After end-users validate the data, it is loaded into SAP. On the SAP side, validation is done by the system during the loading process. Subsequently, after loading has been completed, data owners check and validate the master data and transaction data and, if required, clean it.

In the second case, minimal checking is performed on the legacy side. It is expected that the validation rules enforced by SAP, during loading, will prevent most of the bad data from coming in. After it has been loaded into SAP, the migrated data is cleaned, if required, and validated by the functional team members and key business users.

Who needs to validate migrated data

It should be emphasized that the technical resources, i.e., ABAP™ and legacy programmers, should not be relied upon to check and validate business data. The end-users should be responsible for validating such data because they own, and know, it very well.

Tools available

A number of data conversion tools from companies like Conversion Sciences, which uses a proprietary R/3™ data conversion tool called Proteus, and ETI are available. They can be useful in reducing data migration costs.

INTERFACES, ENHANCEMENTS, AND REPORTS

Interfaces

The introduction of SAP into an enterprise typically results in the retirement of many, though not all, legacy systems. To ensure that the remaining systems and bolt-ons talk to SAP, either in one-way or two-way mode, interfaces need to be built. In some cases, SAP provides a generic interface to its own software. The coding requirements for interfaces are not very complicated or extensive. However, they do require knowledge of the legacy systems being retired. SAP supports a number of technologies including RFC (remote function call), IDOC (internal document format), BAPI's (business APIs), and EDI (electronic data interchange), ALE (application link enabling), etc.

Considerable time and effort is involved in building and testing interfaces. Their development can require highly skilled and technical resources. A significant part of integration testing involves testing interfaces. Therefore, early identification of the interfaces to be built can ensure that their development starts early on in the project, which ensures timely completion. This enables thorough testing and prevents the scope of testing to be reduced that, typically, occurs when interface development falls behind schedule.

Enhancements

In order to accommodate specific needs at every implementation, a number of custom enhancements are needed. These can range from a few for a vanilla implementation to many for a more customized implementation. Some enhancements can be very simple, while others can be fairly complex, especially if an attempt is made to mirror the retiring legacy systems environment.

Enhancements can require significant ABAP™ resources, testing, and SAP source code modifications. A major disadvantage associated with an enhancement is that it will always require special attention and testing every time an SAP release or upgrade is implemented. The advantage is that enhancements can make certain processes run more smoothly. Therefore, every enhancement request should be carefully evaluated before a decision is made to proceed with it.

Reports

Reporting should be an important element in every SAP implementation. However, it is often neglected. The reason is that the primary implementation objective is to make the software run the business. In some implementations, serious consideration is given to reporting only after going live. Consequently, after the system is put into production at these sites, there exists a crisis-like atmosphere because many users cannot work effectively due to the unavailability of critical reports and information.

Reporting requirements need to be addressed as early as possible. The process should be started by listing all the existing legacy reports. These should be grouped by priority. Business critical ones should be identified, and worked upon, as early as possible. If an SAP report that matches a critical legacy report does not exist, then a custom report can be justified and developed. Early identification of these reports enables more efficient allocation and utilization of ABAP™ resources for the development of custom reports.

Creating SAP reports can be very complicated and tedious because the SAP data schema is extremely complex and the relationships between tables are not easy to determine. Using custom ABAP/4® programming to create reports can be very expensive due to the high rates charged by skilled ABAP™ developers. Therefore, custom development of reports should be discouraged, especially those requested due to personal preferences, unless they are justified for business reasons.

Chapter A9
Phase 4—Final Preparation

During the final preparation phase of an ASAP™ project, the following tasks are performed:

❑ Refine the system
❑ Prepare go-live plan
❑ End-user training
❑ Knowledge transfer
❑ System administration
❑ Data migration
❑ Final testing and fine tuning

PREPARING FOR THE HOME STRETCH

Refining the system

During this stage, the system is refined, adjusted and tweaked. Configuration, interfaces, and processes are adjusted. Changes are initiated due to end-user testing and feedback, modifications in procedures and/or processes, unit and integration testing, change in scope and/or requirements, etc.

During this phase, the system continues to undergo testing. As interfaces get completed, they are tested. Every process touched by a change, such as the introduction of a new interface or a configuration change, is tested and/or retested. Every change requires to be tested because it has the potential to create a problem, including breaking a process, due to the integrated nature of the software.

Prepare go-live plan

Cutover plan

In this step, a plan is prepared and implemented to switch over to the SAP system from the retiring legacy systems. This plan, better known as the cutover plan, includes all the major activities and tasks that are required to be executed during the last few weeks prior to go-live. A well-prepared and realistic cutover plan ensures a smooth transition to the SAP production system. A typical cutover plan includes:

❑ Activities and tasks
❑ Schedule and milestones
❑ Data load sequence with estimated time for each sub-load
❑ Assignment of the person responsible for each task
❑ Schedule and procedure for shutting down the legacy systems
❑ Data cleanup procedure
❑ Reconciliation procedure
❑ Checklist for reviewing readiness

Important elements of the cutover plan

The cutover plan lists every type of data load to be executed. It also includes the relationship of each data load item to other data loads items, i.e., successor and predecessor relationships, if applicable.

In accordance with the loading schedule, it needs to be ensured that the business users responsible for data cleanup and validation are made available to the project team. This scheduling is very important for sequential data item loads because the window available, between the completion of one data item load and the start of the next data item to be loaded, can be very small. During the short periods available between various data item loads, the loaded data needs to be checked and validated quickly. If validation is not performed within the allocated time period, it can either delay the overall loading process or, if the checking is incomplete or sloppy, lead to production problems after go-live.

The cutover plan needs to provide a small window between the time data loading is completed and the system is turned on. This window, of half to one day, is required for taking care of any last minute unexpected problems.

Plan approval

The cutover plan must be reviewed by project management, technical team leads, business leads, corporate senior management, as well as by the Steering Committee.

Once it has been approved, its effective implementation as per the plan will ensure that the go-live experience will not be chaotic.

PREPARING USERS AND SUPPORT STAFF

How much to spend on training

A rule of thumb is that training should make up at least 10% of the overall implementation budget. Of this amount, at least 1% should be earmarked for training the company executives. Unfortunately, during SAP implementations, training is often neglected. The results of inadequate training are usually manifested, sooner or later, with serious repercussions at times.

End-user training

This is an important part of an SAP implementation that takes place during the final preparation phase. Training is one of the factors evaluated while making the go/no-go decision prior to going live because it has a considerable impact on:

❑ Smoothness of transition to the new system
❑ End-user acceptance
❑ Overall project success

Why training is required

An SAP project introduces massive changes within an organization. It can force workers to change the way they perform their jobs due to procedure and process changes, role changes, etc. Due to the introduction of SAP, many jobs are eliminated or redefined and new roles are created. Users need to retrain and learn new skills, procedures, and processes. They need to learn how their actions can impact others in an integrated system. Therefore, if training is not provided effectively to the people who will ultimately use the system, it can cause serious operational and morale problems.

End-users needing SAP to perform their jobs start attending Level I and Level II training during this phase. However, implementation team members, who are fairly experienced by now, attend Level II and Level III training during this phase.

Who needs to be trained

There exists a need for training throughout the life of an SAP project. Both project team members and end-users require this training. Project team members start getting their initial training during the project planning and blueprint phases. Their training continues into the realization phase. However, during the final preparation phase, the training focus shifts to the business community—the end-users.

Training scope and cost

The scope of training can be very daunting, especially if the end-users, who can number in the thousands, are scattered across different parts of the country or the globe. Training expenses can be fairly high because:

❑ Users need to learn new procedures and processes
❑ Many job roles and responsibilities change
❑ Practically every user has to be trained

The impact of inadequate end-user training can be very serious. Therefore, training should be approached with a well-planned strategy. The following are some facts that have been observed about end-user training, which need to be aware of by those planning such training:

❑ Training expenses are high
❑ Training cost is consistently underestimated
❑ Training budget gets cut whenever project budgets are squeezed
❑ Training cost can range from 10-15% of the project budget

Training materials

The following are some tips applicable to training materials:

❑ Plan early: have a training plan in place, as soon as possible, for all potential users
❑ Hire professionals to create user-friendly materials
❑ Discard the view that training materials cannot be created until configuration and testing have been completed
❑ Do not use configuration scripts for end-user training
❑ Create focused and targeted training materials that contain very little fluff—should be limited to whatever is required to perform one's job
❑ Rollout training materials on the company website as soon as they become available

Time constraint

The biggest training challenge is to train all the users within a very short period. If the training is staggered over an extended period, the first few groups of end-users who are trained will be unable to use their newly gained knowledge right away. In most cases, they will require refresher training prior to going live. This can be an issue since the number of SAP trainers is limited and there can be hundreds, even thousands, of end-users who need to be trained.

Train-the-trainer is a fairly successful training method. It involves training a group of power users and others drawn from the business community. After they have been trained, these trainers train other end-users within their own functional areas.

The overall training strategy and plan should be publicized as early as possible. This permits efficient scheduling and the creation of high quality, well organized, training materials that are well received by the end-user community.

Knowledge transfer

As implementation proceeds at a site, the consultants thoroughly learn the business processes and configuration specifics for that installation. Unfortunately, from the company's perspective, this knowledge is lost once the consultants leave. Therefore, it becomes imperative for the installation specific knowledge gained by the consultants to be transferred to the company's employees. This needs to be done through a clearly laid out knowledge transfer plan.

Who should perform knowledge transfer

The main technical drivers and leaders during an SAP implementation are the consultants. The client's employees do not have SAP relevant knowledge to fully understand what is going on—till rather late in the project. By that stage, most of the configuration has already been done and new business processes established. Therefore, they have limited knowledge about most areas and, in many cases, end up knowing very little about how the system was configured and implemented. Hence, the only ones capable of transferring knowledge are the consultants.

Why knowledge transfer is ignored

The implementation team at most SAP projects primarily focuses on the implementation, rather than on running the system after go-live—when the lack of knowledge transfer starts to manifest itself in many ways. Therefore, management should make knowledge transfer a high priority item. It should ensure that the consultants consistently and systematically document what they have done throughout the project.

The tendency, at too many projects, has been to assign consultants the task of documenting what they have configured only at the end of the project, which is often too late. The problem with this approach is that during the final preparation and post go-live phases, consultants are too busy resolving issues and fighting fires. At that stage, it is also highly likely that they have forgotten the specific details of what they did months earlier. Therefore, any documentation that they provide at the end of the project contains skimpy details at best which, in most cases, is inadequate for supporting the system after go-live.

What needs to be done

It is imperative that there should be a systematic method for knowledge transfer from the consultants to the client's employees on the project team. The process, methodology and schedule for this should be defined as early as possible during the project. The ideal method is to assign a team member to every consultant right from the start of the project. This buddy system ensures that maximum knowledge is absorbed and retained by the company staff.

GETTING READY TO THROW THE SWITCH

System administration

The technical (Basis) team conducts system tests during this phase. Stress and performance tests are conducted on the servers and other hardware. Auxiliary systems are checked and the system is fine tuned and readied for production.

Data migration

In accordance with the cutover plan schedule, the remaining business data is now migrated, in a step-by-step manner, to the new system. The migrated data is validated after it is imported into the new system. If the legacy system continues to remain in operation for a few extra days after its data has been migrated, any new transactions recorded there are keyed in manually in the SAP system. This duplication of entries ensures that no data fails to be available in the SAP system after it goes live.

Final testing and fine tuning

During final preparation, the system continues to be tested and fine-tuned. The system is subjected to volume and stress tests, performance is optimized, and the system is readied for production. Integration tests are conducted, converted/migrated data is verified, and interfaces are checked. Peripheral equipment, such as printers, bar code readers, etc., are tested.

SAP's Going Live Check can also be performed at this stage. This enables SAP experts to login remotely, analyze the configuration, and make recommendations for optimizing the system.

Chapter A10
Phase 5—Go-Live & Support

FINAL CHECK BEFORE TAKE-OFF

Readiness assessment

An SAP implementation project is long and challenging. It aims to achieve a lot—to get rid of a number of existing legacy systems and replace them by a single system. However, before the switch can be turned on, it needs to be determined whether the SAP system and the business are ready for the big change. For the final decision to proceed, a go/no-go evaluation is required, which depends on a number of factors. The typical factors to be considered, and questions to be asked, before the go/no-go decision can be made are the following:

❑ Are the processes supported?
❑ Has migration been completed and are the interfaces ready?
❑ Has the migrated data been validated and reconciled with the legacy system?
❑ What is the status of the development effort?
❑ Has integration testing been completed satisfactorily?
❑ Are the business critical reports and forms ready?
❑ Have the users been trained and ready to run the system?
❑ Are there any identifiable showstoppers?

Operational support

This needs to be organized well in advance of the go-live date. Typical support encompasses resolution of problems and bugs, requests for enhancements, and training. The largest number of support calls logged immediately after go-live typically deal with authorization issues. To handle support calls, an issue tracking mechanism is required. For this purpose, companies use many third party software such as Remedy.

To ensure an efficient mechanism for handling support issues, they should be segregated into groups such as problems, enhancements, and reports. This permits a focused and methodical approach that can handle a large number of issues, enable prioritization, and also help in tracking metrics.

Change controls

Even before the system is turned on, any requested changes should be put through a strict change control process. Change control procedures ensure that changes to business processes, configuration, and programs are implemented systematically in a controlled environment.

Change control procedures also ensure that any changes made to the system, and released as "transports", pass through a verification process. Such procedures dictate that any changes to be implemented in the production client are first tested elsewhere, in another client, and have the proper release authorization. Having a documented change control procedure ensures that any problem caused by a released transport can be traced quickly and followed by corrective action or, if required, a reversal of the implemented change.

Communication

Where it is required

In an SAP project, which is implemented by scores of project team members, and impacts hundreds of users, there is a lot more to be done than just configuring and implementing the software package. Many other tasks need to be performed including effective and regular communication at every stage of the project. For example, communication is required between:

❑ Project team members
❑ Project management and team members
❑ Project management and the Steering Committee
❑ Project management and business management
❑ Project team members and the end-user community
❑ Business management and end-users

Communications targeted towards the end-users are very important. Typically, most end-users have no idea about the scope and impact of the SAP project. Most of them view SAP as just another software that can be learned on the fly. However, such an attitude can cause serious problems. If this perception is not changed, many users will ultimately find out, after go-live, that they are unable to perform their jobs. Therefore, end-users need to be educated about the impending changes, especially those impacting business procedures, their roles and responsibilities, and individual training requirements.

What needs to be communicated

Communication is required during all stages of the project. For end-users, a special effort must be made to keep them informed. Communications targeting end-users should be focused on, though not limited to, the following:

❑ Why SAP is being implemented
❑ Importance of the software change to the enterprise
❑ Impact of changeover to the new software
❑ Status of the project
❑ Creating awareness about changing jobs and roles
❑ Managing user expectations, especially the view that SAP is a cure-all for the company's problems
❑ Quashing rumors and negative opinions, if perceived, about the project
❑ Need and schedule for new training
❑ Informing them about the impending rollout of the software

Security

Why security is required

The integrated nature of SAP™ R/3® software enables users to have access to information that was previously available in the legacy system to only a few select employees. This creates security and confidentiality issues. For example, personnel and salary data is very sensitive. Therefore, this creates the requirement to provide access to end-users based on authorization profiles that, typically, are based on job functions. The authorization restrictions limit the amount of navigation that a user can perform in the system.

How authorization profiles are created

Authorization profiles are based on a combination of transaction codes or various SAP objects. Typically, a profile is based on a role, which is based on job mapping.

In the first step, the various jobs or roles required to run the business are identified. In the next step, an authorization profile is assigned to each job. Therefore, when a user is assigned an appropriate authorization profile, it permits him to perform only those SAP transactions that are included in that profile. The background work involved in setting up a variety of authorization profiles, for thousands of users, can be significant and requires careful planning.

Balancing security and access needs

The conflicting security and access requirements raise the question of where the line should be drawn between security and empowerment. Having a restrictive security authorization policy makes employees less empowered and less productive. However, having a wide-open policy can create serious problems. Besides sensitivity and confidentiality issues, a lax authorization policy can allow users to navigate to, and change, data that they are not supposed to.

SAP support

A number of avenues are available for obtaining the support of the SAP organization. These include the Online Service System (OSS) and EarlyWatch™ service.

Online Service System

This is the first-level service provided by SAP that can be accessed remotely by its customers. Using a remote login, a user can query a huge database maintained by SAP. This database contains the thousands of issues that SAP users have faced, over the years, and resolved. It also contains the latest news about releases, SAP news, installation and upgrade information, training, etc.

If an answer to a problem is not found in the OSS database, the user can log the issue in the database. SAP experts then address the problem. During the period that a logged issue is open, a user can track its progress. When a problem is finally resolved, its solution becomes available to all SAP users accessing the OSS.

The Online Service System can also be accessed through the Internet. When it is accessed through this mode, OSS is known as SAPNet. Extensive help is available at help.sap.com.

EarlyWatch™

This is a proactive service that allows SAP to diagnose a system so that potential problems can be recognized early on and, consequently, permit them to be resolved before they become real issues.

SAP Customer Services Network

SAP also provides support to its customers through its SAP Active Global Support program, which covers planning, implementation, custom development, operations, upgrades, education, and continuous improvement. Customers can use SAP experts to advise them about selecting and deploying support structures and processes applicable at their implementation in order to optimize benefits and return on investment.

SAP Consulting

SAP provides consulting services to its potential and existing customers that cover various aspects of its IT infrastructure. The services include strategic consulting services, solution delivery services, operations services, and life-cycle management services.

THINKING BEYOND GO-LIVE

Organization structure

The organizational structures required to implement and operate SAP are, due to the nature of their different needs and requirements, quite different. Most enterprises implement SAP projects without seriously thinking about how the post go-live organization should be structured until rather late in the project implementation cycle. The assumption under which many companies operate during implementation, that operations can be handled after go-live in the usual manner with the existing setup, is wrong. After the SAP switch is turned on, life is never the same for the employees who previously ran the business using the legacy systems.

A new organizational structure should be created, as early as possible, to reflect the future operational needs of the company. One such need is the significant support capability that is required to be put in place. This can be created around the nucleus of the project core team and the existing IT support organization. A feature of the new organization is that it is flatter—with fewer managers.

Change control procedure

No SAP implementation can ever remain static. Even after go-live, the software continues to be modified. The changes can be minor if a very customized implementation took place—because relatively few changes are required post go-live. However, the changes can be very extensive at a vanilla implementation site due to the pent-up demand for enhancements, which require customization.

Besides requests for enhancements and the addition of new functionality, a company also has to deal with the periodic release and upgrade cycle of the SAP™ R/3® software. Therefore, a sound change control procedure needs to be defined and implemented. The change control process should clearly layout the procedures for implementing changes to processes, procedures, and systems.

Staffing

One of the biggest challenges faced by organizations after going live is to retain the core team members who picked up specialized skills during the implementation project. Due to high demand for skilled SAP personnel, especially in the cutting edge SAP products (such as APO, SCM and BW), the turnover in this group can be significant after a project is completed. Therefore, a company needs to have a good retention program so that it avoids losing talent at the end of its SAP project. A number of methods have been used to achieve this. These include giving more responsibilities, absorption in other groups who are working on more challenging projects (such as BW and SEM), increased monetary benefits, lateral move within the SAP group, etc. Companies that have recognized the potential turnover issue early on have managed to retain a high percentage of their project team members.

Chapter A11
Project principles, guidelines and tips

All software and/or application projects, such as SAP and Data Warehousing, have some common elements such as planning and preparation, execution and control. Therefore, many of the basic principles of project management can be applied to all of them. However, SAP projects are characterized by many unique elements that set them apart from conventional IT projects. These unique characteristics are described in the following sections.

FACTORS TO CONSIDER BEFORE STARTING A PROJECT

Why is the project being undertaken

It should be understood why the project is being undertaken and what management expects from its implementation. The following are some questions that can provide useful insight into this:

- Is the objective the improvement of already efficient and streamlined procedures and processes?
- Is the objective the replacement of inadequate systems?
- Is everything in disarray or are only a couple of problem systems the drivers for change?
- Is an attempt being made to fix everything simultaneously?

Project justification

Project justification should precede every software project. For all SAP projects, since they are so massive in scope, it is imperative that a thorough cost/benefit analysis be performed. It seems incredible but cost/benefit analysis have been performed after ERP projects have already been awarded, including one on which this author worked. According to a survey[7], only 38% of companies conducted a formal ROI evaluation of its ERP applications.

Cost/benefit analysis should be performed by someone who has high credibility within the company or by a consulting company experienced in SAP implementations. This can defuse any criticism that the project is being implemented due to an executive's personal agenda. A well-justified project ensures that employees will believe that the project is worthwhile. In general, the best justifications match the business objectives of the enterprise to the project goals.

The project justification should be communicated effectively to a selectively targeted audience. It helps to be candid. For example, at one implementation, it was clearly communicated that an important reason for undertaking the SAP project was competition. The company's two competitors had already implemented SAP and therefore, in order to remain competitive, it also had to implement SAP. This candidness did help in getting support from some groups that, initially, had some reservations about the project.

Has the business strategy been defined

This needs to be done prior to software selection and implementation. By performing this task, the company's strategic and business objectives have a greater chance of being met. It also helps to provide a competitive advantage or, at worst, place the company on an equal footing with the competition.

How will the SAP system be used

It needs to be understood how the SAP system will fit in the overall technical architecture and business strategy. The inputs for this analysis can be quite varied. They can include supply chain software, web-enabled remote access, business intelligence roadmap and data warehousing plans, planned mergers and acquisitions, etc. Companies that give higher priority to strategic business objectives compared to software selection and implementation improve their chances of success considerably.

7: Informationweek, March 29, 2004, pg 92

Readiness assessment

An assessment needs to be made that the organization is ready for the SAP system, which will dramatically change the way business is currently being run. It needs to be determined whether the company is up to the challenge. An assessment also needs to be made to determine management objectives and commitment to the project. If commitment is lacking, or the objectives are not in sync with what the SAP™ R/3® software typically aims to achieve, it is advisable to delay the project until such conditions exist.

Skills assessment

An SAP project should not be initiated without thorough preparation and groundwork. Management should determine the skill levels and capabilities of its employees for selecting the software as well as implementing it. Too often, management is less than well informed and has no idea of the considerable impact that an SAP implementation can have on the organization (during and after implementation).

A careful evaluation is required to determine whether sufficient skills exist in-house to implement the project and, subsequently, operate and maintain the system. A widespread view is that external consultants can fill the gap, which is an erroneous assumption. While there exist thousands of SAP consultants, the ones available for the project being considered may not be adequately qualified.

While business needs and requirements drive the push for ERP technology, the role of the support organization, the IT department, cannot be ignored. Since it is critical to the effort to improve and support business process changes, the skills and resources available within this group should be carefully assessed.

Decision making capabilities

During all stages of an SAP project, critical decisions need to be made. These decisions can significantly influence the way business is conducted after the software has been implemented. Therefore, management must assess the background, temperament, and decision making capability of the project staff that will be entrusted with making important decisions. Two critical skills to be evaluated include the ability of these personnel to act quickly and work effectively under stress. In SAP projects, where the stress level is fairly high and teams are highly interdependent, slow decision-making can impact other teams and delay the project.

Specifying the ground rules for decision-making right at the beginning can help ensure success for the implementation. The following are a few rules that can be laid out:

- ❏ Project manager to be assigned specific responsibilities
- ❏ Project manager must approve any scope or program changes
- ❏ Consultants cannot override managers
- ❏ Committees will have override authority vis-à-vis individual managers
- ❏ No decision to remain pending for more than 48 hours (when it gets escalated)
- ❏ No re-direction of blame to third-parties
- ❏ Failure responsibility to be shared by the whole team

IT transition ability

An agile and responsive IT organization must be in place to support the rapid pace and requirements of an SAP implementation. If these characteristics are lacking, it needs to be assessed whether a dynamic team can be quickly put together. The risks associated with having a mediocre IT organization, which cannot transition quickly and effectively to the new technology and infrastructure, are very high.

Corporate culture

SAP, which is the most complex project that a company implements, initiates major changes by:

- ❏ Changing the way business is run
- ❏ Changing confusion into coherence by switching from disparate systems to a single system
- ❏ Changing the way people work
- ❏ Empowering employees

All these factors can cause management as well as lower level staff to resist change. Resistance to change is a natural phenomenon. The way companies deal with it is determined, to a large extent, by the corporate culture.

Corporate culture is a good indicator of whether a requirement for success is present. A negative corporate culture can be powerful enough to reduce the chances of success for an SAP project. Therefore, this factor should be evaluated to determine its contribution to the overall project risk.

It should be realized that corporate culture is an extension of management. If management attitude is not positive, it is highly unlikely that an enterprise will change itself just to make an SAP project succeed. Management must have a good understanding of the culture that permeates throughout the organization. It needs to understand its strengths and weaknesses and, based on its analysis, develop an implementation plan that avoids the obvious pitfalls.

Management and implementation

The degree of success that a project achieves is influenced by a number of key indicators. These include the following:

❑ Project manager: does he have sufficient responsibility and authority? Is he powerful, respected and experienced?
❑ Support: can top management be expected to provide unwavering support during rough times?
❑ Goals: can managers work towards corporate goals with the same fervor as with personal goals?
❑ Responsibility: will both failures and successes be shared?
❑ Resources: can adequate resources be drawn upon?
❑ Conflicts: is quick resolution encouraged?
❑ Teamwork: does the business environment encourage teamwork over individual achievements?

It is not realistic to expect positive answers to all these questions since few organizations will respond positively to all of them. However, what is important for project success is to understand how the company will deal with each of these factors.

Be aware of the cost of failure

A successful SAP implementation leads to many benefits for an organization. However, a failed implementation can be very costly in terms of dollars and morale. Due to its vast reach across the enterprise, such software cannot be easily scrapped after it has been implemented. Also, it can take years before it becomes apparent that an implementation is seriously flawed and that it needs to be scrapped. By the time this is realized, tens of millions of dollars may have been spent. Also, at such a stage, the alternatives are few and, therefore, it is not easy to cut the losses and run. In such cases, the losses can continue to balloon, benefits can be illusionary even after enhancements and rework, and lost opportunities can be significant.

LAYING THE FOUNDATIONS

Defining the guiding principles

These are the basic principles that need to be defined right at the beginning of the project. They provide the project team with a set of goals that can be referred to throughout the implementation. At times of conflict, between team members or with business users, these principles serve as guidelines. Anything out of alignment with these principles should be discarded or implemented only after obtaining special approval—as an exception due to business or other necessity.

Identifying the business drivers

The project business drivers are specific elements that need to be identified at the start of the project. Besides identifying and clarifying project objectives, they can be the basis for metrics used to evaluate the success of the project in meeting its quantitative objectives. Examples of these include increased customer loyalty, revenue and profitability growth, and efficiency improvement.

Obtaining sponsorship

An SAP project requires a sponsor. The project sponsor should be from top management, preferably at the vice president level, and be associated with the department that expects to reap the maximum benefit from the implementation. The sponsor should be an individual who can make things happen and ensure that:

❑ Management stake in the project is conveyed to all levels
❑ Top management support is maintained throughout the project
❑ Necessary resources are provided at critical junctures
❑ Parties at loggerheads are brought together and, if necessary, force compromises
❑ Decisions and compromises are enforced

Obtaining management commitment

Management needs to be involved in all project phases—from the pre-implementation phase through to the acceptance of the system. It has to believe in the project, be supportive, and provide significant commitment for a successful implementation. Management must communicate its commitment and associate its own success or failure with the success or failure of the SAP project.

Recognizing the decision makers

It should be ensured that management personnel who can influence project success are closely involved with the project, with the most important ones being included in the Steering Committee. The tasks that a Steering Committee performs include approving the project scope, prioritizing, resolving conflicts and disputes, committing and making available project resources, and monitoring implementation progress. It can provide a key ingredient for effective decision making by empowering the team.

The Steering Committee interacts with the project on a regular basis and can set the direction, which can make or break the project. If the committee is strong, its support can be crucial for project success.

Choosing the implementation leader

The implementation leader must be a senior executive who is decisive and can make things happen. Besides leadership qualities, such an executive should have a good track record of completing projects on time and within budget. Although it is required that the project be led by a strong project manager, the Steering Committee should have the authority to overrule him.

Chapter A12
Factors impacting project success

Many factors come into play during the implementation of an SAP project. The importance of each variable, which depends on the particular installation, can be influenced by the presence or absence of other variables. The factors that are usually ranked high are described in the following sections.

PLANNING

Organization and management readiness

An organization as well as its management must be committed. They must be ready to introduce changes that, in an SAP project, can be of re-engineering magnitude. Management must be willing to relinquish control. It must be ready to delegate responsibility and empower the project team.

Effective project planning

A realistic project plan is the foundation upon which an implementation is built. It is amazing to find SAP projects being executed without detailed project plans and schedules in place. A project plan with a realistic schedule, milestones, and dependencies must be created and published at the very start of the project. Where possible, resources should be assigned to specific tasks in the detailed project plan, which ensures ownership and specific responsibilities.

Project team organization

Organization of project teams

An SAP project team typically has the matrix type structure. Such a flat organization is usually organized into teams, such as:

- ❑ Functional (FI, MM, PP, etc.)
- ❑ Basis/Infrastructure
- ❑ Training
- ❑ Communication
- ❑ Development

Employees or consultants

When the project team is organized, it is preferred to draft company employees first when filling various positions. Any open positions, after available employees have been drafted, are filled by hiring new employees or by recruiting consultants. Only those consultants should be hired who are available for the full duration of the project, or till the scheduled completion of the tasks they are expected to perform, because consultant turnover can negatively impact the project in many ways.

When hiring new employees for the project, it is recommended that those with previous SAP experience be given preference. This ensures that consultants have experienced employees looking over their shoulders. While consultants bring a lot of experience to the project, too often, they tend to do what is expedient for them rather than what is in the best interest of the company.

Project team characteristics

Characteristics of team members

Team selection is an important element that can influence the chances of project success. Therefore, assembling a dynamic team should be given high priority. The team members, who should be high caliber professionals, must have the following characteristics:

- ❑ Be motivated and ambitious
- ❑ Have good functional knowledge
- ❑ Have good decision making capability
- ❑ Be willing to work long hours
- ❑ Be able to work under pressure
- ❑ Be able to act quickly
- ❑ Work as team players

Ability to think out of the box

During an SAP project, one can frequently hear the phrase "because we have always done it this way." Typically, this is said in response to questions aimed at determining why something had been done inefficiently, or inexplicably, in the past. This type of response requires the ability to think creatively, out of the box, and recommend changes that will significantly improve the way business is being conducted.

Team members should have the capability of challenging the old methods of doing business, processes and procedures, methods and techniques, etc. Their original thinking needs to be encouraged.

CONTROLS

Effective controls

One of the most important elements for keeping projects on track is to have controls in place. These are the tools that prevent a project from going off track: causing delays, cost overruns, and scope creep. For this purpose, standard project management controls can be applied. However, focus on some additional controls can be quite useful during SAP projects. These include control over consultants' turnover, enforcement of escalation rules for decision making, travel costs—which can balloon if a large number of consultants from other locations are assigned to the project, sub-contractor costs, etc. The areas where costs are likely to overshoot, and are good candidates for control measures, include:

❑ Maintenance and updates
❑ Integration and testing
❑ Customization
❑ Data conversion
❑ Data analysis
❑ Consulting
❑ Training

Project manager's background

As in any large IT project, the role of the project manager is important. However, in an SAP project, the stakes are even higher because such a project is critical for the enterprise in many ways.

The project manager needs to be very committed. He should preferably be drawn from an area impacted the most by the implementation, which ensures a strong vested interest. The project manager should be respected and have the experience and capability that is trusted within the company. He should also be powerful, which ensures that things can get done when required.

Scope creep

Understanding scope creep

Scope creep is the bane of SAP projects. The tendency during many implementations is to try to mirror the existing features of the legacy systems, which end-users are used to. Also, small and innocuous requests turn into stealth projects, which end up draining valuable resources. In many cases, such projects create integration problems because the other teams are not in the information loop till rather late in the game. Also, many of the typical requests for enhancements and changes, which involve scope creep, need custom development. Such requests require ABAP™ programming resources, which can be expensive.

Setting rules

The rule for controlling scope during implementation should be very strict: nothing can be implemented unless it is specified in the Business Blueprint document. If a business critical need has not been addressed in the Blueprint document, a scope change request should be initiated and routed through the approval process. At the very least, a scope change request must be approved by the team leaders and, depending on the escalation rules, Steering Committee approval may also be required.

It should be communicated to all concerned that differentiation should be made between needs and wants. Setting initial rules and enforcing them can help keep everyone on track. For example, at one implementation, it was specified in the Blueprint document that the development team would create a total of 20 custom forms and reports in order to cover gaps in SAP. The users were told to prioritize and select for custom development only 20 forms and reports, that they deemed most business-critical, from a considerably larger list.

Months into the project some users wanted additional reports to be developed, which they classified as critical. However, they were informed that new reports could be included in the 20 most critical list only if an equal number of reports, currently classified as critical, were dropped from the development queue. This control mechanism forced the users to think really hard about prioritization and, consequently, scope creep was avoided in this area.

Requests that are important, but not critical, can be placed in a wait-list queue. Such requests can be implemented during a later phase of the project or a few months after go-live (if no additional phase is has been planned).

TECHNICAL

Client architecture

Impact of client architecture

The client architecture should be well planned as it can impact:

- ❑ Data migration plan
- ❑ Data load testing
- ❑ Transport path, which refers to the SAP method of duplicating a change made in one client through to all the other clients
- ❑ Backup and client refresh strategy
- ❑ Development
- ❑ Unit and integration testing
- ❑ Performance
- ❑ Upgrades
- ❑ Interfaces

Undefined architecture

A common problem during implementations is that the SAP client architecture is not clearly defined for too long and, consequently, is not structured efficiently. In many cases, the client architecture gets defined late in the project—when major problems force serious thinking about this issue. At that stage, it becomes very difficult to make major changes without creating major disruption.

If late changes to the client architecture are made, additional work is created due to its impact on data migration and the need to verify that the configuration is still in sync between different clients. This issue requires that a well-planned client architecture be rolled out at the start of the project so that only minor changes and tweaking are required subsequently.

Early start to data migration

Data migration requires a huge effort. It should be started as early as possible so that, ideally, the team gets an opportunity to test data loading at least 3-5 times before the final load is performed in the production client. Starting early has it drawbacks because the configuration is far from being finalized in the early phases of the project. Therefore, the load routines need to be changed frequently in order to keep them in sync with the changing configuration. However, the advantage is that the team becomes more experienced with each test load. Consequently, the final load into the production system, which comes at a critical juncture, becomes a routine task for the experienced developers.

Thorough integration testing

Integration testing is one of the most important phases of an SAP project. The thoroughness and methodical approach used for integration testing is an important factor that determines whether the transition to SAP will be smooth or rocky.

The development effort should be started as early as possible and completed before integration testing starts. One of the worst mistakes that some companies have made is to continue development while integration testing was in progress. Simultaneous testing and development can cause serious issues because every development change has the potential to impact the system and, therefore, cause confidence in the completed tests to be lost. Hence, to reinstate confidence in the completed tests, regression testing is required. If regression testing is performed, it lengthens the testing period and the project can be delayed. If regression testing is skipped, it increases the operational risks following go-live.

Integration testing should be performed using business scenarios that are very comprehensive. They should reflect the way the company's business is going to be run after SAP implementation. Such scenarios can easily expose broken processes during the testing phase. Using scenarios that do not span a complete process should be avoided.

Data cleanup responsibility

The data residing in the legacy systems, both master data and transaction data, needs to be migrated to SAP. There are two places where this data can be checked:

❑ Legacy side (before migration)
❑ SAP side (after migration)

It is very important that the migrated data be validated as it has the potential to wreak havoc—such as shutting down production lines, incorrectly pricing sales orders, generate incorrect invoices, etc. Usually, business users and extended team members are assigned the data validation and cleanup task. However, due to their being unaware of the consequences of bringing bad data into the system, and time constraints, they often perform an inadequate job. It is imperative that the importance of data cleanup be conveyed to the personnel responsible for this effort.

MISCELLANEOUS

Responsibility and ownership

Users need to be involved with the project as early as possible. They need to be made aware of the impending changes for the enterprise. It pays to demonstrate functionality to the power users as it is configured so that valuable feedback, and suggestions for improvement, can be obtained continuously. If they are involved from the start, they will not be surprised when the system goes live. The interaction also gives project team members an opportunity to manage user expectations. Another advantage is that the signoff process becomes relatively smooth.

Knowledge transfer

Why transfer knowledge does not occur

There is little time to relax during an SAP implementation as every deadline and milestone is followed by another. Typically, consultants are too busy to transfer their knowledge to their inexperienced colleagues. As soon as they resolve an issue, or configure something, they move on to the next task or issue. Therefore, throughout the project, consultants transfer very little knowledge to their colleagues—the client's employees.

Repercussions of knowledge transfer failure

Typically, only a small percentage of the company employees working on the project team gain in-depth knowledge about the methods and techniques used to implement SAP™ R/3® software at their site. Consequently, as soon as the consultants leave, there develops a big knowledge gap. This can be avoided if knowledge transfer occurs effectively. Knowledge transfer helps a company retain control over operations as well as future enhancements. Without it, a company's business can become very vulnerable in case of production problems or if, in future, it needs to implement changes or enhancements that require system, process, and/or configuration changes.

Ensuring knowledge transfer

The ideal way to ensure knowledge transfer is to force the consultants to allocate time on a consistent basis, throughout the project life, to specific individuals who are identified for this purpose. This task consumes valuable time, which can be spent elsewhere on important project tasks. However, for the long-term benefit, this compromise is necessary.

Effective communication

Working in close proximity

SAP is a team project. The need for effective communication between teams, and with others within the company, is very high. To ensure good communication between the team members, who are drawn from many departments and may never have worked together previously, they should be located within the same area (floor or building). A common characteristic of such an area, for many SAP projects, is that cubicle partition walls are either removed or decreased in height. Common meeting and lab areas are setup for informal and impromptu meetings or for demos to small groups. This layout architecture, while decreasing privacy, ensures good communication between team members.

Promoting communication

Communication about project status, impending changes, training announce-ments, rumors, etc., needs to be provided to the company employees on a regular basis. There are many ways in which good communication can be promoted, internally and externally, such as:

- ❑ Weekly team meeting where team and project status updates are provided
- ❑ Postings on the company intranet
- ❑ Newsletters, flyers and e-mails
- ❑ Formal and informal information sessions
- ❑ Announcements through normal company channels
- ❑ Meetings for team building

CHAPTER **A13**
HOW TO ENSURE SUCCESS

ANALYZE FAILURES

High profile failures

There have been many high profile ERP and SAP implementation failures in recent years. In 1999, Hershey Foods suffered a major problem in its $112 million SAP™ R/3® system. Problems included lost orders, missed shipments and disgruntled customers. For the third-quarter, revenues were down $151 million from 1998[8]. At Nike, which had estimated $400 million for its ERP implementation, a software glitch cost it more than $100 million in lost sales[9].

While most problems are ultimately resolved, some companies have chosen to scrap problem SAP implementations, in the past few years, despite having spent tens of millions of dollars. For example, Unisource Worldwide, Inc, a $7 billion distributor of paper products, wrote off $168 million in costs related to an SAP implementation[10]. Even on a smaller scale, the losses can be very painful, such as the $10.7 million write-off by Entex Information Services—a $2.5 billion systems integration and outsourcing company[11].

8: CIO, February 15, 2000, pg 71

9: CIO, June 15, 2004, pg 100

10: www.techweb.com, April 22, 1998

[11]: Information Week, March 8, 1999, pg 24

Types of SAP project failures

There are literally thousands of SAP projects that have been quite successful. However, a large number of SAP projects have also been characterized by:

❏ Delays: implementation took much longer than expected
❏ Cost overruns: cost to implement was much greater than anticipated
❏ Cancellations: after spending years and millions of dollars

Additionally, despite making huge investments in SAP™ R/3® software, many companies have found that their business performance did not improve as expected. In such cases, with few exceptions, the software has been blamed. However, professionals experienced in implementing SAP know that despite some software limitations, there are many other failure causes that cannot be attributed to the software itself. These causes are explained in the following sections.

Common reasons for ERP failures

According to an ERP survey of 305 large and mid-size companies using J.D. Edwards, Oracle, PeopleSoft, and SAP, conducted by Peerstone Research[12], the following were identified as the leading failure factors (in descending importance):

❏ Senior executives fail to lead (26%)
❏ Vendor reps over promised
❏ Integrator costs out of control
❏ Software too buggy
❏ Integrator does not know our business
❏ Software lacks key features
❏ Integrator's staff lacks skills
❏ nternal staff lacks skills
❏ Rank-and-file user resistance
❏ Integration with other apps too hard (7.5%)

12: Informationweek March 29, 2004, pg 92

IDENTIFY COMMON FAILURE REASONS AND PITFALLS

There are many reasons for the poor results demonstrated by companies that have been through a less-than-fully successful SAP implementation. The mistakes that are often repeated at various SAP implementations include, but are not limited to those described in the following sections.

Approach and analysis

Many companies implementing SAP do not realize that it is a political project whose scope equals re-engineering. In many cases, they believe that a flawed business strategy and inefficient business processes can be offset by technology. A common mistake is to overextend requirements gathering is over-extended. Another mistake is to relax too early, after a good start to the project, as derailment can occur at any time and during any phase

Team leadership and characteristics

The project can face serious problems if there is lack of leadership. Leadership is required for the project as well as individual teams. Weak people or dead wood should not be picked as team leaders. Project team leaders and members should have the characteristics required for pressure-filled projects, such as independent thinking and leadership, or the project will increase considerably.

Scope

Scope creep is a very serious problem and, hence, there should be strong project controls. Stealth projects, which drain resources, should be nipped in the bud. Lack of scope control and the inability to differentiate between wants and needs can be one of the most serious issues that an SAP project can face.

Data migration

Data cleanup is often not given sufficient importance. It is often done with inadequate resources that, often, do not realize the impact that data that is not clean or validated can have on the business. This effort should be started as soon as possible.

Development and testing

The reporting effort should be started early on. Typically, the requirements gathering and analysis is slow and tends to drag on, leading to a late development start. Another problem is inadequate testing, which is a big mistake. A mistake that also has serious repercussions is when integration testing is started before development is complete. Consequently, regression testing is required, which requires time. If such testing is skipped, it has the potential to cause serious problems in the production system.

Ownership and involvement

Projects suffer when there is lack of ownership. A proven way to have ownership is to select the project manager from a department that stands to benefit the most from the implementation. SAP projects have faced problems when the business users were not included in the decisions that impacted them. The business should have strong and respected functional representatives on the project team, who are empowered.

Customization

Some of the biggest SAP failures have been attributed to excessive customization—when the organization tried to mirror the retiring legacy systems in the new system. Consequently, they retained inefficient processes and, additionally, incurred heavy cost due to the customization, which took considerably longer. Such organizations also built in lack of flexibility in order to accommodate existing processes.

Consulting

Some projects have suffered due to the high turnover of consultants, especially when it occurred at critical times. This problem was severe a few years ago during a tight labor market. It should also be realized that all consultants do not have the same skills, capabilities, and motivation. Therefore, carefully evaluate a consultant's skills for the specific project before a hiring decision is made.

Communication and training

Poor communications and change management are issues at some projects. Training is also a weak link as it is not accorded the importance it deserves. The quality of training is poor and the end-users do not receive appropriate and timely training.

Wrong software selection

When anticipated results do not materialize, ERP software vendors are usually blamed. Are ERP vendors that sold the software the real culprits because business performance did not improve or the implementation was flawed? The fact is that the blame is often misplaced. Certainly, it can be argued that a particular ERP system's logic is sometimes illogical, lacks the required functionality, performs poorly, and so on. However, accountability for ERP software selection needs to be shared by internal staff and external consultants who are involved in the evaluation process.

In the final analysis, the ultimate responsibility for analyzing and selecting an ERP package resides with the company. If it selects SAP, and later finds out that the choice was wrong because it could not support critical business functionality, then the company should not blame SAP.

Inadequate planning

Selecting and implementing a new ERP system, and the process changes that go with it, is unquestionably a complex undertaking. Regardless of size and perceived resources, an SAP implementation should be approached with a great deal of careful planning. Many failures can be attributed to pre-implementation preparation activities that were performed poorly, if at all.

Inadequate controls

Some projects have run into serious problems because either a detailed project plan was not created or followed. Each task on the project plan should have an owner assigned to it. The project should be closely controlled and tasks should be managed as per the plan.

Inadequate organization structure

An organized approach, backed by a well-structured project organization, is a basic requirement for an SAP implementation. In many cases, where an ERP implementation failed to deliver, failure can be attributed to management that did not adequately structure the organization—either before implementation or after go-live.

Lack of understanding

There is a widespread lack of understanding of the unique nature and elements that are involved in an SAP project. This ignorance can extend to all levels of the project hierarchy as well as business/corporate management.

Not appreciating implementation complexity

SAP™ R/3® software cannot be implemented with the approach used to implement a simple, stand-alone, business software. There are too many factors that come into play with SAP implementations, which combine to make them very complex projects. For example, every company and business is unique. Even within the same industry, it will be impossible to find two companies that operate identically. Corporate cultures vary and the level of commitment to a project can vary. Also, the mix of legacy systems and applications in operation at every organization is different. Therefore, the integration effort required, and the complexity of customization, varies at each site. Another unique factor is that all the existing legacy systems need simultaneous replacement in a risky operation.

The level of complexity that can be handled depends on a number of factors including the availability of skills, dedication of project personnel drawn from the company's ranks, and the approach of the integrators and consultants, which can vary considerably.

Unable to understand implementation risks

All software projects, and SAP projects in particular, are exposed to many risks. Therefore, to prevent an SAP project failure, the critical risk element needs to be understood. Failure to identify implementation risks can cause an organization to approach the project in a casual way, which can increase the failure risk considerably.

Being over ambitious

SAP is loaded with features. Therefore, it is not surprising that there is a tendency to be over ambitious and try to implement every feature possible. Consequently, the implementation scope is increased—intentionally as well as unintentionally. Trying to get too much done in too short a period can be very risky. A conservative approach, which works very well, is to get SAP up and running with the minimum functionality required to operate the business. Additional features and enhancements can be added during subsequent phases.

Operating strategy does not drive business process design and deployment

Many manufacturers fail to realize that extensive supply chain improvement requires that management redefine the business in terms of strategic opportunities. The SAP objective is to implement business processes that support the company's strategic objectives. Therefore, business process design and deployment should be driven by the operating strategy that, in many cases, does not happen.

Rush to completion

Many failures have been caused by implementation teams rushing to complete projects with unrealistic implementation schedules. Many rushed implementations occurred in 1999 when the Y2K deadline was looming. In recent years, many implementations have been rushed due to budget and schedule constraints. Some ERP issues have been blamed on vendors, including SAP, prematurely rushing out new products and releases. This can be attributed to stiff competition in the supply chain, e-Commerce, and customer relationship management areas.

Not prepared to accept the new system

For an SAP project to be successfully implemented, an organization and its employees need to be prepared and accept change, which the implementation forces. Failure was the result for companies that did not prepare their employees to accept change and the new system.

WHAT YOU SHOULD DO

Obtain commitment

SAP is a team project that can only succeed if it has the backing of key stakeholders. They, along with executive management, should provide the commitment necessary to make the project succeed. Commitment to the goals, objectives, and project plan is necessary. If the project plan is not committed to, the project will experience problems due to many issues, such as unavailability of resources, at critical times and may even fail.

Start moving quickly

Time is of the essence in an SAP project. While project tasks are spread out over several months, some decisions need to be made, and tasks are required to be performed, as early as possible. The benefits of doing this include the ability to:

- ❑ Identify key users who can make important decisions and influence buy-in
- ❑ Mobilize important resources quickly, when required
- ❑ Better understand the existing business processes and practices
- ❑ Perform data cleanup and validation quickly and efficiently
- ❑ Validate new processes

Be prepared

An SAP project is not easy and can spring many surprises at every stage. But there are not too many surprises for those who are prepared. A number of methods can be used to try and be prepared. These include, but are not limited to, the following:

- ❑ Create a detailed project plan and publish it in a timely manner
- ❑ Work plan, which should be adhered to, should have concrete deliverables with realistic due dates
- ❑ Set milestones and enforce them
- ❑ Track progress with a forward looking focus: focus on what is coming due
- ❑ Project controls and procedures should be effective
- ❑ Ensure accountability; make project team members, and others working part-time on the project, responsible for specific tasks
- ❑ Expect stealth resource drainers such as reports and customized functionality
- ❑ Be prepared to encounter resistance to change

❑ Define roles and prepare job descriptions/task definitions well before training commences
❑ Inform users that initial operations may not be smooth and that the pain could last 3-4 months
❑ Publicize the fact that implementation will be painful
❑ Prepare management to expect only minimal financial benefits during the first year

Build team and end-user commitment

For this objective to be achieved, management needs to be proactive. It can help by assigning high priority to project goals and communicating them throughout the organization. Some of the steps that management can take to obtain commitment and enhance performance include:

❑ Selecting team members with a positive attitude
❑ Linking project performance, such as meeting milestones, with performance review
❑ Specifying individual and team accountability
❑ Imparting a feeling of ownership
❑ Clearly establishing time commitments
❑ Identifying resources early; providing commitment to mobilize extra resources, if required
❑ Making unequivocal public announcement of commitment to the go-live date
❑ Involving end-users in developing procedures

Create and maintain enthusiasm for the project

An enthusiastic and motivated team is required to implement SAP. However, it is difficult to maintain a high level of enthusiasm throughout the course of an SAP project due to its lengthy duration. Most team members have never been previously exposed to a project of this size and duration. Therefore, many of them are surprised to discover that they have to work so hard, and have to meet high expectations, for a very lengthy period.

On the other hand, for experienced consultants, this can be another ordinary project in a long line of projects that they have been exposed to. Another negative factor is that the workload for individual team members is cyclical, which can cause them to lose focus and momentum. Therefore, there is a dual requirement that comes into play:

❑ Creating enthusiasm and motivation
❑ Maintaining enthusiasm

A number of steps can be taken to motivate team members including:

❑ Installing sense of ownership, which is achieved by involvement, from the beginning of the project
❑ Providing challenges throughout the duration of the project, which can sustain enthusiasm and commitment
❑ Avoiding a prolonged decision making process, which can frustrate those who are waiting to proceed, without rushing into premature decisions
❑ Setting high performance standards for implementation team members

Solve problems in a timely and effective manner

During SAP implementations, conflicts occur between the different teams and even between team members, which can prevent timely decision-making. Therefore, a mechanism must be put in place for conflict resolution and solving problems in a timely manner. Some of the steps that can be taken to prevent problems from getting out of hand, and solving them quickly include the following:

❑ Assigning owners to all issues and problems; clearly defining a feedback process that keeps owners in the loop
❑ Including all concerned in the problem solving and decision making process
❑ Identifying the root cause of the problem
❑ Not allowing issues to be dragged on and, if required, escalating them
❑ Documenting decisions and who made them

Understand what can cause budget overruns

Since ERP projects are huge, even a few oversights while planning and budgeting can make costs spiral out of control. These budget overruns are fairly common and need to be anticipated and controlled.

Who should estimate costs

To avoid getting hit with unexpected expenses, costs should be identified upfront by cross-functional teams assembled for this purpose. These teams can be used to question and/or challenge the other teams' numbers, calculations, and assumptions made while budgeting. Such teams should include senior executives, IT personnel, members of other functional groups, and ERP vendor representatives. The inclusion of so many groups can enable a more realistic budget to be prepared.

Controlling costs

Costs need to be controlled for all project tasks. Pressure should be applied for that purpose because a task completed within a budgeted project cost is invariably on time. An area that needs attention is sizing because it can negatively impact costs.

Contingency

Budget consciousness needs to be highly stressed. When budgeting, it should be ensured that there is a contingency built in, which can be based on various criteria. However, while contingency should be applied where needed, there should be a penalty associated with using it up.

Areas to watch

The following are the areas that have the potential to contribute to budget overruns significantly:

❑ Scope creep
❑ Excessive customization
❑ Under-estimation of training requirements
❑ Ballooning of reporting needs

In many projects, especially during the past few years, companies have integrated their SAP system with a data warehouse. In such types of projects, a significant amount of analysis needs to be performed on the SAP side to identify the data sources required for populating the data warehouse. This task has typically been underestimated and, consequently, led to cost overruns.

Build appreciation for inter-dependence

In organizations using legacy systems, people usually work independently or in isolated groups and silos, a practice that changes during and after SAP is implemented. Project members impact each other at every step of the project and mistakes quickly become apparent to others. Therefore, it is very important that:

❑ Team members are made to appreciate inter-dependence
❑ Cross-functional communication is improved
❑ Team coordination is improved and lone ranger efforts are discouraged
❑ Team building efforts are undertaken

Emphasize thorough and effective testing

Testing is a lengthy, but necessary, procedure that is critical to the success of SAP implementations. Both unit and integration testing should be conducted very thoroughly. Testing should be based on a documented plan which must specify the procedures to be followed for testing, bugs resolution, fixing broken processes, regression testing, etc. The following are some guidelines for making testing smooth and successful:

❑ Select the right people for integration testing; they should be very thorough, detail oriented, and able to withstand a high pressure environment
❑ Functional users should be heavily involved, especially during integration testing
❑ Playback demos, for the benefit of users, should be conducted regularly during the course of the project
❑ Test scenarios should be created, or reviewed, by business process stakeholders
❑ Integration test scenarios should be robust and encompass all processes, systems, reports and scenarios; workarounds should not be permitted
❑ Perform integration testing in a stable environment; do not test while the development effort is still under way
❑ Do not combine integration testing and training

Start data migration early on

The development effort on the legacy side, for the data migration effort, is handled by the client's own legacy developers because they are more familiar with their own systems. The initial development effort, which requires extensive field-to-field mapping from the legacy systems to SAP, is spearheaded by the legacy developers. This task should be started as early as possible. Development effort on the SAP side, which requires ABAP™ programming, is performed by ABAP™ developers who, typically, are the implementation partner's employees or sub-contractors.

Most of the data to be migrated from the legacy systems to the new SAP system is typically loaded a few days, and sometimes a few weeks, before going live. However, the actual data migration effort usually starts months earlier. There are exceptions like the company that started its data migration effort just a few weeks before going live.

The first test data load can be performed during the simulation phase, even though only basic configuration may have been completed by then. The reason is that experimental data loads highlight issues early on and make the developers more experienced in data loading techniques. This experience can be very valuable when the final data load, into the production client, is undertaken just before go-live. It is highly recommended that at least two or three test loads be undertaken prior to go-live.

A factor that can impact the smoothness and success of the data migration effort is the comprehensiveness and quality of the cutover plan. It should be ensured that this plan is detailed as well as realistic.

Create thorough documentation

Training budget pruning

In the rush to get the system up and running, documentation gets less attention than it deserves. It is one of the first areas to get pruned when there is a budget overrun. It is typical for documentation quality to be sub-standard in delayed projects because, as expected, the time and budget allocated for creating end-user documentation gets reduced.

Understanding documentation needs

For end-users, there are usually two types of documents that need to be rolled out. The first one is customized end-user documentation based on functional areas and job roles. The second one is the business process procedures (BPPs). Besides being used as reference materials, BPPs, in some cases, can be used for training end-users—if it is decided that comprehensive customized documentation will not be created for them.

System reference documentation

Documenting changes made to the SAP system during the customization process is extremely important. The reason is that consultants ultimately leave the project and, consequently, the knowledge gained during implementation is lost unless there exists adequate documentation. Lack of this documentation can, in some cases, cause serious problems in the future.

Ensuring successful documentation

The following are some tips for ensuring that efficient and thorough documentation is created:

❑ Decide the purpose and type of documentation to be created
❑ Take a systematic approach for creating documentation; for example: have a shared repository, adopt naming conventions, use templates, etc.

❑ Handle creating documentation as a project task, with assigned deliverables, for which specific individuals will be held accountable
❑ Provide adequate time in the project plan for documentation
❑ Force all team members to document all configuration changes, specifications, enhancements, etc.
❑ Coordinate the documentation effort with training
❑ Avoid having documentation redundancies and variations

WHAT YOU SHOULD NOT DO

Do not favor technology over business

SAP is a business solution—not a technology project. The reason why businesses buy software is to improve business processes and functions—not because they want to buy data processing technology. An ERP system should not be an IT project because the end-users belong to other departments.

While the importance of technology cannot be minimized, since it prepares for the company's future needs, leading edge technology is often unnecessary and too expensive. This is borne out by the success of the SAP™ R/3® software, which is based on the more than three decades old mainstream relational database technology and the client/server model. While older technology risks becoming obsolete sooner, state-of-the-art technology can be unstable and risky.

Do not place functionality requirements on the back seat

The key to a productive new system is functionality. If functionality requirements and user expectations are not met, they will react negatively and become disenchanted. Therefore, one of the first steps in an SAP project should be the determination of desired functions. Once the functions have been identified, the system to be implemented must be able to support them. The implemented system also needs to provide the required functionality with flexibility. If it fails to do so, it can become unproductive.

Avoid duplicating old business processes

The tendency to duplicate existing processes should be discouraged. While it allows a much faster implementation because the approval and signoff process is faster, the end result is that the company will retain its existing inefficient processes and issues. The aim should be to implement best business practices rather than configuring processes that most closely match the existing processes.

Do not ignore scope creep

One of the biggest problems with SAP projects is the inability to manage scope. As projects increase in scope, the odds of achieving success decreases significantly. In SAP projects, slowly but surely, more and more requirements pile up due to various reasons that, if implemented, result in scope creep. This requires that a balance be struck between satisfying everyone's functionality requirements and the need to control the implementation cost and limit risk to the project.

Do not ignore risks

Every software project has risks associated with it and ERP projects are no exception. The risk that such projects face need to be identified and prepared for. The basic risks concern time, budget, and planned functionality. The following are some tips for identifying and managing risk:

- ❑ Make business objectives the primary project drivers
- ❑ Do things for the right reasons—for project objectives instead of politics
- ❑ Best hedge against risk is to use a proven methodology
- ❑ Have tight project controls
- ❑ Have realistic milestones and do not change them; communicate that missed deadlines will be penalized
- ❑ Realize that high risk exists with existing applications that are retained
- ❑ Contingency planning is absolutely necessary
- ❑ Make functional managers take ownership and make them accountable
- ❑ Communicate a message to those associated with the project that their future success at the company is dependent on a successful implementation
- ❑ Do not over customize

Do not modify the system unless necessary

Lesser the number of modifications made to the SAP system, greater are the chances of success. However, if no modifications are made, the systems will perform very well but it may fail to support the business. Therefore, every modification request should be carefully evaluated and approved, or rejected, after considering all the pros and cons.

Avoid changing standard R/3™ objects as much as possible

Ideally, SAP™ R/3® software should be implemented with very few modifications. However, each business is unique and, therefore, SAP needs to be modified and customized so that it can support the business. Many requirements can be implemented through configuration changes that modify the database table contents. However, more drastic modifications, such as changing table structures, objects and source code, should not be implemented unless there is a business necessity. The disadvantages of implementing these major changes include:

❑ Increase in risk
❑ Increase in cost during implementation as well as upgrades
❑ Increase in testing requirements
❑ Additional work is required for every software upgrade and release

Do not start development until requirements have been established

At some implementations, development of enhancements, reports, forms, etc., is started without having the specifications in place. This results in change requests that are unnecessary and expensive. By having specs defined before development begins, the number of iterations required to complete the development are reduced.

It should be a part of the development process to have document sign-off on design specifications. This can prevent, or reduce, surprises being sprung by requestors. It is advisable to complete the design walk-through prior to beginning the development effort.

Do not be bypassed

Consultants do not know a company's business as well as its employees. They should not be allowed to take over, especially during the requirements gathering (blueprint) phase. Employees should not let themselves be used for rubber stamping decisions. Key company employees should become co-pilots and fully participate in the decision making process.

The primary reason that consultants have been able to proceed in a certain direction, even though that path may not have been in the best interest of the company, is that usually there are no SAP experienced company employees on the project team. Therefore, when the project team is assembled, try to hire a few SAP experienced employees for the project team. Besides being able to question and/or challenge the consultants, if and when required, such employees can form the nucleus of the post go-live SAP organization.

Do not let consultants loose

Always remember that consultants are not the company's own employees. They will not have any on-going benefits from the implementation. However, this does not mean that the advice of consultants should be ignored or dismissed. They provide a very valuable service by filling gaps, providing expertise, and thinking outside the box. They are specialized and can usually work faster and more efficiently. In many cases, they can be invaluable in implementing a successful system. However, it is imperative that their limitations be kept in mind. When working with consultants, keep the following tips in mind:

❑ Consultants are not the key for success
❑ Monitor consultants closely; do not rely on them to control their costs
❑ Maintain full responsibility for those who work on the project and how much they bill
❑ Hold consultants accountable; however, they should not be made the scapegoat or given credit for project success
❑ Realize that foreign consultants have limited knowledge of country-specific details

Do not underestimate end-user training needs

The proof of the pudding is in the eating. Even if the best SAP system has been implemented, it is useless if the end-users cannot use it easily or effectively. Before they can use it, end-users need to be adequately trained. For most users, the change from the legacy system to the SAP system is drastic and stressful. Therefore, the needs of these end-users should be carefully determined and the training plan created as per their identified needs.

Do not ignore warning signs from partners

Having good partners is an important ingredient for a successful project. On the flip side, a partner that is unresponsive to the client's needs can be a drag on the project. Immediate action needs to be taken if it becomes apparent that a partner does not commit to project scope, milestones, and deadlines. Another warning sign is the unwillingness of a partner to allow the client to screen, or let go, a consultant.

Chapter A14
Market's influence on SAP

ERP GROWTH EXPECTATIONS

ERP market growth rate

SAP initially targeted the Fortune 500 companies. As that market saturated, it shifted its focus to the mid-cap market. In order to continue growth, SAP is now targeting even smaller companies, with revenues as low as 50 million dollars. Starting with release 4.6, it also moved away from the rigid client/server approach to a web-enabled front-end in response to customer demands for easy, convenient, and fast access to data.

According to IDC[13], ERP revenues are expected to grow to $26.7 billion in 2004—a growth rate of under 7%. It has also predicted that the ERP revenues will grow to $36 billion in 2008. This ensures continued growth for SAP in the next few years at least.

SAP growth drivers

For many years, SAP was primarily implemented at new installations, where it replaced legacy systems. However, in the past few years, a higher percentage of implementations have involved upgrades or consolidations across divisions, subsidiaries, etc. According to the 2004 ITtoolbox ERP Implementation survey, 65% of the respondents are considering adding new modules to their existing ERP packages, with the most popular ones being CRM, data warehousing, and supply chain. In the next few years, we can expect more companies with installed SAP systems to add new modules and extend SAP functionality to their:

13: eweek.com of May 24, 2004

❑   Groups/departments/users who were not included in the initial implementation
❑   Subsidiaries and other divisions

Another driver is ERP-to-ERP integration. Companies will continue to improve and extend integration by linking with customers and vendors who already use SAP. In the future, we can expect increased customer demand for implementing additional functionality. This will be widespread at companies that initially implemented a vanilla SAP version, with minor modifications to the software, due to the project requirements for quickly getting the SAP system up and running.

DRIVERS FOR CHANGE

In the market that has matured for ERP, customers now demand a more comprehensive solution that extends the core functionality of vendor products beyond traditional ERP, which was limited to automating the internal processes of companies. Customer demand, to a very large extent, has been influenced by the following five drivers:

❑   Internet
❑   Supply chain management
❑   Customer relationship management
❑   e-Commerce
❑   Business intelligence

Internet

The Internet has been revolutionary. It has fundamentally changed the way many businesses, large and small, are run. SAP has not been untouched by the winds of change. It was somewhat late in recognizing the impact that the Internet would have on its business. However, after SAP realized that it would need to operate in Internet time, it shifted gears and web-enabled the R/3™ software.

Supply chain management (SCM)

SAP integrates a company's various functional areas. However, in order to extend this integration to its partners, suppliers and vendors, additional functionality in the form of supply chain management software is required. SCM manages the flow of products, or services, throughout the processes that typically extend beyond the company to its trading partners.

Previously, a number of independent vendors provided SCM software that was integrated with the SAP™ R/3® software, if SCM functionality was desired by the client. However, SAP has now incorporated this functionality within its own software. Some of the functionality it has introduced includes:

❑ Advanced Planner and Optimizer™ (SAP APO™), which improves demand-forecasting and increases production efficiency
❑ Logistics Execution System™ (SAP LES™), which enables efficient, fast and accurate goods flow through the supply chain
❑ Business-to-Business software, which companies can use to procure goods and services via the Internet.
❑ Built-in radio frequency identification data (RFID) in its latest version of mySAP Supply Chain Management application.

These should continue to be good growth areas for SAP in the next few years. Companies interested in this functionality will evaluate SAP as a serious vendor for their needs, even though it is a relatively new entrant in this field, due to its reputation and success in the ERP arena.

Customer relationship management (CRM)

CRM software manages front-end applications, such as sales force automation, in contrast to the back-end which can be managed by the traditional SAP™ R/3® software. In this fast growing market, despite its late entry in this area, SAP has made good inroads and can manage to grow at a good pace. The competition is tough since other vendors, such as Siebel, are firmly entrenched and have a significant lead. We can expect SAP to improve the available CRM functionality within its core software and, also, attempt to become the preferred, one-stop, vendor of choice. Recently, it introduced integrated CRM services using handheld devices and wireless technology.

e-Commerce

This has been a hot market in recent years. For meaningful e-Commerce, ERP integration with CRM is a critical starting point because companies like to have their front- and back-end software integrated. This reflects the shift in focus from achieving operational efficiency to strategies that are customer-centric and e-Commerce oriented.

Despite its initial mis-steps, SAP has positioned itself well in this area. It has successfully promoted mySAP.com™ as its e-Commerce portal. We can expect SAP to try and establish itself as a major player in this arena, which is expected to continue growing rapidly in the next few years.

Business Intelligence

The need for reporting and analysis, which has skyrocketed in the past few years, has led SAP to address the reporting shortcomings within its software. Besides offering many new reports that run against the transaction system, SAP also created its own data warehouse (BW) so that the business intelligence needs of companies implementing SAP are met.

SAP's RESPONSE TO A CHANGING ENVIRONMENT

Changes in the ERP market have been fast and significant. Since 1997, SAP has introduced new solutions for customer relationship management, supply chain management, and business intelligence. As part of its effort to be responsive to market needs, SAP introduced an Internet-enabled R/3™ in 1996, which was followed by mySAP.com™ in 1999. Some of the new SAP initiatives are discussed in the following sections.

EnjoySAP™

In 1999, SAP rolled out EnjoySAP™, R/3™ Release 4.6, with a new graphical interface and featuring full web accessibility. It aimed to adapt the software to each user's requirements. It sported a role-based personal user interface that is visually different than earlier versions. It was easy to use and interactive. It could be easily tailored to individual requirements such as creating favorite lists of the most frequently used transactions. The benefits included 10-65% efficiency improvements for experienced users and about 50% reduction in the time required to learn new functions.

mySAP™

The Internet has been one of the biggest drivers in SAP's evolution during the past few years. Initially, SAP did not take the Internet seriously. However, market forces forced SAP to do an about face and web-enable SAP. The result was mySAP.com™, which provided an open collaborative business environment of personalized solutions on demand. After the "dotcom" bust, the mySAP.com™ name was truncated and it is now known simply known as mySAP.

Enterprise portal

The SAP Enterprise Portal, which integrates applications and services permit a user to access enterprise-wide data and information from a single location, using role based user interfaces. Access through the portal can be to SAP and non-SAP applications, transaction and decision-support applications, data warehouses, web services, documents, etc. Irrespective of the underlying technology or application, a user can access, create, display/hide, or modify data if appropriate authorization has been provide. The portal also supports workflow and collaboration.

Business intelligence

At most companies, the focus in recent years has shifted, due to the increased competitive environment, from collecting data to using data for decision support. Therefore, instead of relying only on operational (transaction) data, companies now supplement it with data warehouse data, which can be mined with analytical tools, for making informed and sound business decisions.

SAP reporting limitations

SAP has been extremely good at collecting and storing data. However, it has been limited in its ability to retrieve data easily and quickly. To be really useful, data needs to be transformed into information, which is required by companies as a competitive weapon. They need specific, accurate, and timely information for good decision-making. Without it, decision-making can be limited and lead to decisions that can negatively impact the business.

Data warehouse solution

For businesses throughout the world, the need to convert data into information is becoming increasingly important. The need for data analysis has caused an explosive growth in data warehousing. The centerpiece of the data warehousing process is the data warehouse, which is a huge data store formatted and optimized for query processing and decision support. It contains data extracted from the transactions systems of an enterprise, which run the business.

Data warehouse technology provides the means for extracting data, stored in a company's disparate systems, and transforming it into information that can be used for decision-making. Therefore, the logical next step for companies implementing SAP is to implement a data warehouse. In some cases, a data warehouse is implemented in parallel with the SAP transaction system. With SAP being the most important source of a company's transaction data, where it has been implemented, data warehouses at SAP installations will typically obtain most of their data from the SAP transaction system.

SAP™ Business Warehouse

Since 1998, SAP has been providing its own data warehouse, which is known as the Business Warehouse (SAP™ BW), as a decision support tool. It contains many predefined reporting templates, which include industry-specific functionality.

The most difficult and complicated step in creating a data warehouse is migrating data, extracted and converted from disparate legacy systems, into a single database, i.e., the data warehouse. This task is very tedious and time consuming. When both the SAP transaction system and the SAP™ Business Warehouse are implemented at an installation, the extraction and transformation process is simplified and shortened. The reason is that the conversion and loading process, required to migrate data from SAP to the data warehouse (SAP™ BW), are defined by the same vendor—who knows both systems intimately. Therefore, a major task in creating the data warehouse gets simplified.

According to a Gartner analyst[14], 70% of SAP customers will be using SAP BW for decision support. It is also expected that ERP and CRM vendors, such as SAP, will improve the capability of their software to use data generated by their competitors' applications.

mySAP All-in-One (All-in-One)

In an effort to reach out to smaller companies, who needed fast and easy installation, SAP introduced the mySAP All-in-One solution. All-in-One provides prepackaged, out-of-the-box, functionality that SAP clients can use to quickly have a system up and running. It provides broad functionality including financials, supply chain, customer relationships, human resources, and other essential business processes. SAP indicates that implementation is up to 30% faster and 40% cheaper than conventional methods.

14: Informationweek, May 3, 2004, pg 36

The All-in-One solution also has an industry focus, with the development of more than 50 pre-packaged small and mid-size business partner solutions. Industries for whom solutions are being developed include oil and gas, pharmaceuticals, ad agencies, retail/wholesale distributors, etc.

SAP Business One

SAP Business One is an ERP application for small and mid-size companies. It is based on open standards, which integrates with other systems. This affordable, simple, and powerful software solution was first released in Europe in 2001, which was followed by its introduction in the US in 2003. Business One supports companies with as few as ten employees. It can be implemented in about a week and can cost up to $3,750 per user.

Solutions for mobile business

The percentage of mobile workers has increased considerably in the past few years and is expected to continue. SAP has recognized this trend and offers solutions for mobile business. Its solutions include SAP mobile time and travel, mobile sales, mobile service, mobile asset management, mobile procurement, mobile supply chain management, and mobile business intelligence. Using mobile solutions, data or software can be accessed either in connected or disconnected mode.

SAP's three-year roadmap

In early 2004, SAP announced a three-year roadmap[15]. Some of the highlights include:

❑ Approximately half of SAP's $1.2 billion annual R&D budget will be spent on achieving the new Enterprise Services Architecture (ESA) strategy.
❑ Pushing the services-oriented architecture: ESA will use the SAP NetWeaver web services platform to combine components of the mySAP application and deliver them as business-oriented services designed to meet company objectives—rather than making the organisation fit around the technology. Benefits will be more application deployment flexibility, lower cost, and faster response to market demands.

15: Information week, May 14, 2004

- ❑ mySAP will be fully ESA compliant in 2007, with most of the necessary functions available for customers in 2006.
- ❑ Initial focus, in 2004, will be to create an inventory of web services components, and develop the first service to support business collaboration.
- ❑ Customers will be able to decide which functions to implement or outsource as other services will focus on user productivity, process flexibility, and deployment options.
- ❑ Every application SAP to be shipped, from now on, will include a native version of NetWeaver
- ❑ An ESA repository will be included in mySAP by 2005.
- ❑ By 2007, SAP's entire software suite will have been modified to run on NetWeaver and Enterprise Services Architecture.

PART B
Business Warehouse (BW)

Chapter B1
Introduction

WHAT IS THE BUSINESS WAREHOUSE

The Business Warehouse (BW) is an analysis and reporting tool that can be used to analyze current and historical data in SAP as well as non-SAP systems. It is primarily based on OLAP technology, which enables it to analyze data in many different dimensions. It also uses non-OLAP technology to access and analyze data.

Concept and strategic tool

The Business Warehouse is a data warehouse (DWH). It is a strategic as well as operational decision support and reporting solution provided by SAP, which is closely integrated with its flagship product—SAP R/3. The tool is enterprise-centric which, once implemented, becomes the central hub in the information analysis architecture of an organization.

Why BW is popular

The Business Warehouse is a complete data warehouse architecture, with metadata and performance and administration tools, that has been developed on a proven methodology.

It is a superior data warehouse that does not require a top-notch team of professionals to build or maintain it. BW provides all the benefits that are associated with a conventional data warehouse, which are listed in the next section. In organizations that have implemented SAP, BW provides tight integration with its primary source system, the R/3 transaction system that runs the company business, and also helps overcome SAP's reporting limitations.

Benefits of data warehousing

The implementation of a data warehouse provides many benefits to an organization. It can:

❑ Facilitate integration in an environment characterized by un-integrated applications
❑ Integrate enterprise data across a variety of functions
❑ Integrate external as well as internal data
❑ Support strategic and long-term business planning
❑ Support day-to-day tactical decisions
❑ Enable insight into business trends and business opportunities
❑ Organize and store historical data needed for analysis
❑ Provide access to historical data, extending over many years, which enables trend analysis
❑ Provide more accurate and complete information
❑ Improve knowledge about the business
❑ Enable cost-effective decision making
❑ Enable organizations to understand their customers, and their needs, as well competitors
❑ Enhance customer service and satisfaction
❑ Provide competitive advantage
❑ Help generate new revenue (new customers), reduce costs (improved processes), and improve the bottom line (profits)
❑ Help expand the customer base
❑ Streamline business processes and provide decision support for various business processes, such as manufacturing
❑ Provide easy reporting access for end-users
❑ Provide timely access to corporate information
❑ Enable users to analyze data from different angles, using powerful front-end access tools
❑ Reduce users' dependency on IT as they can quickly create their own reports
❑ Generate ROI of 100-400 percent in the first year if the data warehouse is well-designed and implemented

Business Content

The BW is provided with a number of ready-to-run reports, which are widely used as they reflect the standard needs of most businesses. These reports are organized by various functions such as FI/CO, SD, MM, APO, etc. Business content reports need to be activated before they can be used—a task that can be performed through a simple point and click procedure.

Beneficiaries

When data warehouse technology was in its infancy, its primary users were decision-makers, managers and business analysts, who often lacked the technical knowledge required to build reports from scratch. However, at this time, the sophistication of the user community has grown significantly. Data warehouses are now accessed by users across the enterprise, in practically every department, at all hierarchical levels including:

❑ Strategic users
❑ Operational users
❑ Managers
❑ Executives
❑ Novice and casual users
❑ Business analysts
❑ Power users
❑ Application developers

The needs of these users can vary considerably because their information requirements and abilities can vary tremendously. For example, the different needs can be:

❑ Easy-to-use queries and reports, with few parameters, if the user is not technology savvy
❑ Ability to generate periodic reports for analyzing variances
❑ Ability to crunch numbers, slice and dice, and manipulate data and report results
❑ Dashboard type reports for top-level executives

PREREQUISITES FOR IMPLEMENTING BW

Understanding DWH objectives and differences

Before a BW project is undertaken, the objectives of the proposed system, which determines the implementation approach, need to be identified. The reporting and analysis differences between transaction systems and data warehouses need to be appreciated. There are fundamental differences between them that, if not understood, will lay the foundations of failure. Too many data warehouse projects have been undertaken without this prerequisite, with the result that they failed to meet their objectives or had to be scrapped.

Operational systems are primarily used to run a company's business. They are transaction-based and support business applications such as procurement, inventory, sales and order processing, accounting, human resources, etc. Such systems require fast access to the database, which is usually pre-defined. Data warehouses focus on analysis, including multi-dimensional view of the data, and the ability to run ad hoc reports. Such systems supports drill-down and the requirement to slice and dice data. While the operational systems require performance, decision support systems (data warehouses) favor flexibility rather than speed.

The characteristics of operational data and data warehouse data are also quite different. For example, the characteristics that define DWH data include high redundancy, flexible structure, large data volumes, analysis and management oriented, and ad hoc access. This is in contrast to operational data, which is defined by different characteristics such as detailed data that is transaction-driven, continuous updates, small data volumes, no redundancy, as well as high availability and reliability.

Once the differences and uniqueness of a data warehouse are appreciated, it will be possible to plan and implement the project in a manner that will reduce risk and the probability of failure.

Data and reporting environment

A data warehouse touches data scattered in various systems within an enterprise as well as, in many cases, external data. Before a BW data warehouse project is undertaken, the overall environment in which the business is operating, and important external factors, must be studied. The overall system and reporting architecture, current and planned, needs to be studied. Additionally, the systems where the data is currently residing, methods and tools currently employed for reporting and analysis, and the types of users and their high-level requirements must be identified and analyzed before a BW project is undertaken.

Pitfalls

The failure rate for conventional data warehouse projects, as well as BW projects, is very high. A number of mistakes occur frequently, even though they have been well publicized over the years, such as scope creep, poor planning and design, not differentiating between a data warehouse project and a database project, lack of sponsorship and ownership, etc. Before a BW project is undertaken, such common mistakes should be analyzed so that they are not repeated. The most common mistakes and pitfalls have been identified and described in Chapter B17.

CHAPTER B2
EVOLUTION OF DATA WAREHOUSING AND BW

CONCEPTUAL BACKGROUND

Evolution of information processing requirements

The task of getting any meaningful data or information out of the early computer systems used to be very tedious. Consequently, a number of methods, techniques, and tools were developed to solve that problem. They included decentralized processing, extract processing, executive information systems (EIS), query tools, relational databases, etc. The need for timely and accurate decisions also led to the development of decision support systems, ranging from simple to very sophisticated systems. The data warehouse is the latest tool in this evolution.

Consequences of multiple applications and platforms

Traditional business applications were designed and developed with the objective of helping specific departments or functions such as marketing, human resources, finance, inventory management, loan processing, etc. Since such applications were typically developed independently and without coordination, over a period of time, they often contained redundant data. Also, the data residing in these applications, which were often developed on different platforms, was incompatible and inconsistent. Consequently, there was poor data management, enterprise view of data was lacking and, frequently, a query would return different answers depending on the application that was accessed and analyzed. What made the situation even worse, especially after 1981 when the personal computer (PC) was introduced, was the explosion in the number of systems as well as the quantity and type of data being collected. The loss of a central data repository coincided with the widespread demand for timely and more information.

Limitations of transaction processing systems

Online transaction processing systems (OLTPs) were developed to capture and store business operations data. Since their main priority is to ensure robustness, rather than reporting or user accessibility, they suffer from some serious limitations. Their most obvious shortcomings are the inability to address the business users' need to access stored transaction data and management decision support requirements. The OLTPs do not address history and summarization requirements or support integration needs—the ability to analyze data across different systems.

Another problem that limited data extraction and analysis was the limited availability of legacy systems' documentation that could be used effectively and efficiently. Even in modern systems, such as SAP which has more than 9,000 normalized tables, the available documentation leaves much to be desired and, consequently, data cannot be easily or quickly extracted by business users for their reporting needs.

Birth of the data warehousing concept

The failure of OLTP systems to provide decision support capabilities ultimately led to the data warehousing concept in the late 1980s. Its objective, in contrast to OLTP systems, was to extract information instead of capturing and storing data and, hence, it became a strategic tool for decision makers. At this time, data warehousing strives to become the foundation of corporate-wide business reporting by supporting both tactical and strategic decision-making.

In a way, the data warehouse concept involves traversing a full circle. With the advent of the PC in 1981, islands of data had sprouted in an independence move, away from the mainframe centralized concept. The data warehouse, by collecting data stored in disparate systems, is a return to the centralized concept. However, a key difference exists. A data warehouse enables enterprise, and local, decision support needs to be met while allowing independent data islands to continue to flourish. It provides a central point of access where an organization's data is synchronized.

DWH FUNDAMENTALS

What is a data warehouse

A data warehouse is a large analytical database, which typically derives its data from a variety of transaction systems running the business. It is structured for querying, reporting, and analysis. The data warehouse, which can include both transaction as well as non-transaction data, is typically used as the foundation of a DSS that aims to meet the requirements of a large business user community. The data in a data warehouse can be accessed using a variety of front-end, easy-to-use, data-access tools. While data warehouses can be built from scratch, some off-the-shelf products are also available. An example is the SAP BW, which can be implemented fairly quickly after limited customization.

Types of data warehouses

Enterprise data warehouse

An enterprise data warehouse (EDW) contains data extracted from an organization's numerous systems that run its business. A typical company may have 5-10 systems that feed into its corporate data warehouse. Such a warehouse may contain detailed transaction as well as summarized data. The data stored in a data warehouse, which is organized according to subjects such as sales or inventory, can range from a couple of years to 20 years. This period is determined by the requirements for analyzing historical trends across multiple business areas, such as departments or regions. The volume of data stored in a data warehouse typically ranges in the gigabytes. However, many organizations now have data warehouses that contain terabytes of data. The BW can be setup as an enterprise data warehouse.

Data mart

A data mart is a small data warehouse that contains a sub-set of the corporate data. Typically, its scope is limited to a department or business unit. A data mart, like a data warehouse, can include both detailed and summarized data. It can be fed from multiple systems. However, the number of its source data systems is far less compared to a data warehouse. The volume of data stored in a data mart is considerably less compared to a data warehouse. A typical data mart will contain less than 100 GB of data. Nowadays, it is fairly common for organizations to create BW data marts before implementing an enterprise data warehouse.

Operational data store

An operational data store (ODS) is a subject-oriented database that contains structured data generated directly from transaction data sources. Usually, it will contain very little summarized and historical data. An ODS is stored independently of the production system database. It contains current, or near current, data extracted from transaction systems. The objective of an ODS is to meet the ad hoc query, tactical day-to-day, needs of operational users. An ODS is often used as a staging area before data is imported into a data warehouse. In contrast to a data warehouse, which contains static data, an ODS can be frequently updated from operational systems—even in real-time. The ODS is an important component of the BW system.

CONTRIBUTORS TO DWH EVOLUTION AND GROWTH

Data warehousing began to grow explosively starting in the mid-1990s. It is still characterized by high growth and is now considered to be a mainstream and strategic technology that a competitive organization cannot afford to ignore. There are many reasons for the growth and wide acceptance of data warehousing, which are explained in the following sections.

Competitive environment

In the 1980s and 1990s, American corporations faced tremendous pressure to become more competitive and improve their productivity. As part of their effort to achieve a competitive edge, and become lean and mean, companies began to look more closely at the data that they collected over the years. Their need to analyze huge amounts of data, which was stored in disparate systems, and decision support requirements led to the explosion in data warehousing growth.

Globalization

The globalization of the world economy in the past two decades forced American companies to compete with foreign companies who were providing relatively low cost goods and services. Many American manufacturers could not compete in the new environment and, consequently, they had to cease operations or move them to Third World countries. The only way that American companies could compete in the new environment was by becoming more efficient and improving their productivity. To achieve their objectives, they made a serious attempt to use various technologies including data warehousing.

Economic trends

During the economic downturns that took place in the 1980s and 1990s, American companies downsized considerably and made a serious effort to re-engineer their businesses. Continuous and never-ending changes in the environment forced management to become innovative and make the best use of their resources, humans as well as data, which contributed to data warehousing growth.

Key business drivers

The emergence of a number of key enabling technologies as well as many business drivers have fueled the growth of data warehousing. These key business drivers, which were driven by the need to compete more effectively in a very competitive environment, have been:

❑ Shorter product cycles that permitted fewer mistakes and slippages to occur
❑ Need for increasing efficiency and productivity
❑ Growing demand for information at every level in the corporate hierarchy
❑ Need to support a strategy that enabled self-service for information access
❑ Need to leverage corporate data and its hidden value

Rapidly declining hardware prices

An important factor in widespread data warehouse deployment and use has been the sharp decline in the price of computer hardware, especially storage, even as computer processing power and capacity increased tremendously. Prices of processors, disk drives, memory, and peripherals have dropped dramatically in the past few years and, consequently, made data warehouse hardware more affordable.

More desktop power

The power of PC's today is greater than the mainframes of a few years ago. The PC has evolved from a personal productivity tool, which was initially used for word processing and simple spreadsheet calculations, to one that supports sophisticated business applications and heavy-duty multi-dimensional analytical analysis. The development of PC capabilities has led to it being used as the primary tool for accessing data warehouses. Without the PC, the widespread use of data warehouses by end-users would not have been possible.

Technology developments: software and hardware

A number of technology developments have contributed to data warehousing growth including:

- ❑ Server operating software (Unix and Windows NT) characterized by:
  - Powerful features
  - Support for virtual memory, multi-tasking, and symmetrical multi-processing
  - Reliability
  - Easy and fast installation
  - Affordable cost
- ❑ Hardware developments including:
  - Symmetric multi-processors (SMP)
  - Massively parallel processors (MPP)
- ❑ Improvements in relational databases features and technology (RDBMS)
- ❑ Middleware development
- ❑ Widespread growth in networks
- ❑ Graphical user interface (GUI) tools

Proliferation of data

The amount of data being collected by corporations has grown by leaps and bounds due to their desire to analyze as much data as possible. Terabyte data warehouses are quite common now and it is expected that the data being captured will continue to grow. Some of the biggest contributors of data proliferation have been e-Commerce, e-Business, Internet, and clickstream data.

Growth in Internet and Intranets

The explosive growth of the Internet as well as Intranets, which are company networks based on Internet standards, has also fueled data warehousing growth. The ability to access a data warehouse through a web browser, from any location, has eliminated the need to install or learn complex data access software and tools. Consequently, it has significantly increased the number of users, with varied requirements, who also create data as they browse the Internet or the Intranet.

Shift in focus from data to information

In the past, IT focused on capturing and storing data. Therefore, management had to live with standard canned reports that, often, were not provided in a timely fashion. However, with changing corporate needs that required quick decision-making, management shifted its focus from collecting and storing data to extracting information. When it realized that the required information could not be extracted quickly or easily from the OLTP systems, management began to explore various potential solutions including data warehousing.

Availability of application software

The widespread use of ERP software from SAP, PeopleSoft, Oracle, and others has led to the collection of huge volumes of transaction data. However, even though ERP software has been very efficient in collecting data, it has typically been unsuccessful in satisfying the varied reporting needs of its users. Therefore, to meet their need for flexible reporting, many companies have been forced to construct a data warehouse following an ERP implementation.

End-users are more technology savvy

The introduction of the PC has led to business users becoming more comfortable with computer technology. Their level of knowledge and sophistication has enabled them, across the corporate world, to become fairly independent of programmers and systems analysts for their analytical and reporting needs. Such users are able to use sophisticated software tools with minimal training. Additionally, there has also developed a large pool of technology-savvy business analysts who are as comfortable with technology as they are with business. Such users have been instrumental in making data warehouse projects succeed.

DRIVERS FOR BW GROWTH

SAP reporting limitations

There are literally thousands of standard reports that are provided with the SAP R/3 software. However, they do not meet the reporting and analysis needs of many users who want flexibility, multi-dimensional analysis, and powerful features such as drill-down, drill-across, as well as slice and dice capabilities. BW can easily meet these needs.

Cost control for DWH projects

For many years, data warehouses were customized and built from scratch. Such projects were characterized by delayed completions, cost overruns, and failure to meet user expectations. The high failure rates of such projects forced companies to aggressively control costs and build incrementally so that costs and risks could be reduced. In the past few years, a very important BW growth driver has been its ability to help control data warehouse project costs through simplified and phased implementations.

Need to reduce ETL costs

In a data warehouse project, a very large part of the implementation cost is consumed by the extraction, transformation, and loading (ETL) process. The ETL cost can be as high as 75% of the total project cost. With BW, this cost is reduced considerably as it is tightly integrated with the SAP transaction system and, hence, ETL development requirements are minimized. Consequently, BW has benefited significantly from the need to reduce data warehouse implementation costs.

Demand for off-the-shelf DWH solution

There has been a widespread demand for off-the-shelf data warehouse software packages by companies seeking to minimize implementation problems and costs. BW has benefited from this need as it meets the expectations associated with off-the-shelf software, such as reducing implementation time, incremental approach, leveraging standard reports, as well as reduced ETL and consulting costs.

Single vendor preference for OLTP and reporting systems

The desire to have a single vendor for both the OLTP transaction system and the data warehouse, i.e., for operating and analyzing the business, has benefited SAP as it provides both the R/3 transaction system and the BW data warehouse. The move to implement data warehouses in recent years has been a great driver for BW implementations due to the existence of thousands of SAP R/3 installations.

SAP technology roadmap

Market and business-driven innovations from SAP, along with its strategic roadmap, have contributed to recent BW successes in a competitive business environment and will continue to do so for at least the next few years. These include:

□ BW 3.5: Key functional advances include information broadcasting, universal data access, embedded BI integration into NetWeaver, integration of business planning and simulation, and Unicode.

□ SAP BW 4.0: Provides advanced features including active business intelligence. It is expected to ramp up in 2005.

□ Out of the box with a variety of data sources (Business Content).

CHAPTER B3
DWH CHARACTERISTICS AND DESIGN

BASIC CHARACTERISTICS

A date warehouse, including the Business Warehouse, is characterized by four unique characteristics:

- ❑ Subject-oriented
- ❑ Integrated
- ❑ Time variant
- ❑ Non-volatile

Subject-oriented

The data in a data warehouse is organized according to subjects such as customer, vendor, orders, and products. This contrasts with classical applications that are organized by business functions such as loans, finance, inventory, etc. In a data warehouse, the major subject areas are physically implemented as a series of related database tables.

Integrated

The data in a data warehouse is always integrated—without any exception. The source data from multiple systems is consolidated in a data warehouse after undergoing various operations such as extraction, transformation, and loading. The data imported from the source systems reflects integration through consistent naming conventions, data attributes, measurement of variables, etc.

Time variant

Data warehouse data is accurate as of a moment in time while transactional data is accurate as of the moment of access. The data in a data warehouse consists of a lengthy series of snapshots, at various points in time, which can cover a very lengthy period that can stretch 15-20 years. In contrast, typical transaction databases contain data for only a 6-24 month period.

Non-volatile

The data stored in a data warehouse remains static. Any new data, which is typically introduced periodically, is appended. Data warehouse data is subjected to regular access and analysis. However, activities such as insertions and deletions, which occur routinely with operational systems, do not occur in a data warehouse which is initially populated through a massive data load from the source systems followed by periodic appends.

DATABASE CHARACTERISTICS AND DESIGN

Differences in OLTP data and DWH data

An OLTP database contains detailed transaction data, which is collected from the organization's business operations. Though such a database may contain some derived data, which is calculated from the basic data elements, it primarily comprises of basic data elements. For example, the primary element can be the item price while the derived data can be the item's average price over a period of time. The data in an OLTP database is structured and organized so that it favors speed, performance, reliability, data integrity, and security.

A DWH database contains transaction data that has been re-structured for querying and analysis. BW contains both types of data: detailed transaction data in its original OLTP format as well as re-structured data. A data warehouse is also frequently populated with derived and summarized data. The availability of detailed data permits drill-down to be performed if there is a need to dig deeper after the summarized data has been analyzed. For example, a manager can initially analyze the sales performance of his sales force and, subsequently, selectively drill-down into the details of under-performing salespeople. Another key difference is that a data warehouse needs to deal with trends rather than data points. Therefore, its data elements need to have time associated with them, which is part of the key for every record in the database.

Comparing data warehouse and transaction databases

The requirements of OLTP and DWH databases are quite different. Data warehouse data is historical and, therefore, time-dependent. It is primarily accessed on an ad hoc basis, rather than through a pre-defined method. Data warehouse tables are extremely large, which conform to querying and analysis requirements. Such tables are highly interdependent and need to be periodically refreshed from multiple sources.

An OLTP transaction database, which runs a business, is optimized for update functions—not for querying and analysis. It contains small tables because it has to capture data efficiently as performance is an overriding factor. An OLTP database collects a large volume of raw transaction data that cannot be analyzed easily. Such a database does not address decision support requirements of history, summarization, integration, and metadata.

OLTP systems are not used as repositories of historical data, which is required for analyzing trends. Typically, such systems have inconsistent, dynamic (rapidly changing), as well as duplicate and/or missing entries. Also, the data in transaction databases is not in a form that is meaningful to end-users. The important characteristics of data warehouse databases and transactional databases are compared in the following table.

Data Warehouse (DWH)	Traditional Database (OLTP)
Used for data retrieval and analysis	Used to run daily business transactions
Integrated data	Application specific data
Historical and descriptive data	Current, changing, and incomplete data
Organized by subject	Organized for performance
Non-volatile data	Updated data
Relational database structure	Relational database structure
Redundant data	Normalized data
Multi-dimensional data model	Normalized data model
Fewer but larger tables	Greater number of smaller tables
Data for analyzing the business	Data for running the business
Summarized data	Raw data
Contains data about data (metadata)	Contains only data
Queries are unplanned and cannot be easily or quickly optimized	Queries are pre-defined, small, and can be optimized
Time element is contained in key structure	Time element may or may not be contained in key structure

Why DWH and OLTP databases need to be different

DWH and OLTP databases are structured differently due to their dissimilar requirements, which were listed in the previous section. Also, in contrast to an OLTP database, which needs to be updated continuously in real-time by the OLTP applications, a DWH database is updated periodically from the operational systems—typically during off-peak hours when network utilization is low. While OLTP databases require speed and performance, DWH databases require heavy query volumes to be supported. Additionally, DWH and OLTP databases have different requirements for backup, recovery, transaction and data integrity, reliability, and availability.

Database design technique: Star schema

The star schema is the most widely used method for implementing a multi-dimensional model in a relational database. It contains two types of tables, fact and dimension, which are described in detail in Chapter B6. The schema takes its name from the star-like arrangement in which a central fact table is surrounded by dimension tables. The star schema is not a normalized model, as its dimension tables are intentionally de-normalized, even though it is a relational model.

DATA DESIGN

There are a number of design issues that need to be addressed when a data warehouse is being planned and designed, which are described in the following sections. Many business decisions drive these, such as the period for which data is to be stored, the number and type of users accessing the data warehouse, etc.

Levels of data

Data is stored in data warehouses at three levels:

❑ Current detailed data: Transaction level data
❑ Lightly summarized data: Aggregated data, such as revenues by week or by sub-region
❑ Highly summarized data: Aggregated data, such as revenues by month or by region

Each data level targets a different type of user ranging from senior executives to operational users. While an inventory clerk may monitor the inventory of specific items at the detailed level, the chief executive may be more interested in analyzing highly summarized data that can provide insight into the performance of various regions, business units, subsidiaries, product lines, etc.

Current detailed data

The bulk of the data warehouse consists of current detailed data, at the lowest level of granularity (detail), which is extracted from the operational systems. It is organized by subject areas and can be stored as raw or aggregated data. All data items at this level represent snapshots in time. The period for which current detailed data is maintained in a data warehouse varies from organization to organization. Typically, data for 2-5 years is maintained though many companies store data for 10-15 years. The frequency of data refresh also varies according to the business needs. Many companies perform a daily data load, while some prefer to refresh their data in real-time.

Aggregated data

To improve the performance of queries, data can be aggregated or accumulated along pre-defined attributes. For example, car sales data can be aggregated by geography and model by adding the sales dollars for each model within a specific geography. Similarly, overall sales can be cumulated for a week, month, quarter or year. Hence, when a query is run against aggregated data, the response is faster as less data needs to be accessed (since it is already aggregated). The data to be stored in an aggregated format is determined by a number of factors including the frequency of queries.

Lightly summarized data

The requirement for light data summarization in a data warehouse is based upon the fact that most users run queries that repeatedly access and analyze the same data elements at a summarized level. Therefore, by storing summarized data, there can be considerable improvement in the performance and storage requirements.

Highly summarized data

The source for highly summarized data can be lightly summarized data or current detailed data. The primary users of highly summarized data are senior executives and strategic users. While their needs are primarily limited to this level, they can also access lower level detailed data through a drill-down process.

Normalization and de-normalization

An OLTP relational database is a collection of two-dimensional tables, which are organized into rows and columns. In such a database, the design objective is to optimize table structures by eliminating all instances of data redundancy. This is achieved by making database tables as small as possible and, when required, merge selected tables through joins. Therefore, such a system contains a very large number of small tables in which there is minimum data redundancy.

In a data warehouse, the design objective is the opposite—to make database tables larger with more redundant data so that the need for table joins is minimized when a query is executed. The objective is to enable a query to find most of its required data in a single table, which will limit the amount of data that will need to be pulled from other tables. The technique of merging small tables into larger tables with data redundancy, called de-normalization, causes less input/output operations, which improves query performance. *& increases data storage requirements.*

De-normalization provides the flexibility for addressing requirements that are ad hoc and unplanned. However, while it is suitable for a data warehouse, it not appropriate for a transaction database, which emphasizes performance over redundancy. A normalized transaction database limits the queries that can be run against it, since they can severely impact its performance.

Database partitioning

The objective of partitioning is to break up data into smaller physical units that can be managed independently. This technique provides greater flexibility in data management for designers and operations personnel. It overcomes the limitations of large physical units, which cannot be easily structured, reorganized, recovered or monitored. Partitioning enables sequential scanning, if required, as well as ease of indexing. It allows data to be broken up by region, organization, business unit, date, etc., which can be very useful for the purpose of analysis.

Data archiving

The data to be archived, and its frequency, depends on how the data is to be used. If the data warehouse is expected to support operational needs, the requirements may be met by retaining data for a two-year period. However, if the data is to be used for strategic purposes, the retention requirements will be for a considerably longer period, which can extend for 5-20 years. The archived data granularity may be the same as the current detailed or aggregated data.

Granularity

An important data warehouse design issue is granularity because it affects the volume of data to be stored and the type of query that can be executed. If data is highly granular, with a very high level of detail, the volume of data to be stored in the warehouse will be huge. A highly granular data warehouse contains very detailed data, which can include every captured transaction such as individual sales orders and purchase requisitions. A less granular data warehouse contains a higher level of data, such as total purchase orders issued for each month or total monthly sales by region.

If stored data is very granular, practically any type of query can be run against it. However, if the data is less granular, the types of queries that can be executed will be restricted. Usually, senior executives and decision makers require summarized and aggregated data, while operational staff requires detailed data. However, in recent years, this distinction is being blurred as the needs and requirements of these two types of users have overlapped due to changes in the decision-making levels and empowerment of lower-level employees.

Data modeling

The objective of data modeling is to develop an accurate model or graphical representation of the business processes, identify data that needs to be captured in the database, and the relationships between data. A data model focuses on the data required, and its organization, rather than the operations to be performed on the data. It represents data from the users' perspective and is independent of hardware and software constraints. The star schema is the model of choice for capturing data warehouse requirements.

Database design is accomplished in five steps: planning and analysis, conceptual design, logical design, physical design, and implementation. The data model is created in the conceptual design step. It focuses on the data that needs to be stored in the database and how the tables are designed. The functional model focuses on how the data is to be processed and, also, how the queries are to be designed for accessing the database tables.

Logical data model

A logical data model, Figure 1, graphically depicts the information requirements of a business. It combines the business requirements and data structure—the two most important components of application development. If either one of these is lacking or poorly defined, the result will be an application that fails or is not well accepted.

Figure 1: Logical data model

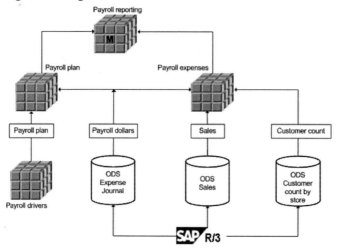

A logical data model is not a database and is independent of a physical data storage device. While a logical database describes the business requirements, the physical database indicates how they are implemented. A logical data model uses an ERD to put together all the data items or information required to run a business. It includes relationships, cardinality, attributes, and keys. Based upon requirements specified by business experts, an ERD is created by a data modeler.

Physical data model

The physical data model is created from the logical data model. Based on the physical data model, the physical database is designed and implemented. The activities in this step include de-normalizing the data, selecting keys, creating indexes, building referential integrity, etc. A well-designed physical data model and database structure ensures system performance and ease of maintenance.

Importance of building a data model

A data model ensures that data required by the database is represented accurately, completely, and is in a format that can be reviewed by end-users before the design is implemented. The data model is used to build the physical database as it contains information for defining the tables, keys, triggers, and stored procedures. Without a data model, database design will be seriously flawed, efficiency and performance will suffer and be less than optimal, data for critical reports may be missed, results produced may be inconsistent, maintenance will be difficult, and supporting business needs will not be easy.

It is imperative that a logical data model be built for every data warehouse project even though it is a labor-intensive and time-consuming activity. A logical data model is the foundation upon which a database for an application is designed. It verifies that the system will satisfy the business needs. The implementation approach and technique is determined to a large extent by the business requirements and the logical data model.

Skilled data architects who can efficiently design data warehouses are difficult to find, especially for smaller projects. Therefore, data modeling for data warehouses is often flawed or less than optimal because it is widely done by inexperienced data modelers or architects.

Chapter B4
Process and Architecture

PROCESS

Data warehouse process components

A data warehouse is an integrated process, shown in Figure 2, that encompasses many technologies. The basic process involves manipulating and moving data from various databases into a central database, where it is stored and subsequently analyzed. The data is moved using a variety of acquisition techniques and tools.

Figure 2: Data Warehousing process

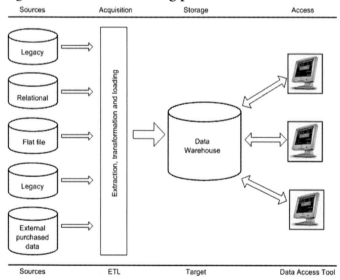

A data warehouse consists of many components, ranging from simple to complex, which can be grouped into three main categories:

❑ Acquisition component: Interfaces with the source databases from where it imports data into the data warehouse
❑ Storage component: Is a large physical database that stores data imported into the data warehouse
❑ Access component: Consists of front-end access and query tools that access and analyze data stored in the data warehouse

Acquisition component

The data fed into a data warehouse can originate from many sources though, typically, it is imported from the organization's transaction database(s). The sources can be mainframe files, relational and non-relational databases, flat files, etc. Many companies also use external sources to feed data into their data warehouses. Most of these sources, internal and external, cannot meet the data warehouse requirement for imported data to be in a specific format—a layout that supports query processing. The reason for this limitation is that most data sources are formatted for transaction processing—not querying and analysis. Therefore, before it can be loaded into the data warehouse, source data typically needs to undergo formatting and transformation operations in order to remove inconsistencies and achieve standardization. For example, gender in three source systems may be coded differently: M/F, male/female, and 1/2. Hence, before data from these three sources can be imported into a data warehouse, at least two must be transformed so that consistent data is fed from all three sources.

ETL components

The overall data acquisition process, called ETL (extraction, transformation, and loading), is at the heart of the data warehousing process. This process is generally grouped into three main components:

❑ Extraction: Involves obtaining the required data from various sources.
❑ Transformation: Source data is subjected to a number of operations that prepare it for import into the data warehouse (target database). To perform this task, integration and transformation programs are used which can reformat, recalculate, modify structure and data elements, and add time elements. They can also perform calculations and a variety of tasks such as summarization and de-normalization.

❑ Loading: Involves physically moving the extracted and transformed data into the target database. Initially, a large volume of data is imported into the data warehouse. Subsequently, an extraction procedure periodically loads fresh data based on business rules and a pre-determined frequency.

ETL operations

All source data may need to undergo some or all of the following operations in the data warehousing process:

❑ Mapping (from source databases to target database)
❑ Cleaning dirty data (for missing, incorrect, or inconsistent data within fields)
❑ Restructuring and reformatting, which can be due to field lengths, sequence, and data types (text, numeric or alpha-numeric)
❑ Recalculation
❑ Selection (using filters such as if/then)
❑ Summarization
❑ Validation
❑ Reconciliation (when data is imported from multiple sources)

Additional ETL tasks can include:

❑ Merge processing when multiple data sources are used
❑ Purge processing when some filtering rules are applied to weed out unwanted data
❑ Staging when source data needs to be placed in an intermediate storage location before it is read by, and imported into, the data warehouse
❑ Back flushing if the clean data warehouse data is to be sent back to the source (legacy) system(s)

ETL tools

ETL tasks are handled by a variety of tools. Some of them, such as file transfer programs, are fairly simple. However, some tools, such as those used for data transformation, can be fairly complex. They can automate data extraction from multiple sources, map sources to the target database, transform and/or manipulate data, and load data into the data warehouse.

The BW system does not need any external ETL tools if SAP is the source system and BW is the target system. However, when the source is a non-SAP system, either BW's internally built ETL capabilities or external third-party ETL tools can be used to load data into the BW data warehouse. Certified ETL tools for BW are provided by a number of vendors including Ascential, Information Builders, WRQ, Hummingbird Communications, Informatica, TSI International, and Business Objects.

Storage component

There are two databases associated with a data warehouse. They are:

❑ Source database
❑ Target database

Source database

The source database feeds data into the data warehouse. In a typical organization, there exist multiple data sources of different types, such as relational and hierarchical, and sizes. In the vast majority of cases, the source database is an OLTP system containing current transaction data. In some cases, the source is a non-OLTP database, such as a data warehouse or a data mart. Examples of source data, which can be from internal as well as external sources, include:

❑ Internal systems: financial, billing, materials management, sales, and manufacturing
❑ External data: industry, economic, demographic, weather, and clickstream

While BW uses SAP R/3 as its primary source database, it also utilizes non-SAP sources (relational and non-relational databases, flat files, etc.) for populating its data warehouse database.

Target database

The core component of a data warehouse system is a very large target database. It holds the organization's transaction and historical data in an integrated format. Due to it's analytical and query processing requirements, data warehouse data is structured in a de-normalized format in contrast to the normalized structure of OLTP databases. The size of a data warehouse can be huge. For example, the Home Depot data warehouse, which was commissioned in 2002, has been designed for storing 60 terabytes of data.

While conceptually, only two databases are required (source and target) for a data warehouse, a third type of database is also used frequently. This is an intermediate database, an operational data store (ODS), into which source data is loaded and stored before being sent to its final destination—the data warehouse (target database).

Operational data stores are supported within the BW architecture. A BW ODS can be the final destination of data imported into the BW system from the source system(s). However, typically, an ODS is used as an intermediate storage location from where the imported data is ultimately sent to the main BW data warehouse object, the InfoCube, after undergoing ETL operations. A BW system can contain many operational data stores. If required, a query can be executed directly against an ODS.

Access component

To access and analyze data stored in a data warehouse, and present it to the users, an access/query component is required. This component can include querying, reporting, and decision support tools. Such tools, which can include data mining software, can typically support queries, calculations, what-if analysis, as well as other advanced functions.

The sophistication of the available data access tools varies significantly. They range from low-end tools, with simple querying capabilities, to high-end tools that can perform sophisticated multi-dimensional analysis. The recent trend has been to web-enable such tools, a feature that provides many benefits. A web-enabled tool is more versatile and easy to use, eliminates the need to install special software on every desktop, provides access through a simple browser, and helps reduce costs as it requires less powerful and expensive hardware.

Most data warehouse users use standard reports and queries. They execute most of their queries using summary views. Only a small percentage of data warehouse users create custom reports, which are often developed by business analysts.

The BW is provided with its own front-end access and analysis tool—the Business Explorer (BEx). It also permits other reporting and analysis tools, such as Cognos and Business Objects, to be used against it.

ARCHITECTURE

Physical architecture and infrastructure

A data warehouse system consists of several physical components that are connected through a network structure, which glues the parts together. The system hardware consists of the acquisition, storage, and access components. The deployment has, in the past, been typically implemented in a 2-tier or 3-tier architecture, or physical configuration, as described in the next section. The 4-tier architecture has become more popular in recent years.

Other components that make up a data warehousing system include the operating system, system utilities, procedures, and middleware connectivity tools. The middleware links different data sources to the data warehouse and provides connectivity between the data warehouse and associated clients.

Data warehouse usage grows exponentially if it is implemented successfully. However, success can create capacity constraints if the system and network are inadequately designed. Hence, a data warehouse should be designed to accommodate growth, exhibit good performance and avoid slow response times, and be scalable.

SAP's BW is built on top of the SAP Web Application Server. However, even though it is closely linked with the SAP R/3 system, it is an independent software package that can be used in SAP as well as non-SAP environments.

Application and deployment architecture

The data warehouse application architecture comprises of the three components, or layers, that make up an application. They are:

❑ Presentation (what the user sees—the client side view)
❑ Functional logic (underlying business rules)
❑ Data (physical data storage layer)

The simplest deployment is a two-tier architecture where a client, such as a PC, interacts directly with a server. In a two-tier system, the first tier (server) hosts the data warehouse database. The client, the second tier, hosts the front-end decision support and analysis tools. The three-tier architecture is more complex as it introduces an intermediate tier between the server and the client. It has the following components:

❑ 1st tier: server tier which handles data processing
❑ 2nd tier: application tier that supports the functional logic and services
❑ 3rd tier: client or desktop tier which handles the decision support and presentation component

A 4-tier architecture is also available for data warehouse implementations. It is characterized by the addition of an additional web component, a web server, as described in an earlier chapter.

Defining the architecture

A data warehouse should not be designed for a particular technology. Its architecture must be designed before the technology is selected. Failure to design the architecture first can prevent the requirements from being supported by the selected technology, which cannot be easily modified or discarded due to the extremely high costs associated with scrapping or modifying a deployed infrastructure. Since many options are available, as many technologies support data warehousing, rarely should an overriding factor force a company to implement a particular technology for its data warehousing needs.

Metadata

Metadata, or data about data, is a key element in the data warehouse architecture. Like a library's card catalog, which helps locate books, metadata provides useful information for locating data stored in a data warehouse. All data about the data, as mapped between the source and target systems, is resident in the metadata. The metadata includes a description of the data warehouse fields and tables, data types, and acceptable value ranges.

The metadata can help determine mapping information, such as where the data warehouse data came from—legacy systems, files, databases, and fields. It provides information about the data structure—tables and columns as well as their definition and descriptions. Additionally, metadata indicates the relationships between the data structures within or between databases. It also provides information about operations performed on imported data such as:

❑ Selection criteria and business rules that were applied
❑ Transformation and integration performed during the data migration process
❑ Filtering and cleansing that was performed
❑ Algorithms used to summarize and derive data

Metadata often resides outside the data warehouse, in a database or a formal repository, and is used to track the relationship between the data model and the data warehouse. It can provide information on how the business definitions and calculations changed over the years. Metadata can also provide a history of extracts and changes in data over time.

There are two types of metadata: structural and access. Structural metadata is used to create and maintain the data warehouse. Its foundation is the data warehouse model that describes data entities as well as their relationships. On the other hand, access metadata provides the dynamic link between a data warehouse and its associated applications. Of the three classes of metadata defined by Inmon, business and technical metadata are commonly referred to as metadata—the data about data. The third type, operational metadata, refers to data about processes.

Chapter B5
Infrastructure and Tools

PLATFORM AND HARDWARE

Platform

A data warehouse can be implemented on various platforms including Unix, Windows, Linux, and mainframe operating systems. Initially, Unix was used extensively but Windows NT has started being used widely due to its lower cost and ease of administration. For BW, typically, the platform is the same as the one being used by SAP R/3 at the implementation site. The BW now sits atop the NetWeaver platform and the Enterprise Services Architecture.

Hardware

A data warehouse system consists of a number of hardware components such as servers, workstations (PCs), memory, disk storage units, networks, etc. The selection of the hardware platform and components depends on a number of factors including:

- ❑ Storage capacity
- ❑ Scalability
- ❑ Performance
- ❑ Number of users
- ❑ Operating system
- ❑ Software
- ❑ Complexity of queries
- ❑ IT skills and maintenance capabilities
- ❑ Budget constraints

Data warehouse usage increases dramatically if users perceive it to be useful. However, past experience has shown that the rapid rise in the number of users usually surprises designers. The underestimation of usage and, consequently, hardware requirements creates problems when the number of users increases beyond expectations and queries start to become more complex.

DATA WAREHOUSE ENGINE

Engine requirements

A data warehouse engine, the database, provides the structure for storing data required to support the analysis requirements. Some of the engine's primary business requirements, and factors that determine its selection, include:

- ❑ Ease of use
- ❑ Flexibility
- ❑ Scalability
- ❑ Reliability
- ❑ Performance
- ❑ Cost
- ❑ Data loading time
- ❑ Ability to support expected data volumes
- ❑ Ease of monitoring and administration
- ❑ Ability to work with various access tools from different vendors
- ❑ Security
- ❑ Vendor (reputation and number of database installations)

Type of database to use

A key data warehouse design decision concerns the database type to be selected: relational database or multi-dimensional (OLAP) database. The characteristics of these database types, and their differences, were explained in detail in Chapter B3. The selection of the database type influences the choice of the data access tool, which can be a simple relational query tool, an OLAP tool that provides a multi-dimensional view of the data, or some other type of specialized decision support tool.

Each database type is characterized by strengths and limitations. Conventional relational databases support the specialized technical requirements of data warehouses such as data extraction and replication, query optimization, bit-mapped indexes, etc. However, they provide limited support for data cleanup and transformation functions. The strengths of multi-dimensional databases include the benefits associated with OLAP as well as fast querying and performance. Their primary drawback is that they are based on a proprietary database solution.

Conventional relational databases provide many of the features that characterize multi-dimensional databases. In many cases, either type of database can be used. However, for specialized or complex analysis requirements, multi-dimensional databases are often preferred.

DATA MIGRATION TOOLS

Role and importance of ETL

An extremely important and difficult task in building a data warehouse is extracting, transforming, and loading huge volumes of data stored in a variety of disparate source systems. The ETL design and development task is also very expensive and can easily consume 50-75% of the data warehouse project budget. The task is very time consuming because it requires cleaning and integrating the organization's data, which is stored in many systems and formats. Hence, it is critical that ETL be accomplished through a well-designed architecture that is reliable and scalable. Such architecture must support the extraction, transformation, and loading of the data elements that need to be fed into the data warehouse.

ETL tools can be very expensive and difficult to use. They have the potential to cause serious problems including project failure and, hence, should be selected very carefully based on the unique needs of each data warehouse.

ETL tasks

Many tools, from a number of vendors, are available for building a data warehouse. The three primary functions that ETL tools, which move data from one location to another, are required to accomplish are:

❑   Read data from a source such as a relational database table, flat file, etc.
❑   Manipulate data (filter, modify or enhance) based on specific rules
❑   Write resulting data to the target database

Specific tasks that an ETL tool may have to perform range from:

❑ Converting data: changing the incoming source data into a unified format and definition
❑ Deriving data: applying mathematical formula to a field(s) in order to create a brand new field
❑ Filtering data: screening unwanted data from source data files before moving it to the data warehouse
❑ Integrating data: merging files from different databases and platforms
❑ Summarizing data: combining tables
❑ Selecting data: selecting and loading data based on triggers

BW ETL tool

The BW system is provided with embedded ETL functionality for loading SAP R/3 transaction data. Typically, data can be interactively selected and moved, from the source system to the target system, using an easy-to-use GUI. The embedded ETL functionality reduces the need for developing custom ETL programs, for loading SAP tables into the BW system, which helps cut ETL costs significantly.

Other ETL tools

The functionality of the available ETL tools varies considerably and their cost can range from minimal to hundreds of thousands of dollars. At the lower end are simple data migration tools whose functionality is limited to extraction and loading. However, the more versatile tools are very sophisticated and can perform many tasks such as enabling transformations, handling a wide range of input formats and sources, etc.

As users clamor for complete solutions, vendors are being forced to provide more functionality and reliability. Some of the desired features include:

❑ Back-end data management and processing including metadata management
❑ Ability to handle real-time, or near real-time, data as batch processing windows become smaller and smaller
❑ Ability to handle greater number of sources and different data sources (XML, HTML, etc.)
❑ Improved administration
❑ Ability to handle greater complexity of mappings and transformations

❑ Improved throughput and scalability for handling rising data volumes even as batch processing windows decrease
❑ Improved capability for capturing changes and updates
❑ Ease of use for loading and/or updating

DATA ACCESS TOOLS

Need for data access

Transaction processing systems have been very effective in capturing and storing operational data. However, historically, they have lacked the ability to effectively utilize the stored data and convert it into information that can be used for reporting and analysis. Therefore, in recent years, this shortcoming led to the development and popularity of tools, such as data warehouses, that enabled users to access stored data and transform it into information.

Requirements

The data access and reporting requirements within an organization vary considerably. At the high end are strategic queries that analyze huge amounts of data across multiple dimensions. At the low end are tactical queries, run against limited data that may be frequently updated, which answer operational questions. The requirements of strategic users, the senior executives, are quite different compared to line managers, front-line workers, and power users. Therefore, an organization's requirements can range from canned status reports, which are most widely used, to ad hoc queries that are developed dynamically and interactively.

The challenge is to create a reporting environment where the needs of all users can be met. This requires balancing the needs of the vast majority of non-technical users, whose needs fall within limited parameters, to the requirements of some users who demand performance and flexibility. The deployment of such a reporting environment, which must be scalable and secure within a controlled environment, must meet the varying needs of business users and also avoid straining IT resources. If the reporting tools are underutilized by the users and do not meet their expected potential, which can be caused by a number of reasons, the data warehouse will end up being viewed either as a limited success or a failure.

Features

Some of the basic requirements of data access products include flexibility to meet the diverse needs of users having a wide range of requirements, scalability, low implementation cost, fast deployment, web access, support for different output types, formatting capabilities, adaptability to changing business needs, ease of use and administration, security, etc.

Categories

The commonly used data access products fall into the following main groups:

❑ Query and reporting tools, which can be deployed cost-effectively for a large number of users. These tools, which have extensive formatting capabilities, cannot answer complex questions that require drill-down capabilities.
❑ Spreadsheets such as Excel.
❑ DSS tools that can perform multi-dimensional analysis against relational databases.
❑ Tools that can access multi-dimensional databases.
❑ Data mining products.
❑ Tools, such as SAS and SPSS, that can perform complex statistical analysis.
❑ Artificial intelligence and advanced analysis tools.

Multi-dimensional tools

A number of multi-dimensional OLAP tools, from different vendors, are available for analyzing data warehouse data. The features and benefits of this technology, which has powerful navigation and presentation capabilities, are described in Chapter B6.

CHAPTER B6
MULTI-DIMENSIONALITY AND OLAP

DRIVERS FOR MULTI-DIMENSIONAL ANALYSIS

Demand for improved data analysis

In the past two decades, organizations invested hundreds of billions of dollars for streamlining their business processes in order to gain a competitive edge. During that period, as Internet usage exploded and many data-hungry applications such as ERP and CRM systems became widely deployed, huge volumes of data began to be collected. However, the captured data was barely analyzed and converted into information because the focus was on collecting data—not analyzing it.

The introduction of data warehousing technology shifted the focus from collecting data to analyzing the gold mine of data buried in corporate IT systems. However, the available analysis tools had some limitations. Consequently, many users felt an acute need for faster and more innovative techniques that would help them answer complex questions and support decision-making. That need led to the development of the multi-dimensional analysis technique and associated tools.

Demand for multi-dimensional views and analysis

Limitations of traditional databases

Traditional relational databases, as well as spreadsheets, are based on a two-dimensional model of rows and columns. Such a model allows a user to view data in two dimensions, such as sales by region. However, data warehouse users rarely want to access data through only one dimension (or column). For example, it will be rare for a telecommunication company analyst to limit his analysis to determining the number of phone customers in a single state, such as Pennsylvania. A typical analyst will perform far more comprehensive analysis, such as comparing

Pennsylvania phone customers through two dimensions—actual versus projected (number of customers).

This scenario can become complicated as more dimensions are added. For example, the analyst might want to determine the number of customers who subscribed to both home and wireless service in the past year. Additionally, he might like to compare the result generated by his query, for the last year, to the historical results in order to determine a trend or aberration. To generate his query using conventional databases, the analyst would be required to access data in different tables and then perform complex table joins—a task that would be beyond the capabilities of ordinary users.

Need to analyze through multi-dimensions

Most data warehouse queries are multi-dimensional, which use multiple criteria against multiple columns, because the two-dimensional view of data limits the type of analysis that can be performed. Two-dimensional views cannot support complex requirements like understanding the relationships between multi-dimensions such as sales, geography (region), and distribution channel. In a relational database, analysis of multi-dimensions would require the setup of a series of tables (sales, regions, and distribution channels). These tables would first be joined and then accessed through complex SQL code in order to perform multi-dimensional analysis, such as determining how costs have trended over time.

The need for joins, which are not difficult for programmers to implement, forces users to consider the data structure. Multi-dimensional analysis overcomes this limitation by enabling data to be accessed through multiple dimensions or columns (criteria), which are presented in business terms and, hence, can be selected easily without knowing the underlying data structure. For example, a user can analyze sales by product by region over time by picking the appropriate dimensions, which are displayed by their business names (sales, product, region, and time).

UNDERSTANDING MULTI-DIMENSIONALITY

The dimensional model overcomes the limitations of relational databases, which are organized in a two-dimensional format. The dimensional model is based on a structure organized by dimensions, such as sales or geography, and is represented by a multi-dimensional array or cube. This model provides an intuitive way of organizing and selecting data for querying and analysis. A multi-dimensional model:

- ❑ Is representative of the company's business model
- ❑ Provides a view that is business rather than technical; users can concentrate on the business instead of the tool
- ❑ Enables slicing and dicing, which provides the ability to analyze data using different scenarios such as sales by products, region, channel, and period
- ❑ Permits data to be easily analyzed across any dimension and level of aggregation
- ❑ Is flexible and permits powerful analytical processing

Dimensions

A dimension represents an attribute such as product, region, or time. All data warehouses have one common dimension—time. A spreadsheet is the simplest example of a two-dimensional model. The spreadsheet row and column names are the "dimensions" while the numeric data in it are the "facts." A time dimension can include all months, quarters, years, etc., while a geography dimension can include all countries, regions, and cities. A dimension acts like an index for identifying values in a multi-dimensional array. If the number of dimensions used is increased, greater is the level of detail that can be queried.

If a single member is selected from all dimensions, then a single cell is defined. A three-dimensional model is represented by a cubic structure in which each dimension forms a side of the cube. In a dimensional model, data is organized according to a business user's perspective with common dimensions being time, region, products, distribution or sales channels, and budget.

Figure 3 represents a three-dimensional model with region, product, and time dimensions. Figures 4 and 5 represent multiple dimension views—by brand and region.

Figure 3: 3-dimensional model

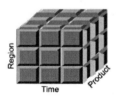

Figure 4: Multiple-dimension views—brand

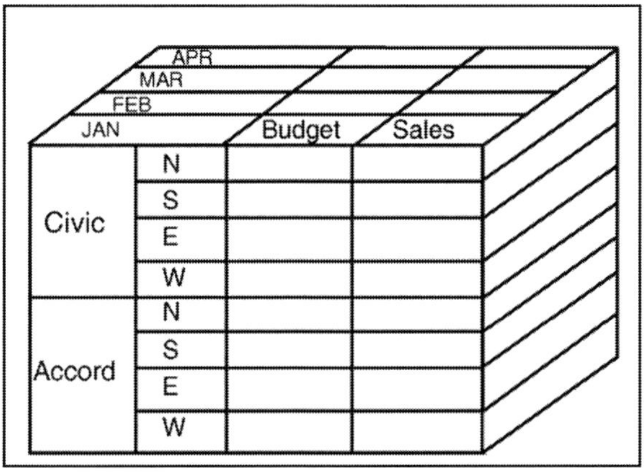

Figure 5 shows the same data sliced along three dimensions (region, product, and time), while Figure 6 shows drill-down to a single cell. Figure 7 provides examples of slicing and dicing along different dimensions.

Figure 5: Multiple-dimension views—region

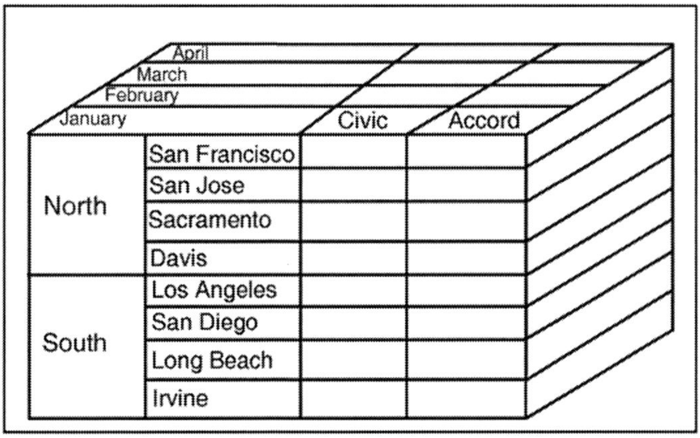

Figure 6: Drill-down to a cell

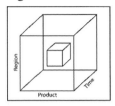

Figure 7: Slicing and dicing along different dimensions

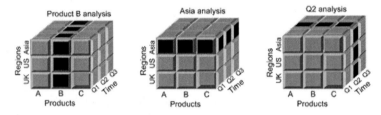

Facts

The values in the array in a dimensional model, which change over time, are called facts. Examples of facts, which are used to measure performance, are sales, units sold, costs, and shipments. Fact tables, which are the focus of dimensional queries, contain two types of fields:

❑ Fields that store the foreign key, which connects each fact to the appropriate value in each dimension
❑ Fields that store individual facts such as price, quantity, and salary

Characteristics of fact and dimension tables

The following are the defining characteristics of facts and dimensions:

❑ Fact table characteristics:
   • Fact table consists of multiple columns and a large number of rows (can be millions)
   • Is the primary table which contains the numeric data—measurements such as price, cost, profit, and salary
   • Holds the "real" quantitative data—the data being queried; typically holds atomic and aggregate data such as the number of cars sold
   • Fact table contains all of the attributes to be measured

- Fact table row corresponds to a measurement
- Measurement takes place at the intersection of all the dimensions such as month, product, and region
- Fact represents a business measure; fact attributes contain measurable numeric values (which are normally additive)
- Numerical measures are restricted to fact tables
- Facts can be operated upon (summed, averaged, aggregated, etc.)
❑ Dimension table characteristics:
  - Reflects business dimensions such as product, region, and distribution channel
  - Contains a primary key that connects it to the fact table
  - Dimensional attributes provide links between the fact table and its associated dimension tables
  - Contains descriptive data reflecting business dimensions; dimensional attributes provide description of each row in the fact table
  - Groups descriptive attributes about the facts; dimension table has many attribute fields; each field describes individual characteristics of the dimension; for example, attributes of product dimension can be description, size, color, weight, and type
  - Are used to guide the selection of rows from the fact table
  - Dimensions permit categorization of transactions; example, customer dimension can be used to analyze procurement by location, frequency, etc.
  - Tables are smaller as they have fewer number of rows
  - Tables are de-normalized but that does not increase storage significantly as the dimension tables are very small compared to the fact table

Multi-dimensional analysis

Multi-dimensional analysis is a powerful analytical tool that can provide insight not possible through two-dimensional analysis. The following example shows how multi-dimensional analysis can be used to analyze the sales for a car dealership using multiple dimensions.

The car dealership is split into two sales regions: North and South. The consolidated total sales for each region are shown in Table 1:

Table 1: Single dimension	
Region	Sales (millions)
North	23.7
South	22.6

In Table 1, there is only one fact (sales) that is related to a single dimension (region). The only dimension in this case (region) is used for aggregating its associated fact (sales). If the car dealer desires to perform in-depth analysis, he can drill-down so that the sales dollars for each region for each quarter, as shown in Table 2, are displayed.

Table 2: Two dimensions		
Region	Time (quarter)	Sales (millions)
North	Q1	56
	Q2	61
	Q3	60
	Q4	60
South	Q1	52
	Q2	57
	Q3	62
	Q4	55

Table 2 relates one fact (sales) to two dimensions—region and time (quarter). It shows the aggregated sales dollars associated with each of the eight combinations of region and time dimensions.

If the car dealer wants to analyze his sales even more comprehensively, he can use a third dimension (model), as shown in Table 3, which relates one fact (sales) to three dimensions (region, time, and model). Table 3 shows the aggregated sales (facts) for each combination of region, time, and model.

Table 3: Three dimensions			
Region	Time (quarter)	Model	Sales (millions)
North	Q1	Accord	23
	Q1	Civic	33
	Q2	Accord	27
	Q2	Civic	34
	Q3	Accord	29
	Q3	Civic	31
	Q4	Accord	24
	Q4	Civic	36
South	Q1	Accord	21
	Q1	Civic	31
	Q2	Accord	23
	Q2	Civic	34
	Q3	Accord	27
	Q3	Civic	35
	Q4	Accord	22
	Q4	Civic	33

Multi-dimensional database

A multi-dimensional database is a type of proprietary database that stores data in an array format, rather than tables. The data is organized and stored by pre-defined dimensions, which permit users to view it in multiple dimensions that correspond to easy-to-understand business dimensions. The enabling of a business view of the data permits users to navigate through various dimensions and data levels, which can help them to perform analysis easily and quickly.

Multi-dimensional databases are designed to support multi-dimensional queries designed for analyzing complex questions. However, while a multi-dimensional database supports slice and dice capabilities, its proprietary solution is a drawback that can prevent or limit the use of available query tools.

Star schema

The star schema design, commonly used for designing data warehouse databases, supports analytical processing. It takes its name from the star-like arrangement of entities. The star schema is the design most frequently used to implement a multi-dimensional model in a relational database. Its structure consists of a central fact table with keys to many dimension tables (Figure 8). The following characteristics are associated with a star schema:

❑ It contains two types of tables: Fact (major) and dimension (minor)
❑ One dimension represents one table
❑ Dimension tables surround the fact table
❑ Dimension tables are de-normalized
❑ Dimension tables are linked to the fact table through unique keys (one per dimension table)
❑ Every dimension key uniquely identifies a row in the dimension table associated with it
❑ A fact table's specific row is uniquely identified by the dimension keys
❑ Uses many ERD components such as entities, attributes, cardinality, primary keys, and relationship connectors

The star schema design has many advantages. It favors de-normalization for optimizing speed. The de-normalization of the time dimension results in a significant reduction in the number of tables that need to be joined when time-based queries are executed. A star schema's performance is superior because one large table (fact table) needs to be joined with a few small tables (dimension tables), resulting in a fast response time. The star schema reflects how business users view data, makes metadata navigation easier for both programmers and end-users, and permits more versatility in the selection of front-end tools.

If a dimension table has subcategories or more than one level of dimension tables, and more efficient access is required, a snowflake schema can be used. The snowflake schema, which is derived from the star schema and is more normalized and complex, adds a hierarchical structure to the dimension tables.

Figure 8: Star schema

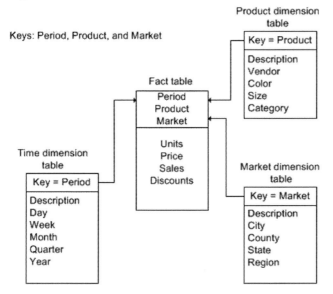

ONLINE ANALYTICAL PROCESSING

What is OLAP

Online analytical processing, OLAP, is a technique that combines data access tools with an analytical database engine. In contrast to the simple rows and columns structure of relational databases, upon which most data warehouses are built, OLAP uses a multi-dimensional view of data such as sales by brand, season, and store. OLAP, which works on data aggregates, uses calculations and transformations to perform its analytical tasks. There are two types of OLAP system architectures:

❑ Multi-dimensional OLAP (MOLAP): It uses a multi-dimensional database in which data is stored in multi-dimensions. The BW InfoCubes are based upon this architecture.
❑ Relational OLAP (ROLAP): It uses a relational database that is accessed directly. This architecture is the basis for accessing an ODS in a BW system.

In 2003, according to the OLAP Report, the estimated total worldwide OLAP market, including implementation services, was $3.7 billion. In 2003, the market share for the top vendors is estimated as follows:

❑ Microsoft: 26.1%
❑ Hyperion (including Brio): 21.9%
❑ Cognos (including Adaytum): 14.2%
❑ Business Objects (including Crystal): 7.7%
❑ Microstrategy: 6.2%
❑ SAP: 5.8%

OLAP database server

An OLAP server stores data as well as the relationships between the data. It is optimized for ad hoc query processing and data manipulation. An OLAP server is designed to work with multi-dimensional data structures, which can be visualized as cubes of data (and cubes within cubes), with the following characteristics:

❑ A cell is a single point in a cube
❑ Each data item is located, and accessed, based on the intersection of the dimensions defining it
❑ Each side of a cube is a dimension that represents an attribute or category such as product, region, channel, or time period
❑ Each cell contains aggregated data that relates the elements along each dimension
❑ Using the dimension numbers that define them, data items can be easily located and accessed
❑ An intermediate server can be used to store pre-calculations

An OLAP server's key characteristic is its calculation engine. It can extract data in real-time from relational or other databases and, when required, manipulate it. However, the more common and preferred method is to physically store the data on the OLAP server in multi-dimensional format. A database that stores data in multi-dimensional format is known as a multi-dimensional database (MDDB). In contrast to a conventional data warehouse relational database, whose size can range in the hundreds of gigabytes to terabytes, an OLAP server is far smaller—typically in the gigabytes range.

OLAP benefits

OLAP technology enables users to access data quickly, efficiently, interactively, and in innovative ways without first having to understand the data structure or technical details. The data, which is presented in dimensions as business users view it, can be queried and analyzed using different views. Compared to data warehouses based on relational database technology, OLAP systems have an additional feature—the ability to perform "what if" analysis, a powerful tool that can simulate the effect of decisions. For example, OLAP can answer a question like, "what will be the impact on airline ticket sales if the price of jet fuel rises by $0.15 per gallon, one hub is closed, and another fuel distribution center is added to the system."

The following are some of the benefits that OLAP technology can provide:

- ❑ Identify key trends and factors driving businesses, which can help users understand changes in buying patterns and customer preferences
- ❑ Ability to perform complex calculations and trend analysis
- ❑ Ability to manipulate data with many inter-relationships
- ❑ Insulate users from SQL language and the relational model
- ❑ Improve query performance; enable massive amounts of data to be analyzed rapidly
- ❑ Improve scalability
- ❑ Support a wide range of tools
- ❑ Automate maintenance of indexes and summaries
- ❑ Decrease demand for reports from IT
- ❑ Enable fast deployment
- ❑ Usage in a wide range of applications such as forecasting, profitability analysis, customer analysis, budgeting, and marketing analysis
- ❑ Increase productivity of individuals and organizations

Desired OLAP features

There are many characteristics and features desired in an OLAP system including:

- ❑ User perspective: data should be transparent to users
- ❑ Ease of use
- ❑ Intuitive data manipulation
- ❑ Easy and fast deployment
- ❑ Seamless presentation of historical, projected, and derived data
- ❑ Reasonable implementation cost
- ❑ Cost-effective maintenance
- ❑ Ability to perform operations against single or multiple dimensions (aggregated, summarized, and derived data)
- ❑ Powerful calculation capabilities
- ❑ Support for statistical and analytical functions
- ❑ Support more than simple aggregation or roll-ups such as share calculations (% of total) and allocations
- ❑ Support for large data sets and unlimited dimensions and aggregation levels

- Time intelligence which supports analysis such as year-to-date and period-over-period
- Secure and concurrent access to data
- Consistent and fast query performance
- Flexible reporting
- Consistent reporting performance
- Integration with desktop tools
- Scalability—large data volumes as well as the number of concurrent users
- Ability to read data while updates are occurring

Types of OLAP tools

The three most common types of multi-dimensional OLAP tools are:

- Spreadsheets, which present data in a cross-tab view that is familiar to business users. The amount of data that can be accessed through such a tool is limited.
- Client-based multi-dimensional databases (such as Pablo), which retain pre-calculated consolidated data in PC memory; the magnitude of data that can be accessed through such tools ranges in the megabytes.
- Server-based multi-dimensional databases (such as Essbase, Express, and Holos), which can handle gigabytes of data and implement various performance and storage optimization techniques. The BW system's database, which uses a multi-dimensional design for its InfoCubes, also falls in this category.

All the tools have certain limitations in terms of functionality, compatibility, scalability, performance, and cost. For example, while ROLAP systems store data in standard relational databases, their schema can be quite complex. A proprietary data structure, despite being stored in a relational database, can make a product incompatible with another product's schema. Additionally, ROLAP systems make a tradeoff in terms of significantly reduced performance and functionality, as well as the cost of implementation, while outperforming in the ability to handle larger amounts of data compared to MOLAPs. Therefore, tool selection should be based on an evaluation of the specific application being considered.

The BW system is versatile in that it supports both MOLAP and ROLAP. MOLAP, used to access InfoCubes, is the primary method for accessing BW (where most of the data is stored in multi-dimensional format in InfoCubes). ROLAP, the secondary method for accessing BW, is used for accessing the ODS (where the data is not stored in multi-dimensional format).

COMPARING OLAP

OLAP versus OLTP

Online transaction processing systems are primarily used to run the business operations of a company. OLTP functions are performed by production applications that routinely capture business transactions in diverse areas such as inventory management, order processing, human resources, production planning, budgeting, etc. In contrast, the objective of OLAP systems is to analyze the data, especially for long-term strategic decision-making even though the recent trend has been to use them for operational purposes. Examples of OLAP applications include trend analysis, sales forecasting, and customer profiling.

| Table 4: OLTP and OLAP comparison ||
OLTP	OLAP
Contains a snapshot of the current data (6-24 months)	Requires a history of transactions spread over many years (5-20 years)
Updated continuously	Static data
Can have errors or missing data	Validated and complete data
Processes millions of transactions per day	Updated periodically through batch processing—usually once per day
Uses Entity-Relationship Diagram	Uses multi-dimensional model

MOLAP versus ROLAP

In multi-dimensional OLAP (MOLAP), data is stored in a special OLAP database server, after being extracted from various sources, in pre-aggregated cubic format. This data remains static until an extract from the source system(s) adds more data to it. In contrast to this approach, relational OLAP (ROLAP) does not require an intermediate server because it can work directly against the relational database. Consequently, it can perform analysis on the fly.

MOLAP performs well with 10 or fewer dimensions while ROLAP can scale considerably higher. BW limits the number of dimensions in an InfoCube to 16, of which three are pre-defined by SAP (time, unit, and data package). ROLAP is unrestricted by the number of dimensions, type or number of users, database size, or complexity of analysis. It can perform ad hoc queries and aggregate data much faster—even with constantly changing and a much larger volume of data. Another ROLAP advantage is that it can leverage parallel scalable relational databases. The disadvantages of ROLAP are that it has limited scalability, places a heavy load on the server, and is expensive to maintain.

MOLAP, which starts seeing performance degradation at about 50GB of data or 10 dimensions, is more suitable for financial applications where the data can be broken down and is smaller. ROLAP is more suitable for applications where a huge amount of data needs to be analyzed, such as marketing and point-of-sale. ROLAP products are provided by a number of vendors including SAP, MicroStrategy, Data Dynamics, IBM, and Information Advantage (Sterling Software). MOLAP vendors include SAP, Comshare, Cognos, Hyperion, and IBM.

Other types of OLAP

Hybrid OLAP (HOLAP)

Hybrid OLAP (HOLAP) combines the features of ROLAP and MOLAP. It takes advantage of the superior processing of MOLAP with the ability of ROLAP to work with greater data volumes. HOLAP stores data in both a relational database and multi-dimensional database (MDDB) and, depending on the type of processing required, either database can be used. In HOLAP, the aggregates are stored using a MOLAP strategy while the source data, which is far greater in volume, is stored using a ROLAP strategy. This configuration enables very fast processing and also minimizes the data storage requirements.

A hybrid OLAP system combines the performance and functionality of an MDDB with the ability to access detailed data, which provides greater value to some categories of users. HOLAP technology, however, is fairly complex to deploy and maintain. Typically, HOLAP implementations are supported by a single vendor's databases, which can be a drawback. Products in this category are provided by a number of vendors including SAP, Microsoft, Crystal Decisions, Oracle, and Pilot Software.

In BW, HOLAP implementation can be provided through a MultiProvider, which joins an InfoCube and an ODS. A MultiProvider permits both types of data, multi-dimensional and relational, to be accessed and analyzed.

Database OLAP (DOLAP)

Database online analytical processing, DOLAP, is another type of OLAP. Its defining characteristic is that an OLAP engine resides in the database, which provides the fastest querying. This technology provides flexibility because users do not have to precisely define their requirements in advance—as required by

MOLAP. Another DOLAP advantage is that it can store more data than MOLAP, while the disadvantage is that it is slower. Products in this category are provided by a number of vendors including Business Objects, Brio Technology, and Cognos. BW does not support this technology at this time.

CHAPTER B7
IMPLEMENTATION APPROACHES

UNDERSTANDING DATA MARTS

Data warehouse limitations and data mart drivers

Data warehouses have provided many benefits that organizations have leveraged to their competitive advantage. However, they have also been characterized by some limitations, which have forced companies to seek alternative solutions for their information needs, including the following:

- ❑ Lag between need and implementation: It used to take a very long time, sometimes years, from the time a data warehouse was requested till the time it was actually rolled out to the users.
- ❑ Huge size and scope of data warehouse projects encompassing the entire organization. Such projects used to be very expensive—costing millions. They also spanned a very lengthy period and, in some cases, took years to implement.
- ❑ For enterprise implementations, which spanned disparate computer systems and numerous departments, complexity and integration proved to be over-whelming for most IT departments.
- ❑ Conflicting requirements, priorities, and the schedules of different depart-ments and business units derailed many projects.
- ❑ Cost overruns and delays were common.

All these problems became the drivers that have led to the development and wide-spread growth of data marts in the past few years.

What is a data mart

A data mart is a small data warehouse, a decision support system, which aims to meet the needs of departments and smaller groups, rather than the complete enterprise. The design principles and objectives of a data mart and a data warehouse are the same. While both are decision support tools and have the same basic characteristics, such as being subject-oriented and integrated, a data mart is far smaller in size and scope. Typically, it is limited to one or two subjects (such as sales and finance), can be implemented within months, and costs less than $200,000.

A data mart has far less users and the size of its database, typically, is only a few gigabytes. This is relatively small compared to the typical data warehouses (storing hundreds of gigabytes) or the larger data warehouses (containing terabytes of data). A data mart requires simpler hardware and supporting technical infrastructure. Hence, it can be implemented by less experienced staff with limited technical skills.

Data mart characteristics

The following is a listing of important data mart characteristics and how they compare to those of a conventional data warehouse:

❑ A data mart aims to meet a department's needs while a data warehouse is designed for the enterprise. Power users and IT staff with limited or no data warehousing skills can implement a data mart.

❑ A data warehouse spans the entire organization, covers most subjects, is designed using an enterprise data model, and is constructed by a central professional team.

❑ A data mart is easy to design and build, which makes it cheaper to implement and maintain.

❑ A data mart, while it can store gigabytes of data, usually contains only a small part of an organization's data.

❑ A data warehouse needs to be planned and implemented as a huge project, which is not the case with data marts.

❑ An organization can build many data marts independently, in a staggered manner, as needs evolve. They need not be based on the enterprise data model structure. If required, data marts can be linked together. However, such a task can be quite challenging.

❑ An organization can have many data marts, built by different teams, without a common design. The result of independent construction is that integration, if required at a later stage, will be difficult to achieve.

❑ While uniformity exists within a data warehouse project, it is missing when data marts sprout within a company because various implementation groups may use different processes, tools, hardware, and software.

❑ A data mart's source can be a data warehouse, another data mart, or an OLTP database.

Extraction and loading

There are two primary ways in which data is usually loaded into a data mart:

❑ Data is fed from an enterprise data warehouse to the data mart(s); any changes to the EDW is propagated to all associated data marts receiving its feeds

❑ Data is fed by direct extract(s) from the operational system database(s)

There are two loading approaches: server-based and PC client-based. In the server-based approach, data extracted from the source system is loaded onto the data mart located on the server. However, the analysis software, used to access and analyze data on the server, is located on the user's PC.

In the client-based approach, both the data and the analysis software reside on the PC. Data is extracted from the source and loaded directly onto the PC. The problem with this approach is that since there can be hundreds of users, they may not update their PC resident databases simultaneously, which can cause their queries and reports to return inconsistent results.

Infrastructure: platforms and vendors

Data warehouses and data marts have been implemented on many platforms including Unix and Windows NT. Implementation of such projects involves many technologies, tools, hardware, and software, which range from the very simple to the very sophisticated. While some vendors dominate in specific areas such as extraction or databases, and some have offerings across the range of products required for implementing a data mart or data warehouse, no vendor dominates in all areas. Some of the products that can be used to create and manage data marts include the SAP Business Warehouse, Oracle Data Mart Suite, IBM Enterprise Data Mart, Sybase Industry Warehouse Studio, PeopleSoft Enterprise Warehouse, and SAS Warehouse Administrator.

Benefits of data marts

Data marts provide many benefits to organizations implementing them. They include:

❑ Easy and fast approval as departmental justification is easier to obtain
❑ Not dependent on IT budget
❑ Faster to build—months instead of years
❑ Cheaper and more affordable—can be built with departmental budgets (hundreds of thousands instead of millions of dollars required for an enterprise project)
❑ Low cost hardware and software can be used
❑ Simpler
❑ More focused
❑ Scalable
❑ Flexible
❑ Political conflicts associated with data warehouse projects are avoided
❑ Fewer and less sophisticated resource requirements
❑ Ability to be linked to other data marts, or data warehouses, to form a distributed enterprise data warehouse
❑ Performance can be improved by storing the data closer to the users

Problems with data marts

While many benefits are associated with implementing data marts, they also have some problems associated with them such as:

❑ Development can be uncoordinated, which creates a hurdle when data marts are used as the building blocks for creating an enterprise data warehouse.
❑ Design is not as thorough as with a data warehouse due to superficial planning and inadequate, or no, consideration for an ultimate upgrade to an enterprise system.
❑ Cannot support a key requirement of an enterprise data warehouse—the ability to analyze enterprise-wide data across business units. Consequently, the age-old problem with legacy systems may also afflict data marts—a query may yield different answers depending on which system was accessed, when it was accessed, and how the query was structured and executed.
❑ Design flaws and the number of data extracts can restrict scalability; may be unable to support massive data volumes associated with data warehouses.
❑ Encourages clandestine development and operations.
❑ More work is required in reconciling terms, definitions, data, and business rules when data is migrated to an enterprise data warehouse.

❏ Designed and built by less experienced personnel, which can affect the quality of the product.
❏ Can be expensive in the long run.
❏ Growth of data marts creates more redundant and inconsistent data that has a cost associated with it and, also, poses problems when there is an upgrade.
❏ Multiple databases are required to be maintained, which can be inefficient and may require greater breadth of technical skills.
❏ Extraction process can be different for each data mart.
❏ Activities such as extraction and processing are not centralized; activities can be duplicated and additional staff can be required for maintenance and support.
❏ Tools, software, hardware, and processes can be different for each data mart.
❏ Knowledge gained by one data mart group may not be shared with the other groups.

IMPLEMENTATION APPROACHES

Implementation approaches

There are three approaches commonly used to build data marts:

❏ Top-down
❏ Bottom-up
❏ Independent

Top-down

In this approach, an enterprise data warehouse (EDW) is built first. In the next step, dependent data marts, which are its highly summarized subsets, are constructed as shown in Figure 9.

The characteristics defining the first approach, the top-down approach, are:

❏ It is methodology-based, which addresses important aspects such as modeling and implementation
❏ Provides an enterprise-wide view of the organization
❏ Avoids integration issues that characterize data warehouses that are derived from data marts

❑ Enterprise data warehouse drives the construction of dependent data marts, which permits better control and quality

❑ Inability to respond to business needs in time, long delivery cycle, high cost, project delays, cost overruns, and other issues associated with large projects

Figure 9: Top-down architecture

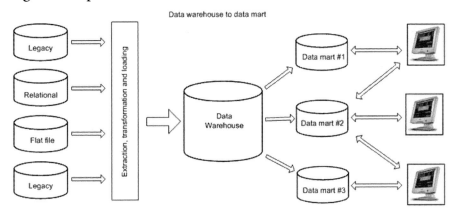

Bottom-up

In the second approach, independent data marts, whose foundation is the enterprise data model, are built first. These data marts can then be used, in the next step, to construct the EDW as shown in Figure 10.

The characteristics defining the bottom-up approach are:

❑ Can meet some enterprise-wide needs as data marts can be combined seamlessly for reporting and analysis purposes

❑ Seamless and transparent integration, while possible, is technologically challenging and performance can be poor, especially if many data marts need to be integrated

❑ Can lead to the sprouting of data marts and data redundancy

❑ Lack of adherence to standards can cause major issues, especially integration problems, when an EDW is constructed from multiple data marts

❑ Fast implementation provides less time for analysis

Figure 10: Bottom-up architecture

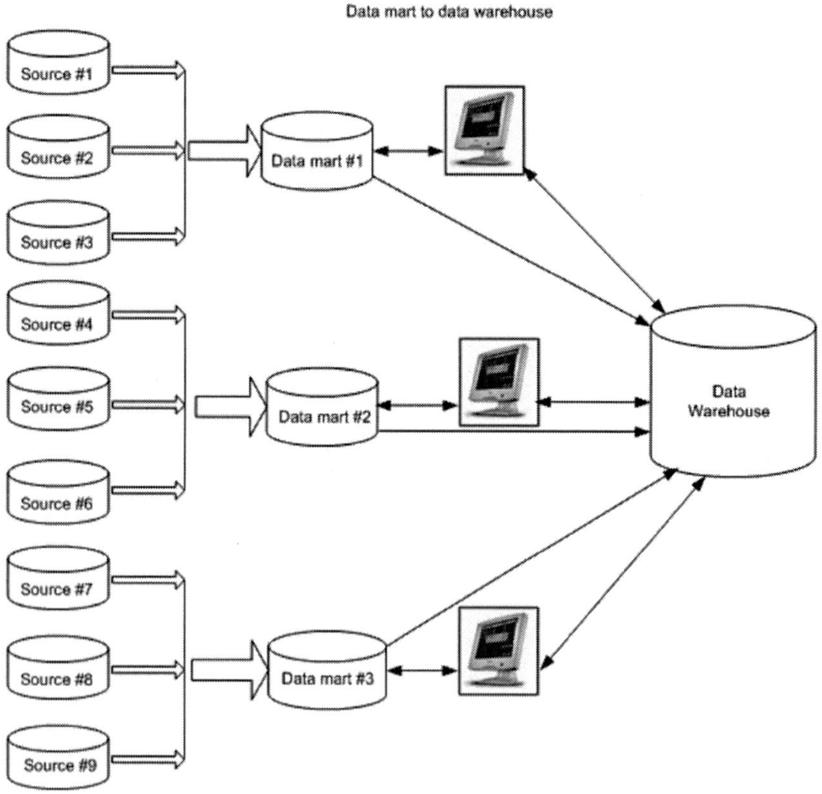

Data mart to data warehouse

Independent

In this approach, data marts are built randomly without any enterprise planning or consideration of a common data model. This approach can lead to anarchy over a period of time.

Which approach to use

The top-down and bottom-up approaches are characterized by various pros and cons. Each approach meets the needs of many different types of users. The decision to select a particular approach is influenced by the relative importance of the various selection variables for the organization considering an implementation. For example, if the objective is to have something up and running quickly, or the budget is limited, the obvious choice is the data mart bottom-up approach. However, if strategic concerns and long-term considerations are driving the requirements, and the company is prepared to spend millions for a well-designed system, the top-down approach for implementing an EDW might be the appropriate choice.

CHAPTER B8
PLANNING A BW PROJECT

PREREQUISITES AND APPROACH

Understand why the project is being undertaken

Before embarking on a data warehouse project, determine why the project is being undertaken as well as management expectations. Is the need departmental or enterprise? Are operational, strategic or tactical needs to be fulfilled by the data warehouse? How urgent are the strategic and operational reporting needs? Answers to these questions will clarify the project objectives and can influence important decisions regarding scope, architecture, methodology, tools, etc. When planning a BW project, study the SAP R/3 cycle, determine if a new implementation or an upgrade is being planned, and evaluate how the results of the investigation can impact the proposed BW architecture and schedule.

Study other ERP projects

A large enterprise may be operating multiple ERP systems, SAP as well as non-SAP, which should be studied before the BW implementation is undertaken. Such ERP systems, existing and planned, can impact the scope of the BW project, technical and business skills required, funding requirements, project ownership, implementation schedule, approach (top-down or bottom-up), methodology, etc.

Perform project justification

Data warehouse projects used to be initiated with R&D budgets, when the technology was immature and unproven, without formal cost justification. However, it is now a mature technology and, therefore, should be approached with the same thoroughness and preparation associated with any application development project. A BW project should not be undertaken unless it has been justified by a cost/benefit analysis. A consultant or someone who is respected within the organization should perform the analysis. A well-justified project improves the probability of success and buy-in, especially if the justification is well communicated.

Project prerequisites

A BW data warehouse project should not be implemented unless:

- ❑ Demand, strategic and operational, has been determined
- ❑ Criteria for valuing the data warehouse has been determined
- ❑ Cost is justified
- ❑ Source(s) and availability of required legacy and external data have been studied
- ❑ Size of the data warehouse has been determined
- ❑ Existing and required infrastructure have been evaluated
- ❑ Location has been determined
- ❑ Operational challenges have been identified

Evaluate potential impact

The implementation of a data warehouse introduces new technologies and retires older ones. The new architecture, which typically is a radical departure from the existing infrastructure, is the foundation upon which the new information architecture is based. It can impact company employees at all levels, ranging from senior executives to end-users, as well as IT staff. Therefore, it is imperative that the potential impact of the BW implementation on the organization be evaluated.

Obtain sponsorship

A typical data warehouse project has unique characteristics, which makes it a risky undertaking sponsorship is lacking. A BW project must have a sponsor who should be drawn from the functional side—not the IT department. The sponsor should have a vested interest in the project. He should be respected and be capable of acting decisively, providing resources when required, forcing compromises, and enforcing decisions. He should communicate his commitment to the project and keep a close eye on its progress and, when required, step in without any delay.

Evaluate readiness for implementation

Data warehouse projects are not easy to plan and implement. An organization considering a BW implementation must be prepared to adopt radical changes that can affect the architecture, techniques, tools, as well as operation and maintenance. Therefore, before deciding to proceed with such a project, management's commitment and the organization's readiness for change must be determined. If management lacks commitment, the project should be delayed until the conditions are more favorable.

Approach

The implementation approach to be used, top-down or bottom-up, should be determined as soon as possible in the planning phase. The approach to be used is one of the most important decisions to be made as it impacts the architecture, risks, budget, schedule, resources, sponsorship, scope, project complexity, implementation, etc.

Scope

The scope must be determined before undertaking a BW implementation project. The subject areas or cubes to be implemented, as well as the user population and access methods, must be identified. Project scope can be managed by limiting the number of subjects to be implemented, number of departments to be included, number of data sources, data source quality, data warehouse size, number or types of users, analysis techniques, and platform to be implemented (existing or new). The scope of custom development and activation of BW business content must be clear as it can impact the implementation cost, schedule, and resources required.

Resources

The technical and functional resources available for implementing the project must be identified and made available. A data warehouse project requires resources who have superior skills, have the ability to work under pressure, and are able to make quick and difficult decisions. If critical resources are unavailable, it is advisable to delay the project until appropriate and required resources become available.

Budgeting

A BW project should be budgeted adequately. Many data warehouse projects have failed as they were incorrectly sized and, hence, inadequately budgeted. If the budget is believed to be inadequate, additional funding should be sought or, if that is not possible or the request is denied, the scope should be reduced.

Consider using a data mart approach

Before a large-scale enterprise data warehouse project is undertaken, it might be appropriate to consider an alternative implementation approach—the bottom-up or the data mart approach. Both methods have pros and cons, which should be thoroughly evaluated to determine the best approach for implementing the data warehouse. If the organization does not have BW experience, the data mart approach will reduce risk and provide an opportunity to gain valuable implementation experience before a very large project is undertaken.

Attend Sapphire and ASUG

The SAP Sapphire conference is an annual event where valuable information and real-world BW implementation experiences can be obtained from those who have already implemented BW. It can help prevent potential users from repeating mistakes made during earlier BW implementations. ASUG is the SAP users group where useful information and experiences can be exchanged with other BW users.

IDENTIFYING BARRIERS, CHALLENGES, AND RISKS

Data warehouse projects are more complex and difficult to implement than conventional application development projects. Before a BW project is started, the challenges and risks associated with deploying a data warehouse should be identified. Failure to understand the unique nature of a BW project, and its impact on the organization, significantly increases risk and the probability of failure. The challenges and risks that typically derail data warehouse projects are discussed in the following sections.

Barriers

An important planning task is the identification of the barriers to implementation. Typically, the barriers are of two types. The first type is political and cultural, which can be attributed to senior executives, functional department managers, data owners, IT, and business users. The second type of barrier is technical, which is comparatively easy to identify, evaluate, and manage. If these implementation barriers are identified in time, the risk to the BW project will be reduced.

Complexity

A BW project is considerably more complex and difficult to execute than a conventional application development project. It is technologically complex, due to the greater number and sophistication of tools required to implement it, and poses integration challenges. Such a project requires many high-level skilled technical resources. It also involves many departments and groups, whose needs and requirements can be in conflict due to different priorities and politics. Consequently, such factors can combine to create a complex project that is under tremendous pressure to be delivered on time and within budget.

Integration

A data warehouse is fed data from multiple sources that can be residing on different platforms and systems. The data from various sources is ultimately integrated inside the BW after undergoing some operations. The overall data warehouse process uses a variety of technologies including databases, ETL tools, middleware, front-end reporting tools, networks, etc. Integrating all of them is a complex task and a challenge—from a technical as well as business perspective.

Financial risk

A data warehouse project is always exposed to two risks: cost overrun and schedule slippage—both of which increase financial risk. They have a negative impact on resources, force scope reduction, lead to competing demand for funds from other successful projects, can cause a window of opportunity to be missed, etc. In the worst scenario, a delayed or over-budget project can be scrapped.

Resource and schedule constraints

The resources for a data warehouse project are made available for a specific period, after negotiations, by various departments and organizations. Any delay in using the resources can, in many cases, effectively mean that they will not be available when required. The complex and time-intensive nature of a BW project, with hundreds of interdependent tasks, requires that schedule constraints must be carefully monitored if project success is to be ensured.

Politics

As a BW project involves many departments including business entities and IT, with conflicting priorities and agendas, it can face serious political issues and associated risks. Major politics can impact such a project at every step including selecting/prioritizing the subjects for implementation, requirements analysis, project team selection, access tool selection, etc. Therefore, someone who is politically savvy and has superior project management skills should lead the project.

Design differences

The design of a data warehouse database is fundamentally different compared to that of an OLTP system database. The primary design objective of a data warehouse, with its decision support and analysis requirements, is querying and reporting. A data warehouse is required to respond to complex and ad hoc queries, rather than provide simple reporting. A data warehouse aims to extract information from a database rather than capture and store data. Hence, it places emphasis on analytical tasks such as drill-down capabilities, slice and dice, etc.

On the other hand, an OLTP system's primary objective is to capture and store transaction data, which leads to its performance requirement that the database be updated efficiently. An OLTP system database stores only current operational data, which typically ranges from six months to two years. A data warehouse contains current as well as historical data that increases its size tremendously and, consequently, impacts its performance. It also contains a time element, which makes it more complex.

Complexity and size of data warehouses

Data warehouse databases contain a large number of tables that are characterized by complex relationships. When a query is executed, the tables required to process it are joined selectively to produce the desired result. To use the data ware-house, non-technical business users do not need to understand the database structure, names of the tables or their relationships, or how to create an SQL query. However, the data warehouse architect has to design a schema that can be presented to the users in an easy-to-understand, non-technical, format that uses business terms. This is a complex undertaking that requires both technical and business knowledge.

Data warehouse databases are very large. In some cases, they are huge, in the ter-abyte range, because they have to store many years' data. The data stored in data warehouses is fed from many sources, internal and external, which makes the database structurally complex. Also, the process to extract, transform, and load data into the data warehouse is very complicated.

Projects are difficult to manage

A BW project cannot be handled like a typical conventional application develop-ment project that is managed and implemented by IT. Due to its nature, a data warehouse project is business-driven—not led by IT. The number and types of users involved with such a project can be quite varied. Stakeholders can be across divisions, geographies, business units, and departments. Personnel involved with the project can include consultants, business analysts, IT technical staff, line managers, senior management, end-users, and ordinary workers. Usually, many project staff members lack data warehouse project experience, which creates a challenging management environment.

Implementation requires many skills

Many types of skills, technical and business, are required to plan and implement a BW data warehouse project. The technical skills span legacy systems, data con-version and migration, operating systems, databases, networking, front-end access tools, client/server and web technologies, etc. Knowledge of the business and decision support systems is also a requirement. Other skills required include organization, the ability to work in a team environment, multi-tasking, working with deadlines and under pressure, and good communications.

Decision making capabilities

During the life of a BW project, many critical decisions need to be made. Therefore, an assessment of the decision-making capabilities of the project staff must be made. If the staff is unable to make decisions, due to lack of delegation of responsibilities or inability to make decisions (due to the corporate culture or personality), it will be difficult to complete the project on time. The project team members must be able to act quickly and decisively.

GETTING READY FOR THE PROJECT

Determine project principles

The guiding principles, which are a set of goals, must be defined at this stage. They can be referred to and used throughout the project, especially when conflicts arise over misinterpreted objectives. The project business drivers also need to be defined at an early stage. They provide the means for quantitatively measuring success against metrics. Examples include revenue growth, customer retention rate, improvement in efficiency, decrease in product failure or returns, etc.

Perform skills assessment

The start of a data warehouse project should be preceded by skills assessment. The skills levels and capabilities, of the potential project team members and ultimate end-users, need to be determined. Both technical and business skills assessment must be performed. The skills assessment exercise helps pinpoint deficiencies and indicates the areas where external resources may be required for implementation and/or providing support after the BW becomes operational.

Select implementation partner

Three common approaches are used for implementing a data warehouse:

❑ Using in-house staff
❑ Using a vendor
❑ Teaming with a partner

Unless the company staff has data warehouse or data mart implementation experience, the first option can mean a longer implementation time and considerably higher risk (cost and time). The lack of technical know-how can lead to a flawed design, poor performance, extraction and loading problems, selection of the wrong tools, other technical issues, etc.

In the second option, with an experienced vendor, the implementation can be faster and smoother. However, maintaining the system can be an issue after the vendor leaves due to inadequate knowledge transfer to the operational staff. Therefore, upgrading such a system will be more expensive compared to a system implemented by in-house staff. Also, there will be a greater need for ongoing and future consulting/training costs.

Typically, the third approach is the best because a skilled consulting partner implements the BW in close collaboration with company employees, who pick up both business and technical skills. The key to a successful implementation is to select a partner who, besides designing and implementing the BW, can also provide on-going support, if required.

Select project leader

A BW implementation leader should be one who possesses the qualities associated with a successful project manager. The person selected for such a position should have a reputation for completing projects on time and within budget. The project manager should be a decisive leader and must be given adequate authority so that the project does not suffer due to the lack of adequate decision-making authority.

Determine project team requirements and roles

The implementation of a BW data warehouse project requires many skills— technical and business. The typical positions that are associated with such a project include:

❑ Sponsor: Senior executive responsible for the overall project who, typically, is the chairman of the Steering Committee
❑ Steering Committee: Responsible for ensuring that the project runs smoothly and is in sync with the corporate business and IT strategy; consists of functional staff drawn from various business areas as well as IT representative(s)
❑ Project Manager: Responsible for project's strategic direction and ensuring that budget and schedule are adhered to; manages the project and project team; provides progress reports

❑ Functional sponsor: Executive responsible for the business within the specific functional area

❑ Functional representatives: Functional business users and end-users associated with the project in various capacities; may be working full-time or part-time during various project phases—from planning through user acceptance

❑ Project team: Implements the project and executes specific project plan tasks; includes business team members (subject matter experts, business analysts, functional staff, etc.) as well as technical team members (architect, developers, data warehouse administrator, etc.)

❑ IT support staff (during implementation): Responsible for the IT infrastructure and software requirements

❑ IT support staff (after go-live): Responsible for maintaining the system and infrastructure

Select project team members

The project team members required to fill the identified roles within the project are selected keeping in mind the following:

❑ Team members should have suitable characteristics that can enable them to meet the requirements of a challenging project; they must understand the company's business, needs, and requirements

❑ Should be capable decision-makers

❑ Must be able to allocate time to the project; team members should not have dual requirements that interfere with their project tasks

❑ Preferably have a stake in the implementation

Project team training

The members of the project team need to be trained in various BW courses before they start to implement the Business Warehouse solution. SAP offers a number of courses that cover data warehousing fundamentals, data modeling, configuration, Business Explorer, ABAP/4 programming, etc. The roadmap for various tracks, as well as specific courses offered by SAP, are listed on its website at www.sap.com.

CHAPTER B9
BUILDING A BW DATA WAREHOUSE

METHODOLOGY

In the past decade, as data warehouse technology has matured, the approach to implement it has also changed. Instead of an iterative methodology, structured methodologies are being used to implement data warehouse projects. The various methodologies reflect the experiences that implementers have gained over the years. The important point to note is that an implementation must not be carried out without a formal methodology—the roadmap for ensuring that a project is executed according to sound project principles.

The most commonly used methodology for implementing BW is the ASAP methodology, which was described in detail in earlier chapters. The BW implementation, using either the ASAP or other methodologies, is executed in a series of steps that need to be clearly identified in a project plan. The work plan must be diligently adhered to or the project will be jeopardized and the potential to incur delays and cost overruns will increase significantly.

In the following sections, various implementation phases for a BW project using the ASAP methodology are described. Appendix A shows a generic ASAP project plan.

PROJECT PREPARATION

An unplanned project is a blueprint for disaster. Before a BW implementation is started, it should be preceded by detailed planning, as described in the previous chapter. Such planning must define the scope, specifications, as well as specific responsibilities for the client, vendor, and consulting partner(s).

The project plan, which is created in the project preparation phase, contains the project schedule and identifies the activities to be performed for implementing the BW. The project deliverables are identified in this phase and the resource requirements, internal as well as consulting, are also defined.

In many projects, a number of tasks listed in the business blueprint and realization phases are performed at a preliminary or high level in this phase even though, logically, they should be performed during later phases. These include tasks such as database selection, capacity planning, data refresh and update strategy, archiving strategy, etc., which can impact the implementation as well as routine operations and maintenance.

BUSINESS BLUEPRINT

In this needs assessment and requirements gathering phase, i.e., the analysis phase, a very comprehensive study of the business is conducted. It involves interviewing executives, managers, business analysts, and functional experts from various business units being considered for the BW implementation.

In the blueprint phase, the information needs of the business users, the requirements, are determined. The first step involves analyzing the business to determine the current environment—the 'as-is" situation. In the next step, the high-level business requirements are converted into specific requirements of what the new system must do and what its characteristics should be.

This phase leads to the definition of the architecture as well as the processes for linking the data sources, the data warehouse, and the front-end access tools. It can result in scope modification (increase/decrease). The results from the blueprint phase also have the potential to impact the implementation approach (top-down or bottom-up), which may or may not have been selected previously.

Some of the other important items that are typically determined or defined in the analysis phase include:

❑ Subject areas (customers, orders, sales, bookings, etc.)
❑ Desired features and functions
❑ Logical data model
❑ Dimensional business model (facts, dimensions, hierarchies, and relationships)
❑ Dimensions of potential interest

- ❑ Operational/Other data required to be moved into BW (customers, bookings, sales, external data, etc.)
- ❑ Data sources and elements (legacy and other sources—external or internal)
- ❑ Data requirements (which data is to be used)
- ❑ Data levels (detailed versus summarized, granularity)
- ❑ Historical data requirements
- ❑ Data flows: how the sources (OLTP systems/other data marts/EDW) feed the BW
- ❑ Sizing
- ❑ Range of queries expected
- ❑ Query and reporting requirements
- ❑ Existing and planned platforms and processes
- ❑ Impact on existing infrastructure (hardware, software, networks, etc.) and personnel

REALIZATION

The realization phase includes design as well as development activities. In this phase, a determination is made of "how" the system will be implemented. The primary design consideration is to develop an optimal solution within various constraints, such as cost, schedule, and infrastructure.

Design

The impact of every major design issue, on the implementation as well as future operation and maintenance, is studied. Some of the common design issues addressed in this phase include the following:

- ❑ How much data is to be extracted and transformed
- ❑ Should complete files, or only changes, be imported
- ❑ Should update frequency be event or time driven
- ❑ Aggregation
- ❑ Backup and recovery procedures
- ❑ Data distribution and replication (to ensure that when data is changed, all copies of the database reflect the changes and remain in sync)

During realization, the logical and physical data models are developed. The high-level data model identifies the major subject areas as well as the relationships between the major subjects. The mid-level data model identifies attributes, groupings of attributes, as well as the relationships of groupings of attributes. The low-level data model, which is ready for physical database implementation, includes the physical characteristics of attributes.

The physical database design involves designing the database, fact and relationship tables (based on the star schema), data de-normalization, indexing, etc. The data source physical data models are mapped to the physical model of the data warehouse (source to target). The data mapping and transformation tasks involve:

❑ Defining the sources
❑ Determining the logic and rules
❑ Determining the file layouts
❑ Data formatting and translation; creating the transformation specifications
❑ Mapping the source(s) to the target

Construction and testing

Before the construction step is implemented, various components of the BW system and its supporting IT infrastructure, such as servers and third-party tools, need to be evaluated and selected based upon a timeline specified in the project plan. Some components may already be installed within the existing IT infrastructure while others, including hardware and software, may need to be procured.

In the realization phase, the BW is constructed as per specifications and project scope. The physical data warehouse, the database that will hold all the imported source data, is created from the logical and physical database designs in a number of steps. The important steps include data extraction, transformation, staging, loading, validation, and testing. An important task that precedes ETL is the development of programs that perform a variety of tasks such as:

❑ Normalizing and building tables
❑ Modifying/refreshing the warehouse
❑ Extracting, transforming, and loading data
❑ Summarizing and aggregating data

The development and testing activities performed in this phase include some or all of the following:

❑ Connecting the BW system to R/3 and other sources
❑ Mapping to source systems
❑ Writing extraction programs (extractors)
❑ Creating InfoCatalogs

- ❏ Creating ODS
- ❏ Creating InfoCubes and MultiProviders
- ❏ Writing transfer rules
- ❏ Creating workbooks, templates, and queries
- ❏ Activating business content
- ❏ Integrating the BW with the Portal, if required
- ❏ Data conversion
- ❏ Creating authorizations
- ❏ Building the QA system (where integration testing is conducted) and training system (where end-user training is conducted)
- ❏ Implementing security
- ❏ Unit testing
- ❏ Integration testing
- ❏ User acceptance testing

FINAL PREPARATION

In this phase, the system is refined and adjusted for optimal performance. Additional testing is performed as interfaces are completed and changes are implemented to incorporate feedback received from end user testing and integration testing. Some of the tasks completed in this phase including:

- ❏ Installing/upgrading the physical infrastructure (network, PCs, desktop tools, etc.)
- ❏ Configuring PCs
- ❏ Installing the front-end access tool
- ❏ Creating starter queries and reports
- ❏ Training for end-users, power users, strategic users, and operational users
- ❏ Developing a user support structure

A cutover plan that lists the tasks required to switchover to the BW system consists of all major activities including tasks, schedule, data conversion and loading sequence, and data validation. The cutover plan can be executed over a period that can very from a few days to a few weeks.

Before the BW can be rolled out, a support infrastructure needs to be in place and the end-users must be adequately trained. The level and depth of training varies as the skill levels of the users can vary considerably. Casual users, who typically run canned reports or create simple reports, can be trained with minimal or self-paced training. However, heavy-duty users, such as business analysts and power users need more in-depth training as their requirements and dependence on the BW is considerably higher.

GO-LIVE AND SUPPORT

In this phase, a number of activities are carried out including readiness assessment to determine if the users are ready and the BW is ready to be rolled out. A number of communications need to go out about the project and the rollout in the period leading up to go-live. At this time, change controls are also put into place to deal with expected change requests.

After the BW becomes operational, the data management process including extraction, transformation, staging, and load scheduling is automated, wherever possible. The loading is scheduled based on one of two common procedures: bulk download (which refreshes the entire database periodically) and change-based replication (which copies the differences in data residing on different servers).

Once a BW is up and running, it will continue to require attention in different ways. A successful data warehouse will see the numbers of users rise considerably, which can affect its performance—if it has not been properly sized. Also, support and enhancement requests will roll in. Some other common issues that need to be dealt with while operating a BW include:

- ❏ Loading new data on a regular basis, which can range from real-time to weekly
- ❏ Managing batch loading jobs; resolving loading errors
- ❏ Ensuring uptime and reliability
- ❏ Ensuring query performance
- ❏ Managing the front-end tools
- ❏ Managing the back-end components
- ❏ Updating data to reflect organizational changes, mergers and acquisitions, etc.
- ❏ Applying fixes (OSS notes and patches)
- ❏ Requests for modifying reports
- ❏ Reconciling reports due to changes in existing reports
- ❏ Modifications generated due to changes in the source (SAP or other systems)

Chapter B10
BW Architecture and Objects

PLATFORM

NetWeaver

The BW system is now supported by an infrastructure based on the recently introduced NetWeaver platform and the Enterprise Services Architecture (ESA). This platform supports the integration of BW with other non-SAP systems and platforms. NetWeaver components, starting with the '04 release, are delivered in a single package that includes BW 3.5. The Business Warehouse, just like the other SAP NetWeaver components, operates on the SAP Web AS.

Business Framework Architecture (BFA)

The BW is a central component of SAP's Business Framework Architecture, Figure 11, which is a component-based architecture. Within this environment, BW acts as a data recipient as well as a data provider—from and to other mySAP components.

Figure 11: BW and the BFA

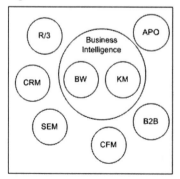

The BW system integrates into the Enterprise Portal, through which SAP and applications from non-SAP systems can be accessed through a single point of entry (Figure 12).

Figure 12: BW/Enterprise Portal integration

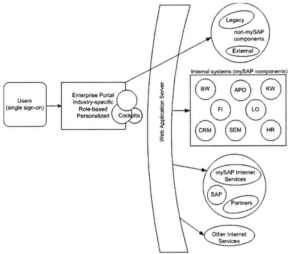

Source: Adapted from SAP AG documentation

Relationship to R/3 hardware

In the past, BW has been installed as a separate SAP instance, with its own application servers and database, independent of an associated R/3 SAP system. With the introduction of NetWeaver, tight integration has been introduced between various components. Therefore, BW can be run on the same servers as the SAP ERP Central Component (SAP ECC), the new ERP core component within mySAP ERP 2004, as SAP BW no longer requires its own physical system.

BW PROCESS

The BW data warehouse process is the same as the conventional data warehouse process, with some subtle differences. Like the conventional data warehouse process, the high-level BW process includes the following:

Source

There are two main types of sources for BW:

❑ SAP systems: Includes mySAP components, which provide data to BW via extractors. Source can be another BW system.
❑ Non-SAP systems: They can include external databases and data providers.

ETL

BW can read flat files in ACSII or CSV format and also process XML data. It can directly access data in relational database tables using DB Connect. The prerequisite for the loading processes from an SAP system into BW is a connection using Remote Function Call (RFC) and a plug-in. A plug-in is an ABAP programming language component that enables a mySAP component to exchange data with an SAP system. The two transfer methods used are the IDoc method and the PSA transfer method. Interfaces are also supported through the following technologies:

❑ BAPI (Business Application Programming Interfaces): used to communicate between BW and external systems
❑ SOAP (Simple Object Access Protocol): used to read XML data and store it in BW
❑ SAPI (BW Service Application Programming Interface): an internal SAP component used to communicate between mySAP components and BW

Access

The SAP Business Warehouse tool for accessing and analyzing data, which uses OLAP, is the Business Explorer, which is covered in detail in a Chapter B14. It consists of the following three components or tools that can be used to perform Excel and Web-based analysis:

❑ BEx Analyzer
❑ BEx Web Application
❑ BEx Mobile Intelligence

ARCHITECTURAL COMPONENTS

A simple BW architecture is depicted in Figure 13, which shows a system fed by multiple sources (SAP and non-SAP), while Figure 14 shows the important components of a BW system.

Figure 13: BW architecture

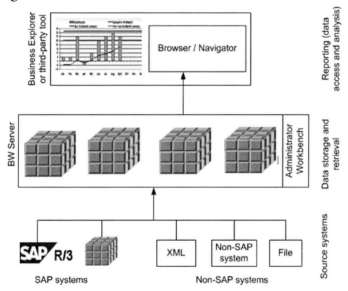

Figure 14: BW components

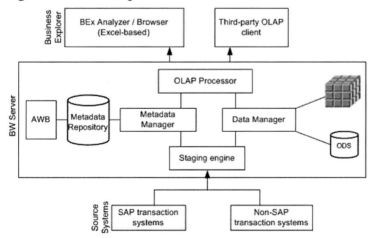

BW information integration architecture

Figure 15 depicts BW's information integration architecture, which encompasses various components such as source systems, PSA, ODS, InfoCubes, metadata, master data, and data access.

BW information access architecture

Figure 16 provides an overview of BW's information access architecture. It graphically displays the access direction—from the front-end tools to the R/3 system and external systems via the intermediate objects (ODS and InfoCubes).

BW web reporting process

The BW is a central and important component, the reporting hub, in the reporting environment of an organization. As shown in Figure 17, it provides the ability to store, access, and analyze data using a variety of techniques and technologies.

Figure 15: Information integration architecture

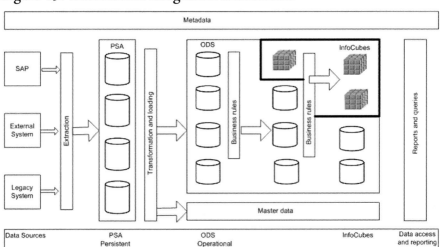

Figure 16: Information access architecture

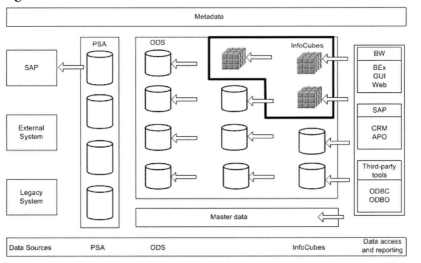

Figure 17: BW web reporting process

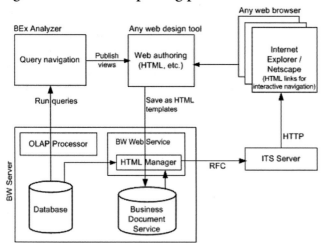

BW layers

BW organization has been defined in terms of layers or components. The 3-layer BW architecture is shown in Figure 18.

Figure 18: 3-layer architecture

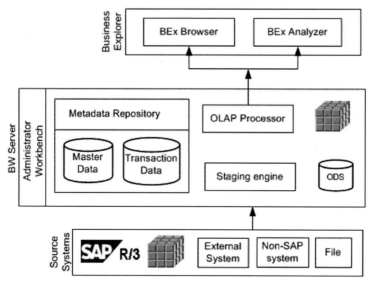

6-LAYER ARCHITECTURE

In addition to the 3-layer architecture, the BW has also been described in terms of an architecture that has 6-layers or components (Figure 19), which are:

- ❑ ETL services
- ❑ Storage services
- ❑ Analysis and access services
- ❑ Presentation services
- ❑ Administration services
- ❑ Metadata services

Figure 19: 6-layer services architecture

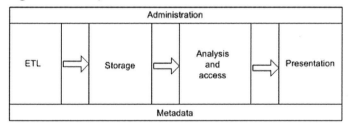

ETL services

This is the extraction, transformation, and loading component of the BW system. The staging engine manages the staging process for the data extracted from various source systems. Some of the highlights of this component include:

- ❑ Provides open interface for:
  - • Exchanging metadata with BW
  - • Uploading data to BW
- ❑ Staging area for intermediate data storage; staging is managed by the Staging Engine
- ❑ Staging Engine:
  - • Implements data mapping and transformation
  - • Generates and implements transformation programs
  - • Executes transfer and update rules
  - • Requests source systems to load data, which move it into the BW
  - • Implements same staging process for SAP and non-SAP data

Another components of the ETL services is the DataSource Manager, which:

❑ Supports the Staging Engine
❑ Manages the capture and intermediate storage of uploaded data in the Persistent Staging Area (PSA)
❑ Supports various types of interfaces such as BW Service API, file interface, Staging BAPI, DB Connect interface, and XML interface

Figure 20 shows the BW data extraction process, while Figure 21 depicts the BW data transformation and loading process.

Figure 20: BW data extraction process

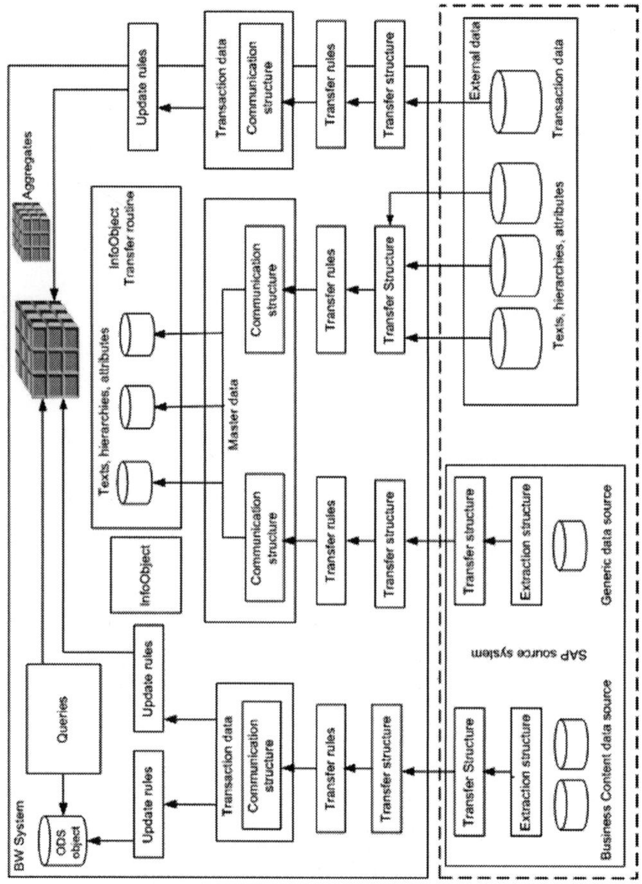

Source: Adapted from SAP AG documentation

Figure 21: BW data transformation and loading process

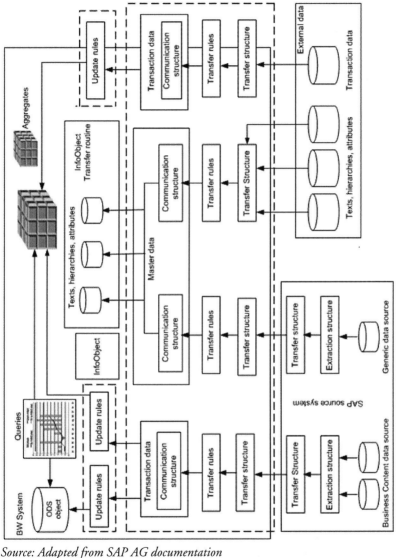

Source: Adapted from SAP AG documentation

The PSA, which is a set of database tables, is a data staging area of BW that stores data in the original source system format before any transformations are applied (Figure 22). The objective is to check the quality of the loaded data before it is moved to its final destination—an ODS or an InfoCube. The PSA provides an option for saving the transaction and master data, temporarily, before they are transferred into an InfoSource. If required, data in the PSA can be modified before it is loaded into an InfoCube.

Figure 22: PSA and ODS

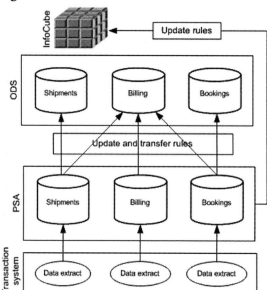

Storage services

This is also known as the Data Manager, which maintains data in the ODS objects and InfoCubes. It also provides information about the availability of data for queries to the OLAP processor. The Data Manager contains the following components:

❑ Master data manager, which:
- Generates the master data infrastructure
- Maintains master data
- Provides access to master data

❑ InfoCube manager, which:
- Generates the InfoCube infrastructure
- Maintains InfoCube data
- Provides access to the InfoCube data

❑ ODS object manager, which:
- Generates the ODS object infrastructure
- Maintains ODS object data
- Provides access to ODS object data

❑ Aggregate manager, which:
  ● Generates the aggregate infrastructure
  ● Monitors updates to objects that can impact the aggregate (associated InfoCube and master data used in the aggregate)
❑ Archiving manager, which:
  ● Manages the archiving of data
  ● Monitors associated metadata

Analysis and access services

The key component in this layer is the OLAP engine, which uses multi-dimensional analysis to retrieve data from the database and then, as requested, present it to the user. It provides both analysis and navigation functions. The three components are BEx Analyzer (MS-Excel-based), BEx Web Application, and BEx Mobile Intelligence. This layer also includes InfoProviders, which are of two types:

❑ Physical InfoProviders, which contain basic InfoCubes, master data tables, InfoSets, and ODS objects
❑ Virtual InfoProviders, which contain remote InfoCubes and MultiProviders

Presentation services

This layer contains the components required to display information, extracted from the database, in:

❑ BW's BEx Analyzer
❑ Third-party front-end tools, such as Cognos and Business Objects

The other components included in this layer are the BEx Browser, BEx Query Designer, BEx Web Application Designer, and BEx Web Services.

BW is provided with standard reports that can be easily accessed though the click of a mouse. Standard reports include procurement and human resources department reports as well for individual roles such as product managers, controllers, etc.

Administration services

The administration services include a number of services required to administer the BW system. These services are accessed through the Administrator Workbench (AWB), which is the most important component. The AWB is the starting point for accessing different services and functions such as development, administration, control, monitoring, and maintenance of objects and processes. It includes various components including:

- Modeling: Creates and maintains objects relevant to the ETL process
- Monitoring: Used to monitor and control various processes, such as data loading
- Reporting agent: Used to perform background scheduling and execution of reporting functions
- Transport connection: Manages changed or new objects for transport to other BW systems
- Documents: Provides links to various documents for BW objects
- Business Content: Provides ready-to-use information models that can be used without customization
- Translation: Provides the ability to translate BW objects' texts
- Metadata Repository: Provides central management of all BW meta objects and associate links

Other defining features of the AWB include the ability to:

- Maintain all BW objects and metadata: predefined metadata (or Business Content) and client-defined metadata
- Create and maintain the BW data warehouse: logical source systems, InfoObjects, InfoSources, ODS, InfoCubes, InfoProviders, MultiProviders, and aggregates
- Assign InfoSources to data targets (InfoCubes and ODS objects, collectively, are called data targets)
- Perform metadata modeling:
  - Model and maintain business and technical metadata using BW meta-data objects
  - Generate operational metadata from data warehouse processes
- Define the extraction processes
- Execute transformations required to move objects from sources to targets—from data extraction from the source system (s) to saving data in the InfoCube(s)
- View and activate re-defined models (Business Content)
- Schedule data transformation, data loading, and other tasks through the BW Scheduler.
- Monitor batch processes via the BW Monitor. Other tasks supported include troubleshooting, activating objects, indexing, loading processes' statistics, etc.
- Execute queries in batch mode using the Reporting Agent

❑ Collect objects that need to be moved from the development system to the desired system (QA or production), using the Transport Connector, and then assign them to the transport request

Metadata services

The BW Metadata Services component comprises of:

❑ Metadata Repository:
  • Stores metadata
  • Contains business metadata such as definitions and descriptions
  • Contains technical metadata such as structure and mapping rules
❑ Metadata Manager:
  • Maintains Metadata Repository
  • Manages metadata (add, change, delete, and retrieve requests)
  • Manages metadata exchange with other systems

BW OBJECTS, STRUCTURES, AND RULES

Source systems

A source system feeds data to the BW system from a variety of sources, SAP and non-SAP, listed earlier. The steps needed to create an R/3 source system are the creation of logical systems for the R/3 client and the BW client, naming the background users, and creating the R/3 source system in BW.

DataSource

The DataSource provides the field structures for the source system (Figure 23). It comprises of:

❑ Extraction source structures, with all source system fields provided by extractors, which collect data from source systems
❑ Transfer structure, with selected fields from the extraction source structure

DataSources are available for transaction data, master data, and hierarchies.

Figure 23: Data sources

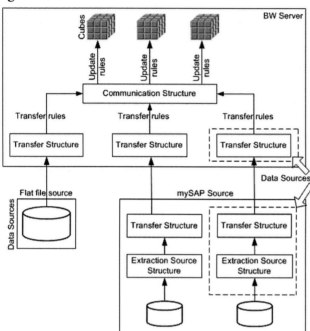

Source: Adapted from SAP AG documentation

Data target

A data target refers to an object into which data is loaded, such as InfoCubes, ODS objects, and InfoObjects. There are two types of data targets:

❑ Pure data targets: queries cannot be created or executed against these data targets
❑ InfoProvider: these are data targets against which queries can be defined

InfoObject

Key figures and characteristics are collectively known as InfoObjects, which are the objects used to build structures (extract, transfer, and communication), tables, and InfoCubes. InfoObjects, which represent the lowest level business objects, or fields, can be of the following types:

❑ Key figures
❑ Characteristics
❑ Units
❑ Time characteristics

The technical name of standard InfoObjects provided by SAP within Business Content starts with the number 0, such as *0Customer* and *0Amount* (for customer and amount). The technical name of user-defined InfoObjects starts with a character between A and Z, with a length of 3-9 characters. InfoObjects are used in InfoCubes, ODS objects, and InfoSources.

Key figure

A key figure is a data field that stores values or quantities, such as quantity and amount. For example, units sold, gross revenue, quantity, profit margins, costs, and amount can be key figures. Key figures are the facts in the fact table. There are six types of key figures recognized by BW:

- ❑ Amount
- ❑ Quantity
- ❑ Number
- ❑ Integer
- ❑ Date
- ❑ Time

Characteristics

In the BW star schema, the dimension attributes are known as characteristics. They describe the objects used in business processes and are used to analyze key figures. Examples of characteristics are:

- ❑ Vendors (*0Vendor*), customers (*0Customer*), cost center, and products, which are objects in business processes
- ❑ Weight and color, which are attributes

An attribute is an InfoObject, characteristic or key figure, which describes a characteristic in further detail. For example, if Vendor ID is a characteristic, its attributes can be vendor name and vendor address. Attributes can be defined as display or navigation attributes. A display attribute provides supplemental information, when combined with the characteristic, but does not enable navigation. However, navigation attributes permit defined attributes to be used for report navigation. They enable navigation from characteristic to characteristic during query execution. A negative aspect of using navigation attributes is that they impact performance.

Restricted key figure

Restricted key figures are an InfoProvider's key figures that have been filtered, or restricted, through the selection of one or more characteristics. They are used by BW queries to analyze specific data, such as period sales (Q1 or Q2). The key figure to be restricted can be a basic key figure, already restricted key figure, or a calculated key figure. In contrast to a filter, which places a restriction on the entire query, a restricted key figure limits its restriction only to the selected key figure's characteristic value (or interval).

Calculated key figure

A calculated key figure is a value that is determined by using calculation rules or formulas within a report, such as average sales price. It can consist of basic, restricted, or other calculated key figures in an InfoProvider. The calculated key figures are stored in the metadata repository—not in database tables.

Variable

Variables are query parameters, which are defined in the Query Designer, that enable queries to be flexibly customized. Variables, which can be processed in various ways, are global, reusable objects. They can be used in all other queries. When a query or a web application is executed, the appropriate variables are filled with values. When a query is executed, BW determines variable values by executing a user exit or by requesting user input.

Master data

In BW, master data, which refers to additional information about characteristics, is stored in separate tables. It consists of attributes of a characteristic. Master data consists of three data types: attributes, texts and hierarchies (external). SID (surrogate-ID) tables connect master data tables to an InfoCube and to the key figures of its fact table. They change a long InfoObject key into a 4-byte integer, which improves performance.

InfoObject catalogs

This is an InfoObjects' directory that can be used to organize InfoObjects. Separate catalogs exist for key figures and characteristics. Since an InfoObject can be used in many different areas, such as HR and Finance, it can be simultaneously assigned to multiple InfoObject catalogs.

InfoCube

InfoCubes are the central objects, the data containers, in a BW system. An InfoCube is a multi-dimensional data structure consisting of a number of relational tables. It is based on the star schema and contains key figures and characteristics organized in dimensions. Key figures, such as sales and costs, are linked to characteristics such as materials and cost centers (i.e., the master data). An InfoCube consists of a fact table and associated dimension tables. There are two types of InfoCubes:

❑ Basic InfoCubes
❑ Virtual Cubes

A virtual cube is a logical, not a physical, cube. Only a basic InfoCube contains data. Data can only be loaded into a physical cube, which is a data target. In an InfoCube, characteristics can be organized to a maximum of 16 dimensions of which three are predefined by SAP (time dimension, unit dimension, and data packet dimension). Other basic InfoCube features include the following:

❑ Has only one fact table, which cannot contain more than 233 key figures
❑ Usually has four dimension tables: units dimension, time dimension, data package, and one or more user-defined dimension

ODS objects

An ODS object is a file containing transaction data or master data, which has been consolidated and cleansed. ODS objects, which contain key figures and characteristics, are used to build the ODS (which does not have fact or dimension tables). An ODS object can be transactional or non-transactional. An ODS object acts like an InfoCube when it is made available for reporting, despite some differences. It enables drill-down to the source document without accessing the OLTP system. The ODS provides reporting benefits such as enabling drill-down, from an InfoCube to the ODS, as well as direct reporting against it.

The structure of ODS objects permits responses that are similar to the OLTP source from where they are copied (transaction systems). ODS objects cannot be used for multi-dimensional analysis as their structure is not based on the BW schema. Hence, they cannot be aggregated like InfoCubes. However, they can be included in MultiProviders, which can perform multi-dimensional analysis. Physically, the ODS is a data store from where data must be loaded into the InfoCubes. It lies between the InfoCubes and the PSA.

InfoProvider

An InfoProvider is a data object, such as an InfoCube (basic or virtual), ODS object, or an InfoSet for which queries can be executed in BW (Figure 24). An InfoProvider is an object or view that is relevant to reporting. An InfoProvider can be physical or virtual. It can include remote InfoCubes and MultiProviders (which combine two or more InfoProviders). Physical data stores include InfoCubes, ODS objects and InfoObjects. Logical views of physical data stores include RemoteCubes, Virtual InfoCubes, MultiProviders, and InfoSets.

A MultiProvider is an InfoProvider, which accesses data in various InfoProviders and then makes it available for reporting. Physically, a MultiProvider does not contain any data. It pulls any data that it requires from its InfoProviders—such as InfoCubes, ODS objects, InfoObjects, and InfoSets.

Figure 24: InfoProvider architecture

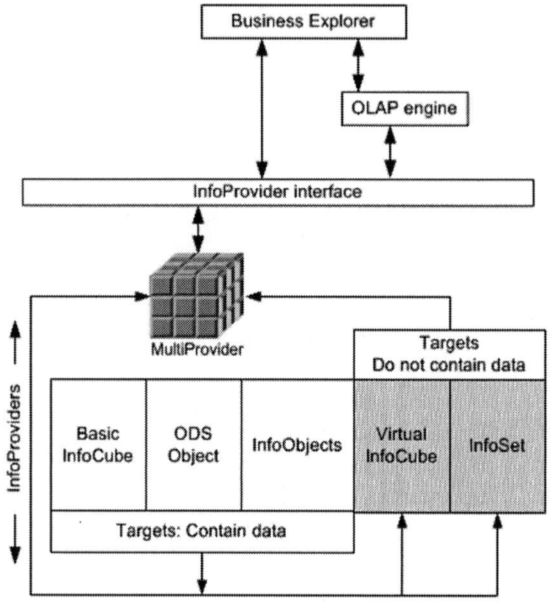

InfoAreas

InfoAreas are used to organize various BW objects, such as InfoProviders and InfoCubes, in a tree structure or directory. Every InfoObject is assigned to an InfoArea through the InfoObject catalog.

InfoSource

This object refers to a set of logically associated information and InfoObjects (Figure 25). The field structure in which they are stored is called the communication structure. An InfoSource structure groups InfoObjects logically and contains, in separate tables, the following:

❑ Transaction data, which is stored in InfoCubes and ODS objects
❑ Master data (attributes, texts and hierarchies)

Figure 25: InfoSource

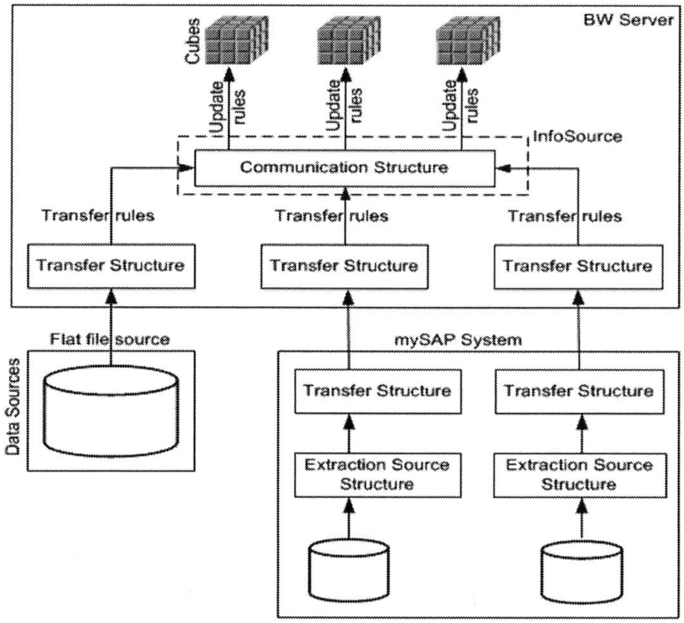

Source: Adapted from SAP AG documentation

An InfoSource does not store data. It comprises of transfer and communication structures between the source systems and the InfoCubes. There are two types of

InfoSources: with flexible update and direct update. To obtain the source system data, InfoSources interface with InfoCubes and characteristics.

InfoPackage

An InfoPackage is a BW object that is used to schedule and monitor data loads (Figure 26). It defines how to select, transfer, and load data. It defines the conditions for requesting data from a source system, such as data update options, triggers, selection conditions, etc. Some of the functions performed by an InfoPackage include selecting and restricting data, supporting processing options and update parameters, selecting data targets for updates, scheduling, etc. The InfoPackage needs an InfoSource to determine the structure of the object where the data is being sent (such as an InfoCube). InfoSources and InfoPackages are organized in a tree structure called an application component.

Figure 26: InfoPackage

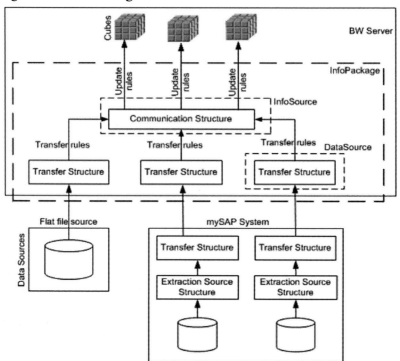

Source: Adapted from SAP AG documentation

InfoSets

An InfoSet is a virtual InfoProvider that supports the joins of ODS objects and master data tables. It does not support InfoCubes in contrast to MultiProviders, which support the union of multiple InfoProviders of all types. No data is stored at the InfoSet level. An InfoSet can be accessed via an OLAP engine and use the Business Explorer as the front-end tool.

Transfer rules

Transfer rules and InfoSources are used to define the mapping of fields (from a specific DataSource to an InfoSource) and transformation rules for the extraction, transformation, and loading process. A transfer structure, which is a data structure, ensures how and which data is to be transferred between the source and the BW system. It maps DataSource fields to InfoSource InfoObjects. It transforms data from transfer structures into a communication structure, if required. BW proposes a transfer structure based on the information contained in the communication structure.

Update rules

An update rule is the mechanism for connecting an InfoSource to the data target, such as an InfoCube, and applying any additional transformations. It specifies how the data, such as key figures and characteristics, is updated in a data target (a physical storage location) from a communication structure. An update rule specifies how data is transferred into a data target(s) from a communication structure. Multiple data targets can be updated from a single InfoSource. Also, multiple InfoSources can update a single data target.

Authorizations

BW supports authorizations, which grant BW system users specific rights to display, modify, or delete data. Only authorized users can logon to the BW systems. The rights accorded to users are based on roles, which correspond to the functions that they perform. For example, purchasing staff will not be able to view or modify HR or planning data. A user can either be an individual or a process, which can perform certain functions like loading data into the BW system.

BUSINESS CONTENT

The Business Content is a pre-configured information model, containing standard reports and associated objects, which helps SAP customers to avoid re-inventing the wheel. The idea is that many business processes are fairly standardized and follow best business practices, which are incorporated in the Business Content and, hence, available to SAP BW customers.

The objects contained in Business Content include standard BW objects such as DataSources, InfoObjects, InfoSources, InfoProviders, InfoCubes, ODS, Workbooks, Queries, SAP and non-SAP extractors, Crystal reports, Web templates, roles, etc. The Business Content can be used without any modification. However, if required, they can be modified or enhanced.

The prerequisite for using the Business Content is to activate the appropriate objects, reports, queries, and analyses. The activation can be selective. For example, activating the Business Content for a sales manager will only activate the objects, queries, etc., required by that role. Some of the standard Business Content reports include sales values, returns (values and quantities per customer), sales comparison, deliveries by period, profitability analysis, and comparisons (planned vs. actual, variance, etc.). The Business Content can be activated by individual scenarios, such as:

❑ FI/CO: A/R analysis, A/P analysis, G/L analysis, AA analysis, CCA analysis, CO-PA analysis, PCA analysis, etc.
❑ SD/MM: Sales analysis and purchasing analysis
❑ APO: Demand planning and APO resource and operation data analysis

What it contains

The Business Content is structured according to applications as well as industries. Applications include Financials, Human Resources, Supply Chain Management, Customer Relationship Management, Supplier Relationship Management, and Product Lifecycle Management. A number of industries are supported including automotive, chemicals, healthcare, retail, media, pharmaceuticals, apparel and footwear, and consumer products.

The Business Content includes the following scenarios:

❑ Financials: Accounts Receivable Analysis, Accounts Payable Analysis, General Ledger Analysis, Asset Accounting Analysis, Asset Accounting Analysis, Cost

Center Accounting Analysis, Product Cost Controlling Analysis, CO-PA, and Profit Center Analysis

❑ Customer Relationship Management: Sales Analysis, Cross-Functional Analysis (Financial and Sales data), Billing, Booking, Backlog report, Work Force Management, CRM Lead Analysis, CRM Activities Analysis, and CRM Customer Interaction Center (CIC)

❑ CRM Opportunities Analysis, CRM Sales Order Complaints Analysis, and CRM Service Quality Analysis

❑ Supply Chain Management: Purchasing Analysis, Manufacturing Analysis, Demand Planning Analysis, Resource and Operation Data Analysis, and Inventory Analysis

❑ Product Lifecycle Management: Project System—Controlling and Dates

❑ Human Capital Management: Cross-Application Time Sheet, Time Management—Time and Labor, Personnel Development—Qualifications, and Travel Management—Travel Expenses

Activating procedure

The Business Content activation process is fairly simple, which can be performed using a simple drag and drop procedure for the applicable objects. The activation is carried out in three steps:

❑ Select the selection level: option is available to select individual objects or complete scenarios; levels available include roles, InfoProviders, InfoObjects, InfoSources, and Object types

❑ Select the Business Content objects and grouping procedures, which enable all the objects to be collected for a single area

❑ Install the Business Content objects

BW also provides Demo Content, which contains sample data in addition to the Business Content metadata. The DemoCubes provided include DemoCube for Sales, DemoCube for Purchasing, and DemoCube for Profitability analysis. Appendix B and Appendix C list the objects contained in two pre-configured InfoCubes provided by SAP.

CHAPTER B11
BW DESIGN

THE DESIGN PROCESS

Objective

Data warehousing is a process that encompasses many components and tools. The ultimate aim is to create a data warehouse against which queries can be executed. In the BW system, this translates into creating an InfoCube from which the front-end access tool can extract and analyze data. A typical installation will be based on a complex design, as shown in Figure 27, with numerous InfoCubes and other objects connected through a complex relationship. The design architecture can be fairly dynamic and change over time due to additions, enhancements, and changes to objects and flows.

Process for creating a star schema

In order to perform its access and analysis functions, a query has to access various objects in an InfoCube. Therefore, before it can be designed, the various key fields and characteristics that are to be included in it need to be identified in a requirements gathering process. This process involves in-depth meetings and discussions with the end users to determine their needs and, consequently, the key fields and characteristics required to be incorporated in the InfoCube. After these requirements are finalized, they become the basis for creating the star schema. Figure 28 is an example of a star schema developed for the finance-accounts payable transaction data.

Figure 27: Complex enterprise design architecture

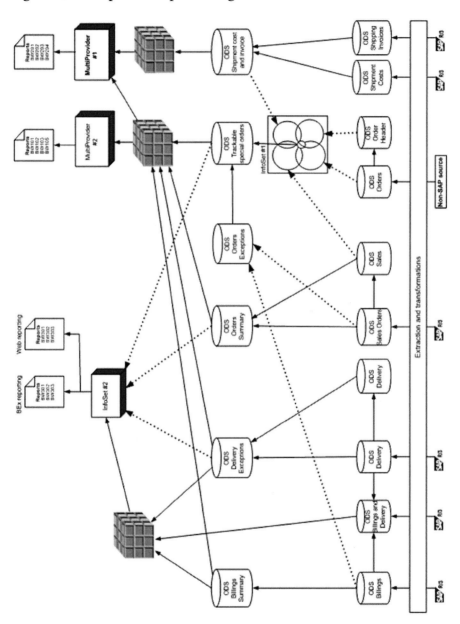

Figure 28: FI-AP star schema

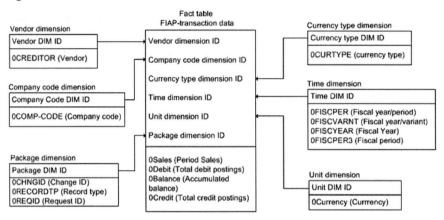

The BW star schema is a modified version of the classic star schema (Figure 29). In the BW schema, master data is not contained in the dimension tables. Instead, it is stored in master data tables. The characteristic values also are not stored in the dimension tables. For each characteristic, a numeric SID key is generated, which replaces the characteristic as the dimension table component. SID tables connect master data tables to InfoCubes and, hence, to the fact table's key figures.

Figure 29: BW star schema

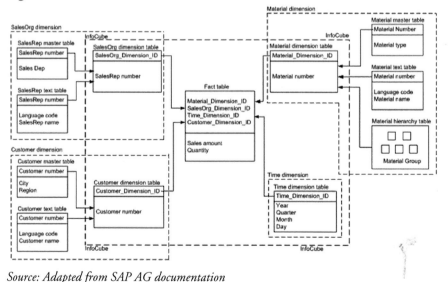

Source: Adapted from SAP AG documentation

Creating design documents

A number of design documents, the foundation upon which the BW is constructed, need to be created before the build process can start. The title of these individual documents, as well as their content, varies from organization to organization. However, when taken together, the overall content within these documents is similar. The following sections describe some of the commonly used documents and what they, typically, contain.

Functional report specifications document

This document lists the basic requirements of the query or report, such as results required, report type and delivery (BEx, web, etc.), KPIs (key performance indicators) measured with the report, filtering parameters, selection criteria, exceptions, conditions, report layout, report navigation, sorts, totals, drill-down and drill-across requirements, frequency, aggregation requirements, etc.

Architecture design document

This document provides an overall, high-level, architectural design. For example, it can include the following information (which is based on the accounts receivable and deductions data mart analysis requirements):

- Overview
- Logical data model
- Data flow
- One A/R and one deduction cube will be created
- One data source will feed item details
- Data loading will be daily for the deductions cube and monthly for the A/R cube
- Object details:
  - Data sources: name, description, granularity, data extraction frequency, fields (with technical name, description and source information), as well as mapping and transfer rules
  - ODS tables: name, description, granularity, extraction frequency, fields (with description and source information), and update rules
  - InfoCubes: name, description, granularity, extraction frequency, dimensions, key figures, navigation attributes along with their InfoObject names
    - Master data: name, description, extraction frequency, fields (with description and source information), and update rules
    - MultiProviders: name, description, granularity, extraction frequency, dimensions, key figures, and navigation attributes along with their InfoObject names

❑ Object relationship: loading sequence and configuration
❑ Data load details
❑ Star schema
❑ Aggregates

Design specifications document

This document contains the design specifications. The information included in this document is more specific and detailed than in the architecture design document. For example, for a cube design, the following information will typically be included in the design document:

❑ Business overview
❑ Design approach
❑ Star schema
❑ Data flow
❑ Appropriate and relevant object details such as name, description, technical name, mapped object, source field, source table, characteristics, key figures, navigation attributes, type, length, decimals, units, and data elements for structures such as:
  • Data sources
  • ODS tables
  • Cubes
  • InfoProviders or MultiProviders
❑ Update rules for ODS and InfoCubes
❑ Data loading details
❑ Aggregates
❑ Performance information including details for aggregates, InfoCube partitions, indexes, and archiving

Functional specifications document

This document contains the functional specifications for the proposed development. It will typically document the following information and requirements:

❑ Business requirements
❑ Scope
❑ Risks
❑ Alternative solutions
❑ Gaps
❑ Assumptions
❑ Flow diagrams

- ❑ Operational and maintenance requirements
- ❑ Data volume estimates
- ❑ Load frequency
- ❑ Error handling procedure
- ❑ Security and authorizations
- ❑ Integration requirements
- ❑ Testing requirements
- ❑ Functional test scenarios

Technical specifications

This document contains details for implementing the proposed solution, program components, inputs and outputs, program logic flow, program controls, transfer rules, test scenarios, error processing, report specifications, string testing, job specifications, security, etc.

Query design document

This document provides details about the specific report to be built such as:

- ❑ Report objective and description
- ❑ InfoProvider
- ❑ Role
- ❑ Global components (shared)
- ❑ Local components (query specific)
- ❑ Variables, characteristics, and key figures
- ❑ Filters
- ❑ Free characteristics
- ❑ Column and row items (with business rules and any restrictions)
- ❑ Exceptions
- ❑ Conditions

Importance of documentation

Some of these documents are combined into a single document at some organizations, while others prefer to keep them separate. The important point to note is that the content in these documents does need to be captured and documented, which ensures many benefits such as documenting assumptions and logic for implementing a particular solution. It ensures efficient handling of future enhancements and modifications by analysts and developers who may not have been involved with the original project.

TYPICAL DESIGN ISSUES

Source types

The number and variety of sources feeding the BW impacts its design. Consideration has to be given to the types of sources, which can include mySAP components, external databases, and flat files. They can impact the protocols, the amount of customization required, need or modification of extractors, update and transfer rules, implementation time and cost, data quality and verification, technical skills requirements, etc.

Access

The access method influences BW design and implementation because the requirements will be different for conventional access, to BW reports and queries, compared to web-based access using a simple browser. The access method can impact query development, functionality, network traffic, processing power, maintenance and support, authorizations, security, required tools, etc.

Number of users

The number of users expected to access and use the system, and the type of queries that they are expected to execute, impacts the design. The number and types of users expected to use the system, and their geographic distribution, will influence the type of access to be provided (conventional or web-based), summarization requirements, granularity, authorizations, security, network requirements, tools selection, etc.

Navigation

The requirement for navigation and the ability to slice and dice, drill-down, and drill-across can influence BW design. The requirement for navigational attributes, which are not physically stored in the InfoCube, can impact the development effort and performance. The ability to jump, or navigate from the current query results to another query, can increase complexity and be an important design consideration.

Hierarchy

A hierarchy is a structured and grouped method of displaying characteristics according to individual evaluation criteria. A hierarchy structure is arranged in successive levels, where the elements in the different levels are interdependent. Hierarchies are external to InfoCubes and form the basis for aggregation and drill-down criteria within reports. They enable users to analyze data at different levels of detail. The hierarchy design has many implications for reporting and analysis and, therefore, is an important design consideration that needs to be studied. Setting up and maintaining hierarchies can be a complex undertaking, especially if they do not remain static.

Performance

Performance is one of the most important design considerations. A poor design can lead to slow and/or inflexible queries, which can lead to many issues such as dissatisfied users, overloaded networks, analysis limitations, sizing issues, etc. In the worst case, dissatisfied users will simply stop using the BW queries.

Authorizations

The task of implementing authorizations in the BW system is tedious and can be quite complex, depending on the variety of roles that need to be supported. There can be considerable complexity in implementing the task of mapping roles to objects and authorizations because roles are unique. Each role is restricted to specific objects and queries and hence, in its ability to view specific data or execute authorized queries and reports.

Refresh

The data in BW is updated periodically from its various sources. The design has to consider the data refresh frequency (daily, real-time, etc.) and refresh timing (night, day, peak or off-peak), which can be impacted by the granularity, aggregation, delta uploads, data volume, uptime requirements, and other factors.

Upgrades

A BW project never ends as new subjects continue to be added, cubes continue to be built and/or modified, and enhancement requests never stop. Additionally, new releases and upgrades also continue to roll in at a regular pace. Hence, any design needs to plan for future changes to the system, which may or may not be currently identified.

Changing data sources

The data sources feeding a BW can change over time due to many reasons. Two of the most common reasons are mergers and acquisitions and the rollout of BW to more divisions or departments. The changes can impact the interfaces, loading process, loading times, communication methods, etc. A well-designed system can handle such changes with relative ease.

Changing business

No business remains static and the changes an organization may face, which can impact the BW system, include mergers, reorganization of business units, organizational and reporting structure changes, changes in definitions, changes in key figures or dimensions (which can be slow or frequent), new metrics, etc. The potential for changes need to be evaluated, and planned for, during the design process.

Database selection and administration

The database is one of the most important components of a data warehouse, which needs to be selected very carefully after a thorough evaluation. The features and capabilities of various databases can vary significantly. For example, Oracle is very robust, scalable, reliable, and well-proven over the years but it is difficult to administer. On the other hand, while SQL Server is not as highly rated, it is easy to administer and is considerably cheaper. The design needs to consider various constraints, such as cost and maintenance, as well as features (desired and mandatory). The design needs to consider the DBA skills required and the availability of personnel for administering the data warehouse database.

ADVANCED FEATURES

Virtual cube

A virtual cube provides a logical view, physically contains no data, and is not a data target. The data it requires is retrieved from the relevant source system after query execution. Virtual cubes are of three types:

❑ SAP RemoteCube: supports queries that can directly access transaction data in other SAP systems.
❑ General RemoteCube: supports queries that can access non-SAP data, which is accessed using BAPI.
❑ Virtual InfoCube with Services: cube that uses a remote data source; a user-defined function module is used as a DataSource.

The term multi-cube refers to a cube that combines multiple basic cubes and/or remote cubes (Figure 30). Such a cube does not contain any data. It is setup with the objective of enabling analysis across multiple areas and cubes. To a user, a multi-cube is just like a basic cube.

Figure 30: MultiCube

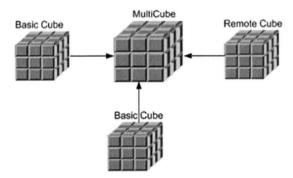

Aggregates

The objective of creating aggregates, subsets of InfoCubes, which provide frequently accessed data such as monthly or annual sales, is to improve performance by reducing the amount of data to be read by a query. Aggregates enable faster navigation as well as faster query run times. An InfoCube can have many aggregates and the determination of which aggregate to choose is made by the query that is being executed. If an appropriate aggregate does not exist, data will be retrieved from the original InfoCube. BW provides a mechanism for automatically updating the aggregates when the underlying data is updated.

An aggregate operates differently from a multi-cube because:

❑ An aggregate creates smaller InfoCubes from the original cube and, hence, reduces the amount of data to be retrieved
❑ A multi-cube acts in the reverse because it combines multiple cubes, which results in a larger amount of data being retrieved even though the multi-cube itself does not contain any data

The goal of aggregates is to balance reduced retrieval cost with the cost of aggregate maintenance. While aggregates reduce query cost by reducing the amount of data to be retrieved, it generates a significant overhead in updating the aggregates. The reason is that aggregate rollup is required when new data is loaded, changes to master data and hierarchies require recalculation of dependent aggregates, and additional storage is required.

MultiProviders

A MultiProvider is a special type of InfoProvider, which combines data from many InfoProviders (Figure 31). A MultiProvider does not contain data. Instead, it obtains its data from InfoProviders that are feeding it. The InfoProviders that combine to create a MultiProvider can be an InfoCube, ODS object, InfoObject, or an InfoSet. Any combination is possible such as an InfoCube combined with an InfoCube or an InfoCube with an ODS object.

Figure 31: MultiProvider

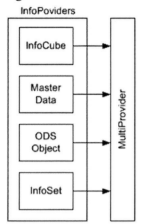

A MultiProvider avoids the creation of huge InfoCubes, which would be required if the data in two different objects were to be stored and maintained in one object. With a MultiProvider, the data can be kept separately in smaller cubes or ODS until the query is executed (Figure 32). At that time, the MultiProvider can first combine data from the two sources and then provide data to the requesting query.

Figure 32: Querying a MultiProvider

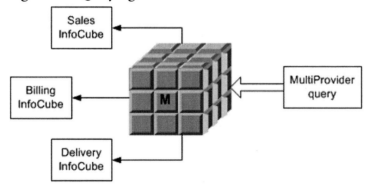

CHAPTER B12
CREATING AND LOADING INFOCUBES

PREREQUISITES

The SAP R/3 and BW systems are separate, though they interface and communicate with each other. They can also be run on the same servers. However, typically, they have been installed with their own dedicated servers. The BW system can first be installed independently and, subsequently, be connected to the R/3 system (if it is the data source that will be feeding the BW). Some of the steps involved in installing BW and connecting it to an R/3 system include:

❑ Installing BW, which can include the following steps:
   • Loading the software on the BW server
   • Creating file system/directories at the operating system level
   • Installing the BW central instance
   • Installing the BW database instance
   • Installing Java core
   • Configuring the transport management system
   • Creating users and granting authorizations in client 000
   • Installing the license key
   • Applying latest support packs
   • Creating client for data loading and extraction from R/3
   • Creating users and granting authorizations in client 100
❑ Connecting to the R/3 system, which can include the following steps:
   • Creating logical systems on BW and R/3 (source)
   • Assigning logical systems, BW and R/3, to the clients in both BW and R/3

- Creating source system in BW using transaction code RSA1
- Executing transaction code SB1W on the R/3 system

CREATING AN INFOCUBE

Objective

In this chapter, a step-by-step procedure for creating a basic InfoCube (data mart) will be demonstrated. The InfoCubes used in business applications range from very simple to extremely complex objects and, hence, can contain a few or scores of key figures and characteristics. In the step-by-step procedure to be demonstrated in this chapter, only a few key figures and characteristics will be created and incorporated in the InfoCube to be created.

It should be noted that only the minimum requirements for creating an InfoCube, including creating objects and making appropriate settings, will be demonstrated in this example. Despite this vanilla approach, the following procedure will provide a good demonstration of the steps involved in creating an InfoCube and, additionally, reinforce data warehousing concepts introduced in earlier chapters.

The first steps

Figure 33 shows the high-level procedure that needs to be followed for creating a basic InfoCube.

Figure 33: How to create an InfoCube

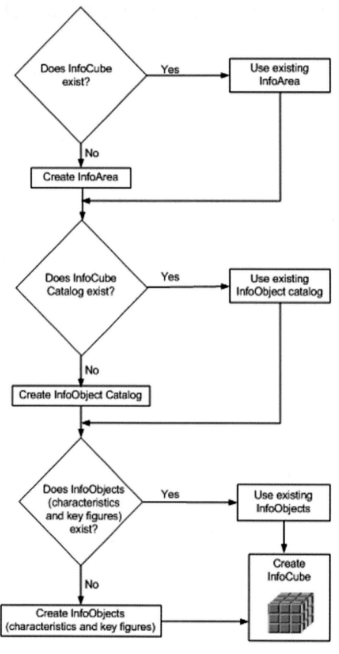

Create schema for the InfoCube

The prerequisite to creating an InfoCube is to identify the objects, key figures and characteristics, upon which it will be based. The schema that will be used to design the InfoCube to be created in this chapter is shown in Figure 34. The objects to be created for the new InfoCube include:

❑ Characteristics
- Sales order number (*ZOrder*)
- Customer number (*0Customer*)
- Material (*0Material*)

❑ Key Figures
- Order quantity (*ZTOrderqty*)

Figure 34: Star schema for exercise

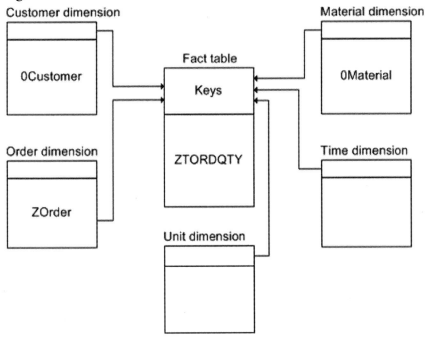

Navigate to the Administrator Workbench

The procedure is initiated by starting BW, which can be launched through the SAP/BW launch pad, as shown on the next window (Figure 35):

Figure 35

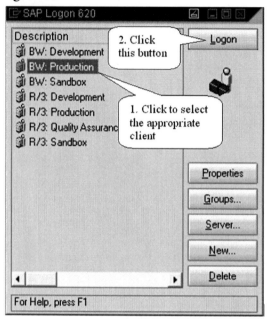

Copyright SAP AG.

The appearance of the launch pad varies from installation to installation. Hence, the selections available on your launch pad may differ compared to the launch pad shown in Figure 35. To start the BW system:

❑ Click the appropriate client (in Figure 35, *BW Production* client has been selected)
❑ Click the *Logon* button

This will cause the next window to pop-up (Figure 36):

Figure 36

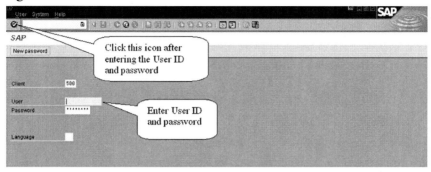

Copyright SAP AG.

The client field will be populated by the system and can be changed, if required. As instructed in Figure 36:

❑ Enter the appropriate *User ID*
❑ Enter the password
❑ Click the highlighted checkmark

This will launch BW and lead you to the next window (Figure 37):

Figure 37

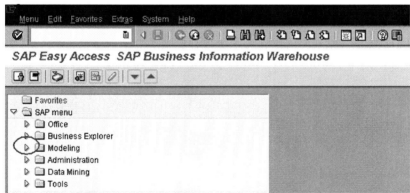

Copyright SAP AG.

❑ Click the arrow next to *Modeling*, which is highlighted in Figure 37, in order to drill-down to the lower level selections

The drill-down will lead you to the next window, where the Administrator Workbench is highlighted (Figure 38):

Figure 38

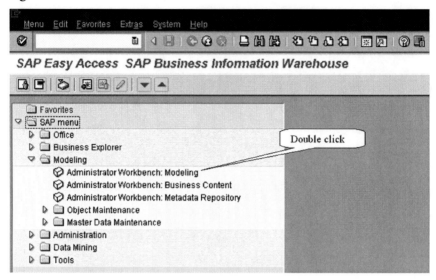

Copyright SAP AG.

All the base objects, as well as the InfoCube, will be created in the Administrator Workbench tool. To start the Administrator Workbench:

❑ Double click the cube to the left of *Administrator Workbench: Modeling,* which is highlighted in Figure 38

This will launch the Administrator Workbench, which is shown on the next window (Figure 39):

Figure 39

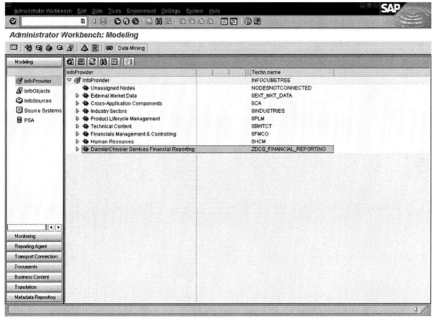

Copyright SAP AG.

Create InfoArea

The next step in the procedure requires creating an InfoArea. To create an InfoArea, navigate to the InfoObjects area by:

❑ Clicking the *InfoObjects* button, which is displayed in the left window of the Administrator Workbench (Figure 39)

This will lead you to the next window, where InfoObjects are displayed (Figure 40):

Figure 40

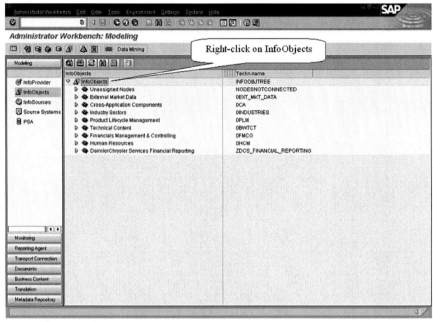

Copyright SAP AG.

☐ Right-click on *InfoObjects*, as instructed in Figure 40

This will lead you to the next window, Figure 41, where a pop-menu lists *Create InfoArea*:

Figure 41

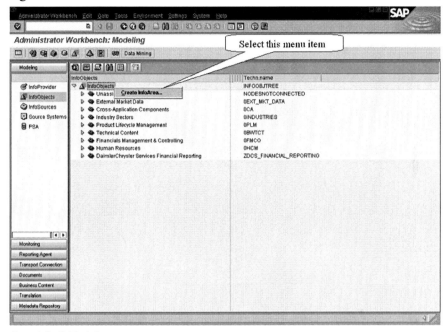

Copyright SAP AG.

❏ Select *Create InfoArea* from the pop-up menu

This will cause the next window to pop-up, where entries in two fields are required to be made (Figure 42):

Figure 42

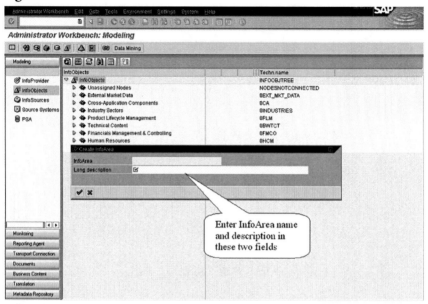

Copyright SAP AG.

On Figure 42, enter the *InfoArea* name and long description in the appropriate blank fields. Figure 43 shows the pop-up window after the two entries have been made:

Figure 43

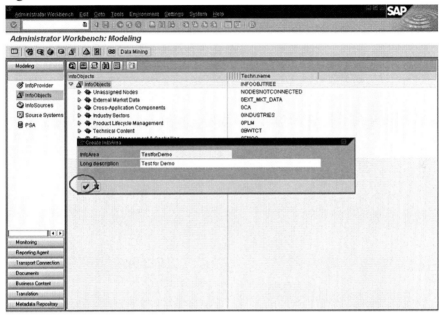

Copyright SAP AG.

Note: The demo InfoArea is to be named *A test for Demo*. Hence, the *Long description* entry in the Figure 43 pop-up box will need to be modified slightly, by adding the character *A*, before the next step is executed.

❑ Click the circled checkmark

This will create the InfoArea, which is displayed on the next window (Figure 44):

Figure 44

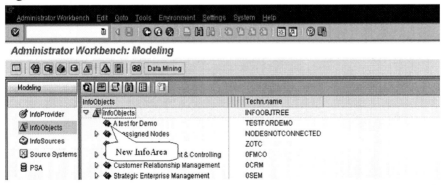

Copyright SAP AG.

Create objects

In the next step, we will create *InfoObject Catalogs*, which are like folders, for characteristics and key figures. This task is described comprehensively in the following sections.

Create InfoObject catalog for characteristics

To create an InfoObject catalog for characteristics:

❑ Click the *A test for Demo* InfoObject, which will highlight it as shown on Figure 45
❑ Right-click the selected InfoObject (*A test for Demo*)

This will cause a menu to pop-up, which is shown on the next window (Figure 45):

Figure 45

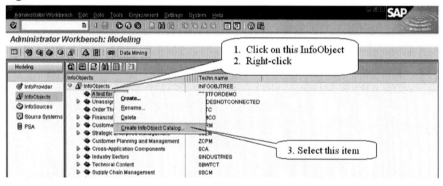

Copyright SAP AG.

❑ Select *Create InfoObject Catalog*

This will lead you to the next window, Figure 46, where characteristics can be created.

Create a characteristic

We will now create a characteristic *ZOrder*. On Figure 46 (which pops-up with blank fields):

❑ Enter the *InfoObject Catalog* name (as shown)

Figure 46

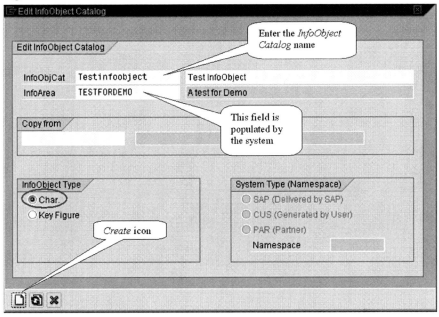

Copyright SAP AG.

On Figure 46, note that InfoObject Type *Char* (characteristic) has been selected, because a characteristic is to be created in this step.

❑ Click the *Create* icon

This will cause the next window to be displayed, Figure 47, where the characteristics can be defined:

Figure 47

Edit InfoObject Catalog
List of characteristics
Create icon
Move scroll bar up/down to display hidden characteristics

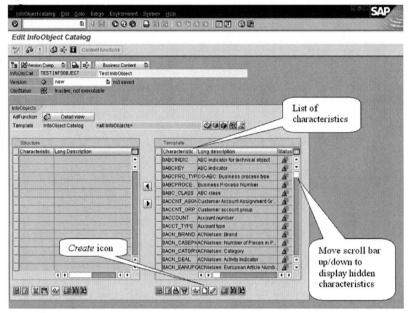

Copyright SAP AG.

- ❑ Click the *Create* icon

This will cause the next pop-up window, Figure 48, to be displayed with blank fields:

Figure 48

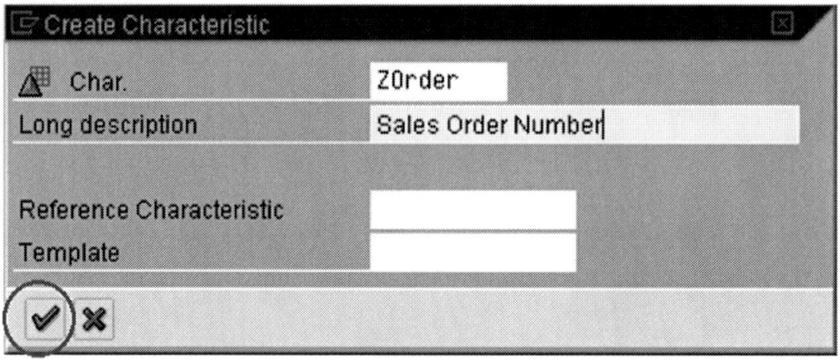

Create Characteristic
Char.
Z0rder
Long description
Sales Order Number
Reference Characteristic
Template

Copyright SAP AG.

On Figure 48, make the following entries, as shown:

❑ Enter the characteristic name (*ZOrder*)
❑ Enter the Long description (*Sales Order Number*)
❑ Click the circled checkmark

This will lead you to the next window, where the *General* tab is selected (Figure 49):

Figure 49

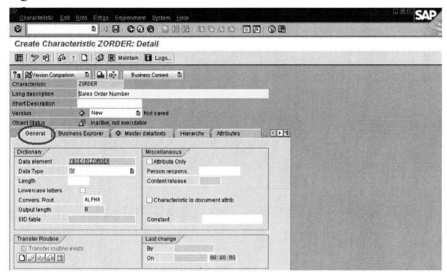

Copyright SAP AG.

❑ Enter the appropriate data in the blank fields in Figure 49

The next window, Figure 50, shows the required *General* tab fields after they have been keyed in.

Figure 50

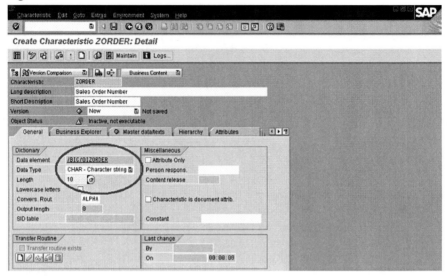

Copyright SAP AG.

To move to the next tab:

❑ Click the *Master data/texts* tab

This will lead you to the next window (Figure 51):

Figure 51

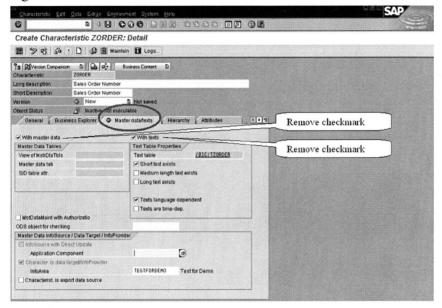

Copyright SAP AG.

❑ Remove the two checkmarks ("with master data" and "with texts"), as instructed on Figure 51

The next window, Figure 52, shows that the checkmarks have been removed.

Figure 52

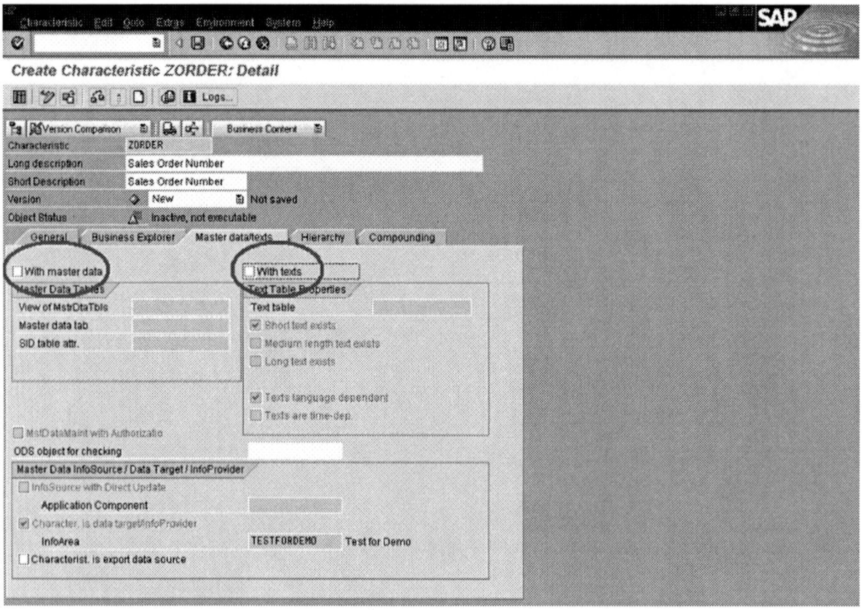

Copyright SAP AG.

Activate characteristic

We now need to activate the *ZOrder* characteristic, which can be done by:

❑ Clicking on the *Activate* icon, which is highlighted on the next window (Figure 53)

Figure 53

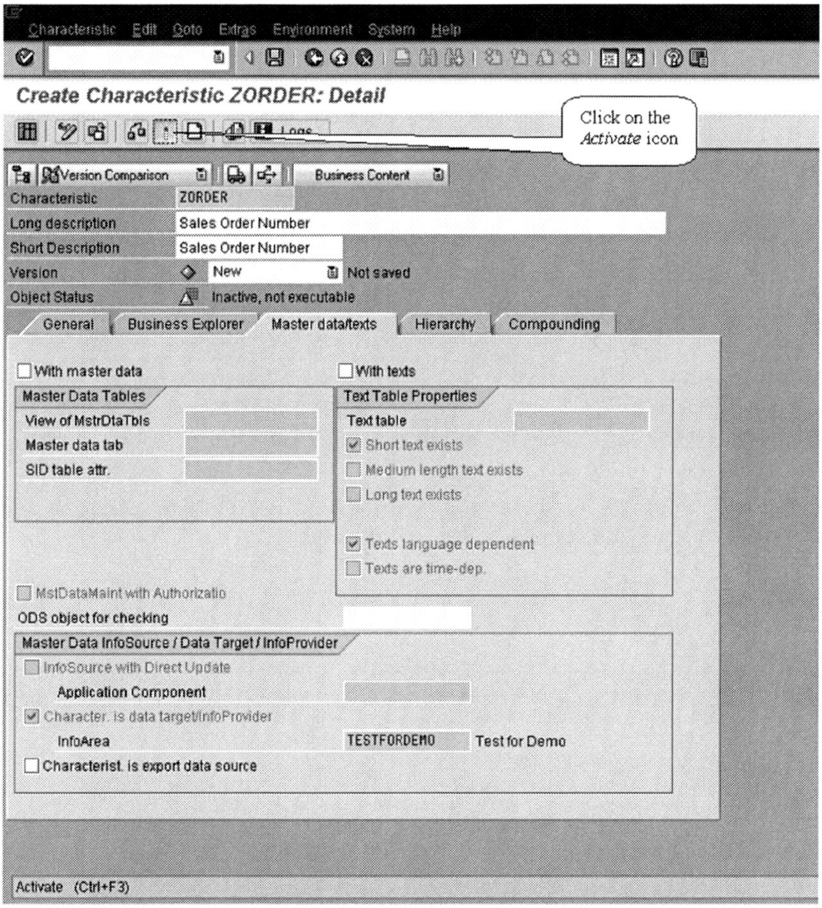

Copyright SAP AG.

This will cause a pop-up window, Figure 54, to appear:

Figure 54

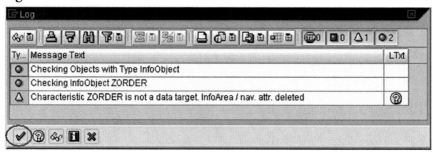

Copyright SAP AG.

❑ Click the circled checkmark

This will cause a warning message to be displayed (Figure 55):

Figure 55

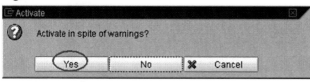

Copyright SAP AG.

❑ Click the *Yes* button

This will cause the following window, which contains a system message that the activation has been performed, to be displayed (Figure 56):

Figure 56

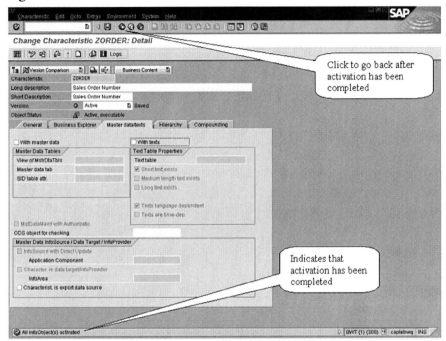

Copyright SAP AG.

After the activation task has been performed:

❑ Click the back arrow, as instructed in Figure 56

The newly created object, *ZORDER*, is highlighted on the next window, Figure 57, by a circle:

Figure 57

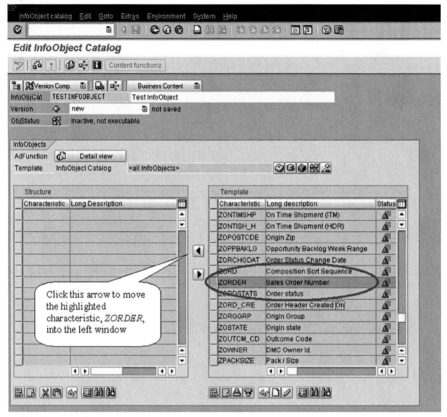

Copyright SAP AG.

We now need to move *ZORDER,* the newly created characteristic that is highlighted in Figure 57, into the structure (in the left window).

❑ Highlight *ZORDER* in the right window, as shown in Figure 57
❑ Click the left-pointing arrow

This will move the selected characteristic, *ZORDER*, into the structure, as shown in the next window (Figure 58):

Figure 58

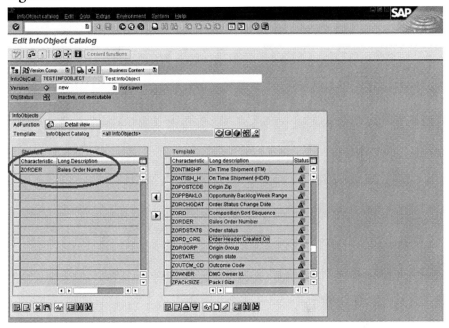

Copyright SAP AG.

Select additional pre-existing characteristics

In addition to the newly created characteristic, *ZORDER*, we will now add two pre-existing characteristics into the structure. The system typically contains a very large number of characteristics and only a few are displayed within a window, as shown in Figure 58—where 14 characteristics are displayed.

To view a pre-existing characteristic, which is not currently displayed in the window, move the scroll bar up/down until it gets displayed, as instructed in Figure 59:

Figure 59

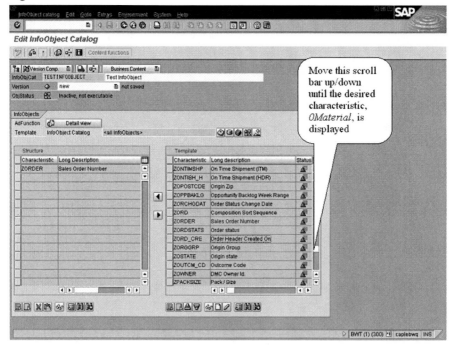

Copyright SAP AG.

We will now select the *0Material* characteristic in Figure 59.

❑   Scroll up/down until the *0Material* is displayed within the list of characteristics
❑   Click the desired characteristic, *0Material*, when it is displayed

The next window, Figure 60, shows that the *0Material* characteristic has been highlighted and selected:

Figure 60

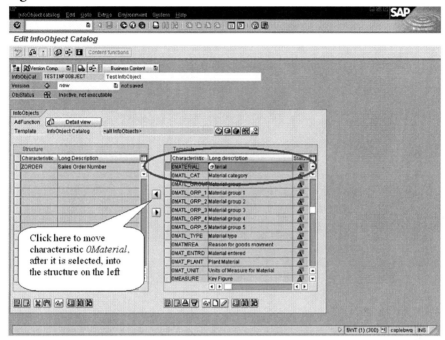

Copyright SAP AG.

To move the characteristic into the left window in Figure 60:

❑ Click the left arrow, as shown

Similarly, another characteristic, *0Customer*, needs to be moved into the structure in Figure 60:

❑ Select characteristic *0Customer* (in the right window in Figure 60)
❑ Click the left arrow

The three selected characteristics, after they have been moved into the structure in the left window, are highlighted on the next window (Figure 61):

Figure 61

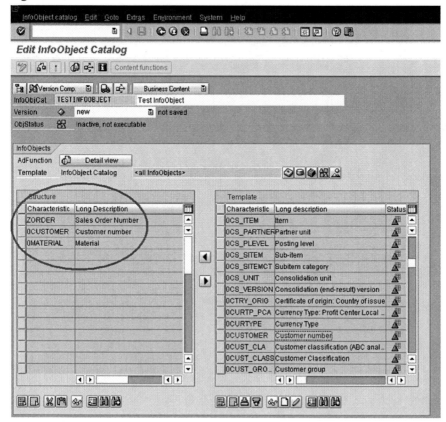

Copyright SAP AG.

Activate InfoObject catalog

We will now activate *TestInfoObject*—the InfoObject Catalog. On the next window, Figure 62, the *Activate* icon is highlighted:

Figure 62

Copyright SAP AG.

❑ Click the *Activate* icon

This will activate *TestInfoObject*, the InfoObject Catalog, which is confirmed on the next window (Figure 63):

Figure 63

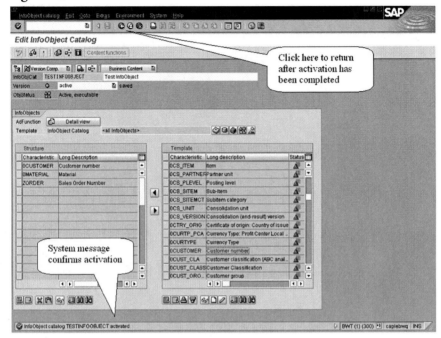

Copyright SAP AG.

❑ Click the highlighted back arrow, as instructed in Figure 63

This will lead you to the next window (Figure 64), where the new InfoObject Catalog, *TestInfoObject*, is highlighted.

Figure 64

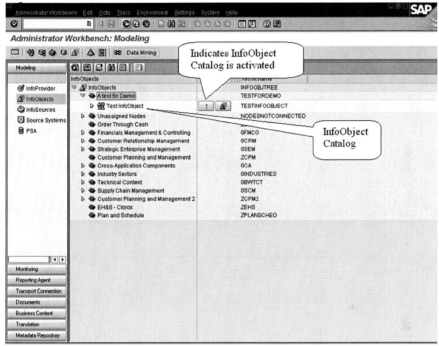

Copyright SAP AG.

Create InfoObject catalog for key figures

The next step is to create an InfoObject Catalog for key figures, just like an InfoObject Catalog for characteristics that was created in the previous section. The starting point for this task is the next window (Figure 65):

Figure 65

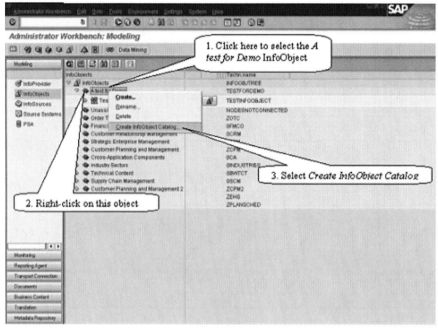

Copyright SAP AG.

As shown in Figure 65:

☐ Click the *A test for Demo* InfoObject, which selects it
☐ Right-click the mouse, which will pop-up a menu (shown in Figure 65)
☐ Select *Create InfoObject Catalog* from the menu

This will lead you to the next window, Figure 66, where the InfoObject Catalog can be edited and the process started for creating a key figure.

Figure 66

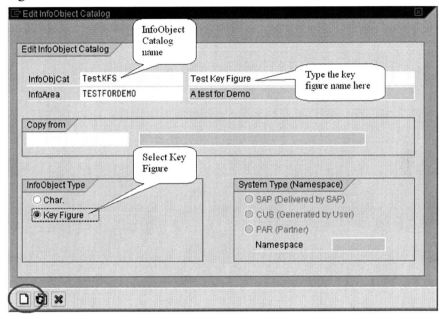

Copyright SAP AG.

Create key figure

We will now create the key figure *ZTORDQTY* (order quantity). On the previous window (Figure 66):

❑ Click the *Key Figure* (InfoObject Type) radio button (note that the default radio button is *Char*)
❑ Make the appropriate field entries, as shown
❑ Click the *Create* icon, which is circled

This will cause the next window to be displayed (Figure 67):

Figure 67

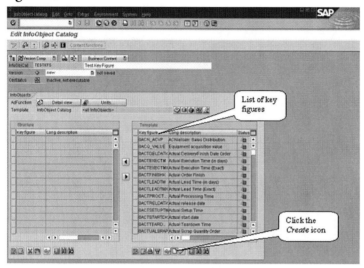

Copyright SAP AG.

❑   Click the *Create* icon

This will bring up the next pop-up window (Figure 68):

Figure 68

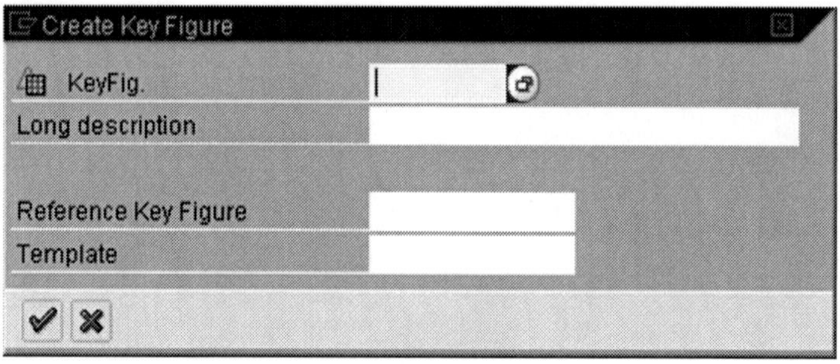

Copyright SAP AG.

❑   Enter the appropriate data in the blank fields

Figure 69 shows the pop-up window after the blank fields in Figure 68, *KeyFig* (key figure) and *Long description*, have been populated:

Figure 69

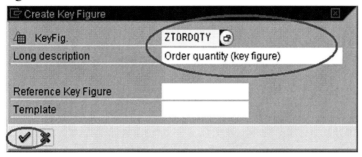

Copyright SAP AG.

❑ Click the circled checkmark

This will cause the next window to be displayed (Figure 70):

Figure 70

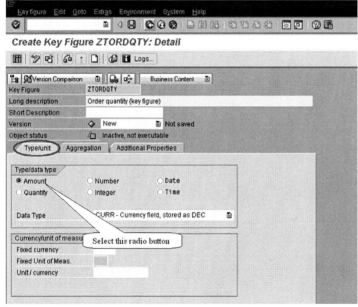

Copyright SAP AG.

On the previous window, Figure 70, you will note that the *Type/unit* tab has been selected and displayed. Also selected is the *Amount* radio button.

❑   Click the *Quantity* radio button

This will select *Quantity*—a selection that is displayed on the next window (Figure 71):

Figure 71

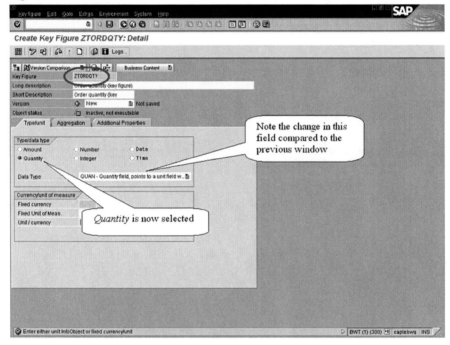

Copyright SAP AG.

The next two windows display the two other tabs, *Aggregation* (Figure 72) and *Additional Properties* (Figure 73), where no data is to be changed for this exercise. They are only being displayed to make you aware of the variables contained in them.

Figure 72

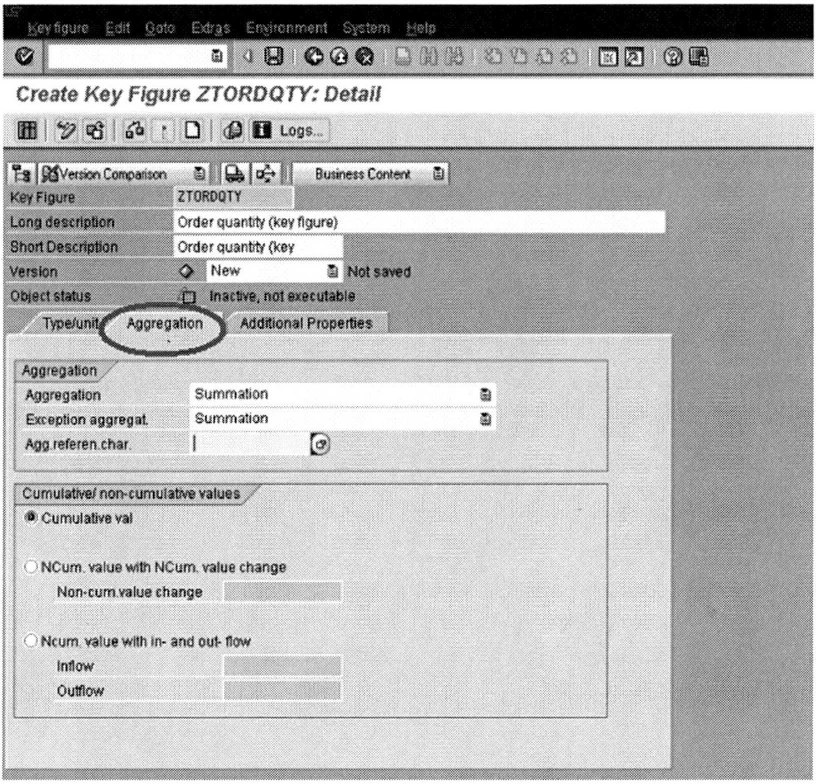

Copyright SAP AG.

Figure 73

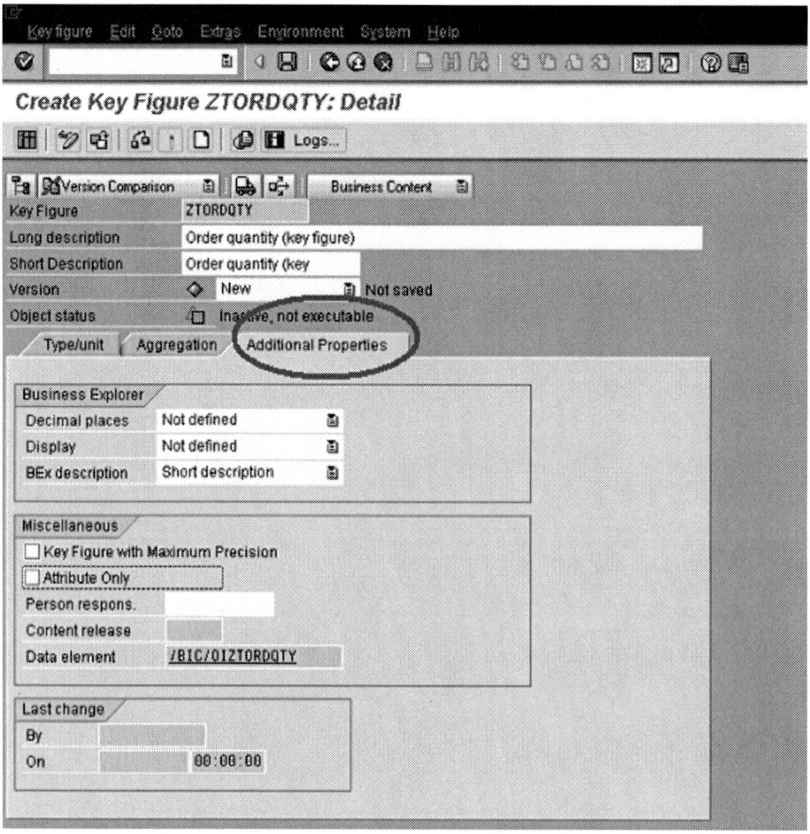

Copyright SAP AG.

To return to the *Type/unit* tab:

❏ Click the *Type/unit* tab in Figure 73

This will lead you to the next window (Figure 74):

Figure 74

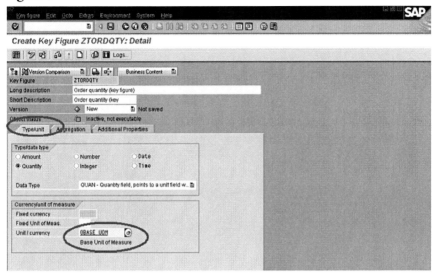

Copyright SAP AG.

❑ In the *Unit currency* field, enter the base unit of measure (as shown in Figure 74)

Activate key figure

In the next step, we will activate *ZTORDQTY*, the newly created key figure. To activate:

❑ Click on the *Activate* icon, which is circled on the next window (Figure 75)

Figure 75

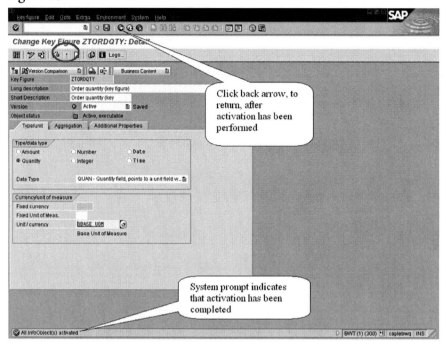

The callouts in the figure read:

"Click back arrow, to return, after activation has been performed"

"System prompt indicates that activation has been completed"

Copyright SAP AG.

After activation:

❏   Click the back arrow, as shown on Figure 75

This will lead you to the next window, Figure 76, where the newly created key figure, *ZTORDQTY*, is highlighted.

Figure 76

Copyright SAP AG.

Select key figure

On the previous window (Figure 76), we will now move the key figure, *ZTORDQTY*, from the window on the right side into the window on the left side.

❑ Click the circled left arrow

This will lead you to the next window, Figure 77, where the key figure is now displayed in the left window:

Figure 77

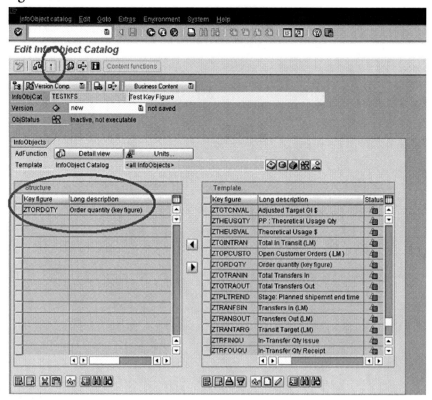

Copyright SAP AG.

Activate InfoObject Catalog

In the next step, we will activate *TestKFS*—the InfoObject Catalog. To activate:

❑ Click the *Activate* icon, which is circled in Figure 77

This will lead you to the next window, Figure 78, which displays the system prompt indicating that activation has been completed.

Figure 78

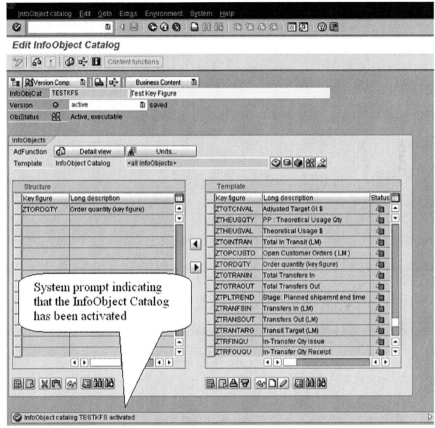

Copyright SAP AG.

Create InfoCube

The InfoObject can now be created because the required objects are now available, having been created in the previous sections. To create the cube, which will be named *Test InfoCube*, proceed as follows:

❑   Launch the Administrator Workbench

This will take you to the next window (Figure 79).

Figure 79

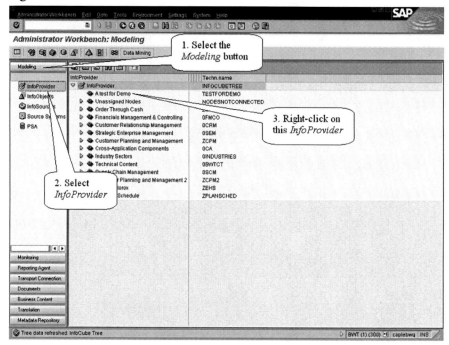

Copyright SAP AG.

Now execute the following instructions, which are also displayed on Figure 79:

- ❑ Click to select the *Modeling* button
- ❑ Click to select *InfoProvider*
- ❑ Right-click on the *A test for Demo* InfoProvider

This will cause a menu to pop-up, which is displayed on the next window (Figure 80):

Figure 80

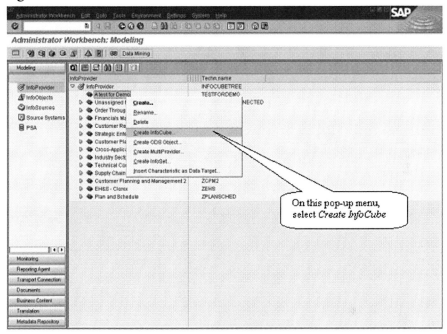

Copyright SAP AG.

❑ Select *Create InfoCube* from the pop-up menu

This will lead you to the next window (Figure 81):

Figure 81

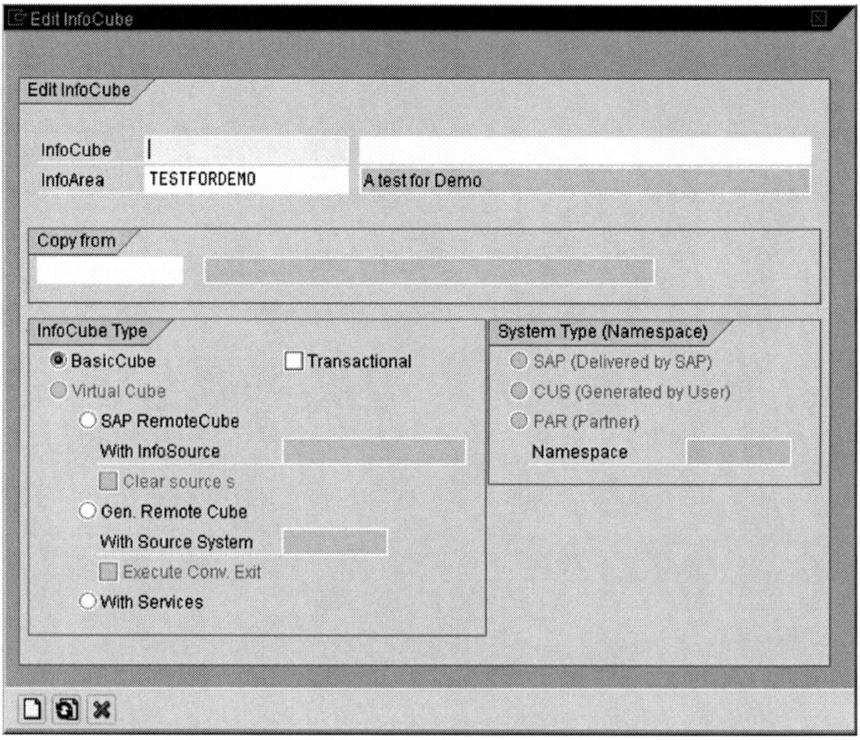

Copyright SAP AG.

Now enter appropriate values in the blank fields in Figure 81:

❑ Enter the InfoCube name (*Z TestCube*)
❑ Enter the InfoCube description (*Test InfoCube*)

These entries are displayed on the next window (Figure 82):

Figure 82

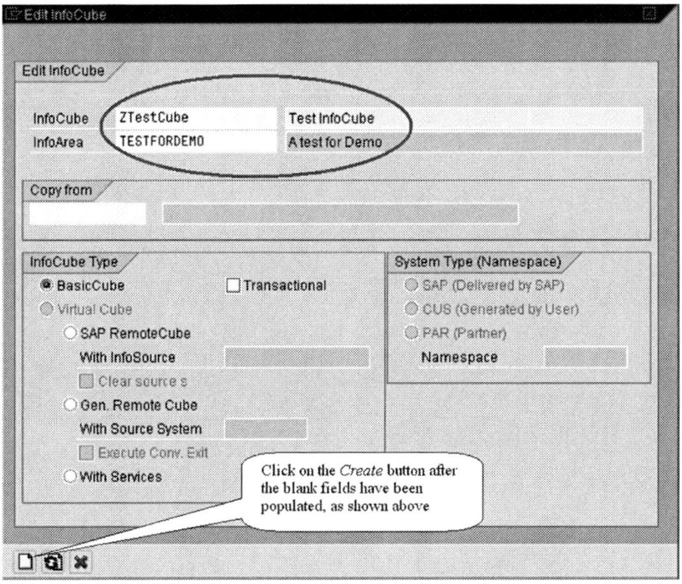

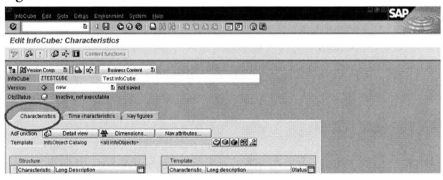

Copyright SAP AG.

❑ Click the *Create* button

This will lead you to the next window, Figure 83, where the key figure and characteristics required by the InfoCube will be selected.

Figure 83

Copyright SAP AG.

Notice that the characteristics tab has been highlighted in Figure 83.

Select characteristics for InfoCube

We will now select the characteristics, which will be used in the InfoCube, from the list of characteristics in the right window (Figure 84). To view a required characteristic that is not currently displayed, the scroll bar can be used (by moving it up or down).

Figure 84

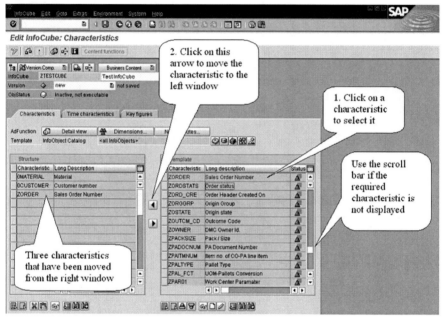

Copyright SAP AG.

Using the steps highlighted in Figure 84, proceed as follows:

❑ Click the *0Material* characteristic, in the right window, to select it
❑ Click the left arrow to move *0Material* into the left window

Similarly, select and move the other two characteristics, *0Customer* and *ZOrder*, from the right window into the left window. Figure 84 shows the three characteristics, in the desired structure in the left window, where they were moved from the right window.

Select key figure for InfoCube

We will now select the key figure required for the InfoCube. On the previous window (Figure 84):

❑ Click the *Key Figures* tab

This will lead you to the next window, where the key figures tab is highlighted (Figure 85):

Figure 85

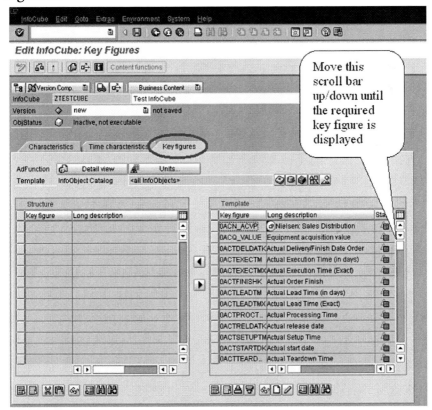

Copyright SAP AG.

❑ Move the scroll bar up/down until the desired key figure, *ZTORDQTY*, is displayed (Figure 86)

Figure 86

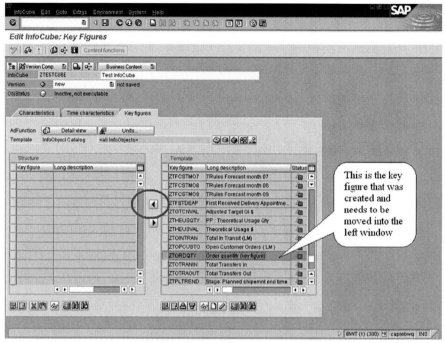

Copyright SAP AG.

To select and move the desired key figure from the right window into the left window in Figure 86:

❑   Click the key figure, *ZTORDQTY*, to select it
❑   Click the circled left arrow

This will move the key figure (*ZTORDQTY*) from the right window into the left window, where it is displayed in Figure 87:

Figure 87

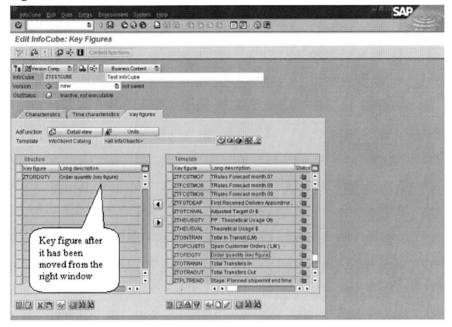

Copyright SAP AG.

Select time characteristic

The next step requires identifying the time characteristic. On the previous window (Figure 87):

❑ Click the *Time characteristics* tab

This will cause the next window to be displayed (Figure 88):

Figure 88

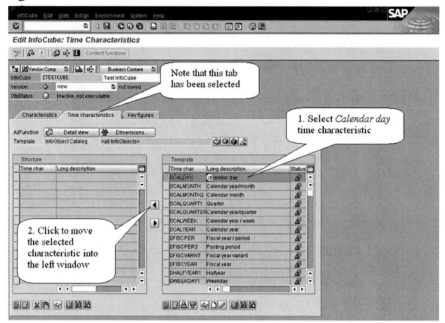

Copyright SAP AG.

Now execute the following instructions, which are also displayed in Figure 88:

☐ Click the time characteristic *Calendar day* (*0CALDAY*)
☐ Click the left arrow

This will move the *Calendar day* characteristic from the right window into the left window, where it is displayed in Figure 89.

Figure 89

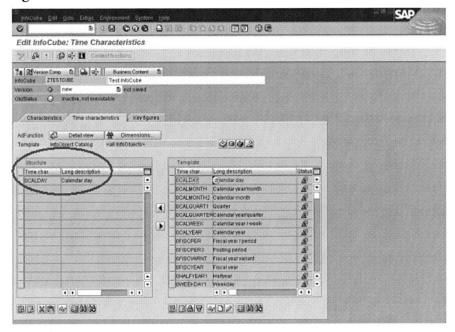

Copyright SAP AG.

Creating dimensions

The next step in the procedure for creating an InfoCube requires creating the dimensions. We will start with Figure 90, where the *Dimensions* button is highlighted.

Figure 90

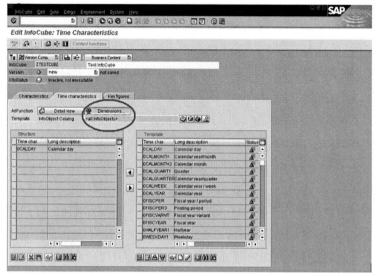

Copyright SAP AG.

❏ Click the *Dimensions* button

This will cause the following pop-up window to appear (Figure 91):

Figure 91

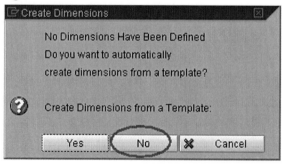

Copyright SAP AG.

❏ Click the *No* button

This will lead you to the next window (Figure 92):

Figure 92

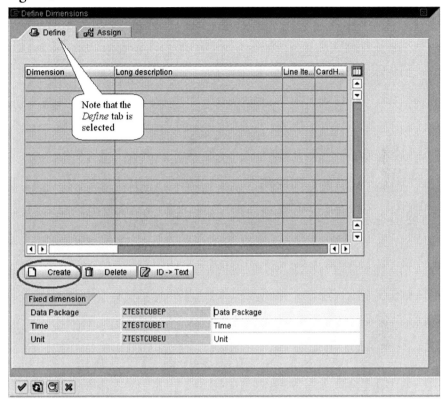

Copyright SAP AG.

Defining dimensions

On the previous window (Figure 92):

❑ Click the *Create* button, which is circled

This will lead you to the next window, Figure 93, where the dimensions are defined. To create the required three dimensions:

❑ Enter the three dimensions (*Material, Customer and Order*), as shown in Figure 93

Figure 93

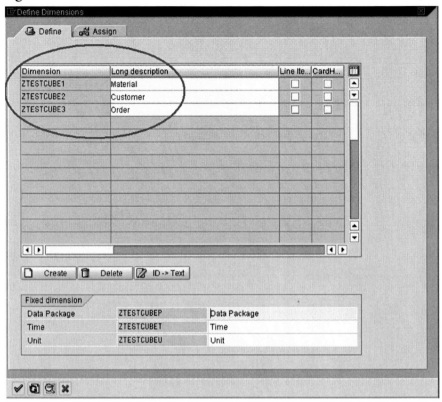

Copyright SAP AG.

Assigning dimensions

The next step requires assigning the three dimensions. This task is performed as follows:

❑ Click the *Assign* tab in Figure 93

This will select the *Assign* tab, as shown in the following window (Figure 94):

Figure 94

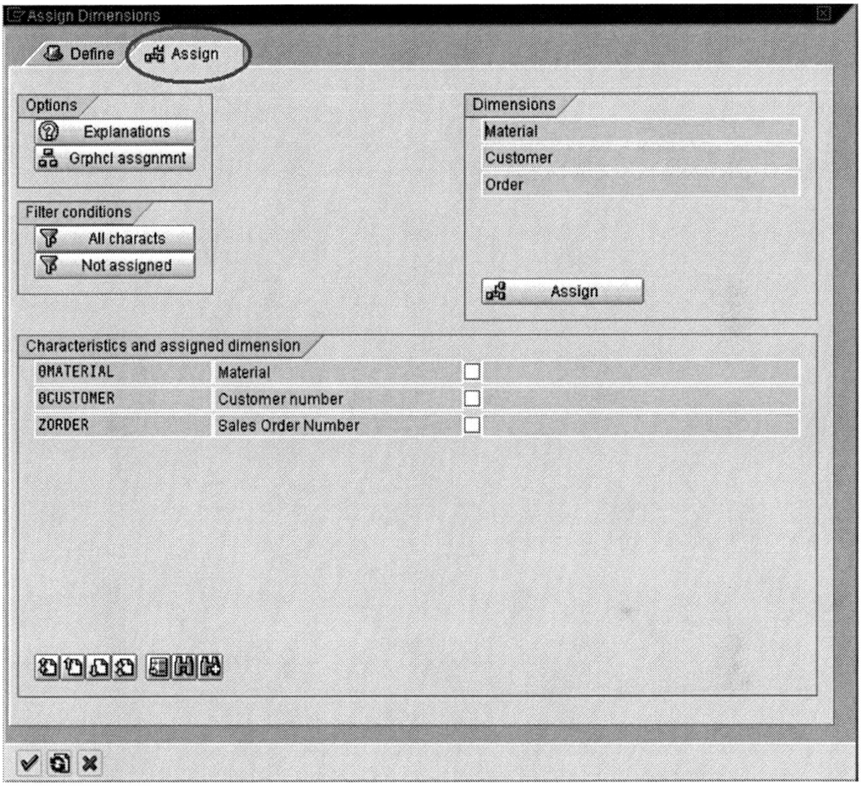

Copyright SAP AG.

To assign the first dimension, *Material*, execute the following steps, which are also highlighted on the next window (Figure 95):

❑ Click the *Material* dimension
❑ Place a checkmark in the box for *0Material* (under *Characteristics and assigned dimension*)
❑ Click the *Assign* button

Figure 95

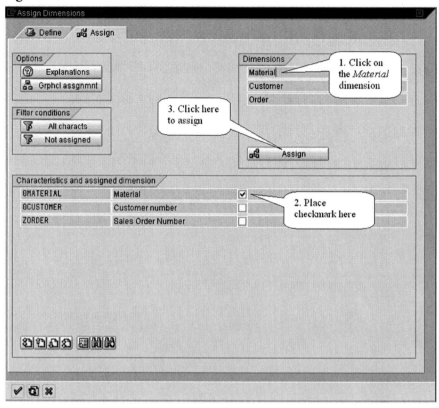

Copyright SAP AG.

To assign the second dimension, *Customer*, execute the following steps, which are also highlighted on the next window (Figure 96):

❑ Click the *Customer* dimension
❑ Place a checkmark in the box for *0Customer* (under *Characteristics and assigned dimension*)
❑ Click the *Assign* button

Figure 96

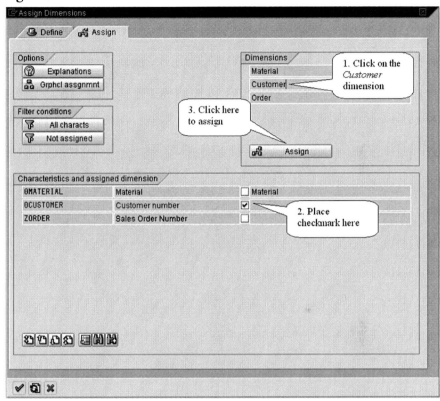

Copyright SAP AG.

To assign the third dimension, *Order*, execute the following steps, which are high-lighted on the next window (Figure 97):

❑ Click the *ZOrder* dimension
❑ Place a checkmark in the box for *ZOrder* under (*Characteristics and assigned dimension*)
❑ Click the *Assign* button

Figure 97

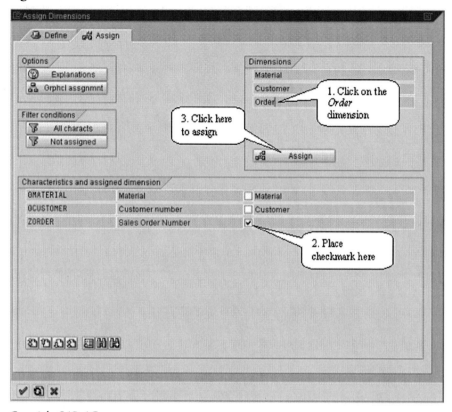

Copyright SAP AG.

This will lead you to the next window, Figure 98, where the three assignments are displayed:

Figure 98

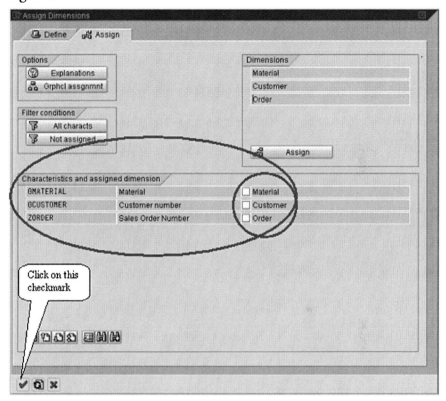

Copyright SAP AG.

❑ Click the checkmark

This will take you back to the next window (Figure 99):

Figure 99

Copyright SAP AG.

Checking and activating the InfoCube

Check InfoCube

At this stage, we will perform a check on the InfoCube.

❑ Click the *Characteristics* tab (Figure 99)

This will lead you to the next window, Figure 100, where the icon used to perform the check is highlighted:

Figure 100

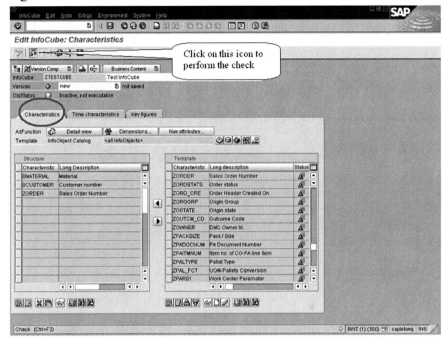

❑ Click the *Check* icon

The system response, highlighted on the next window (Figure 101), indicates that the check was successful.

Figure 101

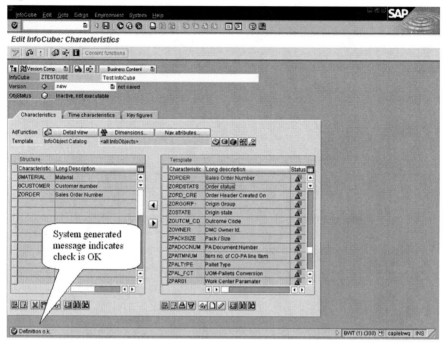

Copyright SAP AG.

Activating InfoCube

In the final step, we will activate the newly created InfoCube (*Test InfoCube*). The icon used to perform the activation is shown on the next window (Figure 102):

Figure 102

Copyright SAP AG.

To activate the InfoCube:

❑ Click the *Activate* icon

The activated InfoCube is shown on the next window (Figure 103):

Figure 103

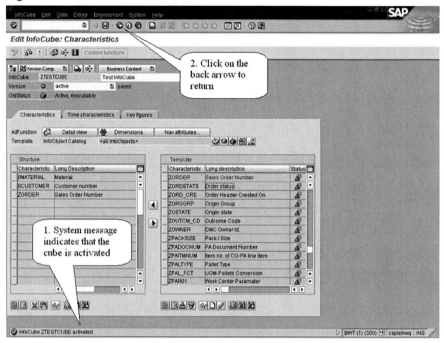

Copyright SAP AG.

After the cube has been activated:

❑ Click the back arrow, which is highlighted in Figure 103

This will take you to the next window, Figure 104, where the activated InfoCube is displayed in the list of InfoProviders.

Figure 104

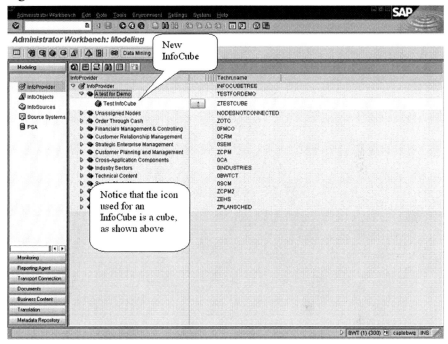

Copyright SAP AG.

Displaying the results

Displaying InfoCube contents

To display the objects contained in *Test InfoCube*, the newly created cube that is displayed in Figure 104, navigate through each of its three tabs (Characteristics, Time Characteristics, and Key Figures). Figures 105-107, the next three windows, respectively display the contents of each of these three tabs.

Figure 105

Figure 106

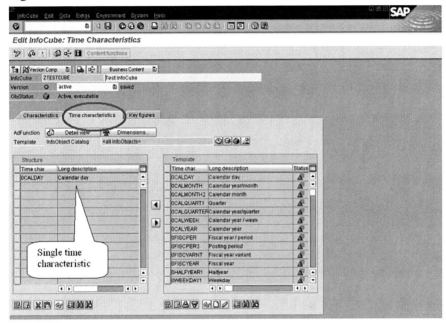

Figure 107

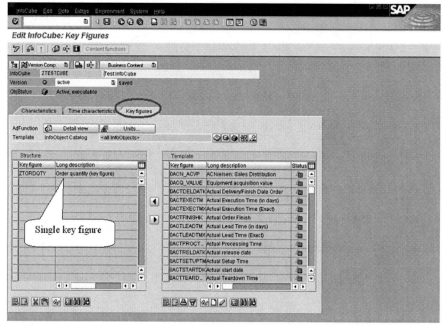

Copyright SAP AG.

Display InfoObject overview

To provide an overview of the InfoObjects associated with the *Test* InfoCube, in a single window, proceed as follows:

❑ Launch the Administrator Workbench (shown in Figure 108)

Figure 108

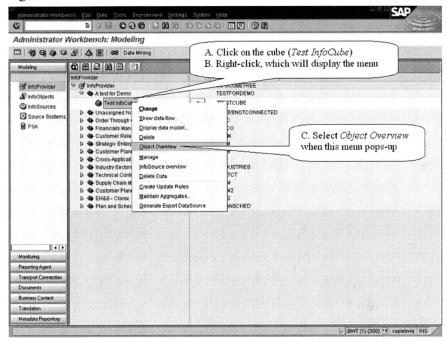

Copyright SAP AG.

- ❑ Click the *Modeling* tab
- ❑ Click on *InfoProvider* in the left window
- ❑ Drill-down to the InfoCube (*Test InfoCube*)

Next, as shown in Figure 108:

- ❑ Click on *Test InfoCube* to select it (step A)
- ❑ Right-click, which will display a menu (step B)
- ❑ Select *Object Overview* from the displayed menu (step C)

This will lead you to the next window, Figure 109, which displays the objects associated with *Test InfoCube*:

Figure 109

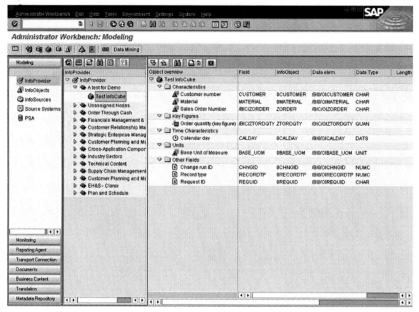

Copyright SAP AG.

Loading an InfoCube

A number of steps are required to load data into an InfoCube. The following sections provide an overview, not the details, of the process for loading data into an InfoCube.

Create Source System

A cube needs to be populated with data before any analysis can be performed on it. Such data can potentially be loaded from a variety of source systems. Therefore, the BW system needs to know which system(s) to extract the data from. It also needs to know how to do it as the procedures can differ for loading data from different systems, such as a flat file, R/3 system, legacy system, data warehouse, or another data mart. For loading data from a flat file source, the following steps will be required to create it as a BW source system:

❑ Navigate to the *AWB*
❑ Select *Modeling*
❑ Select *Source Systems*
❑ Right-click on *Source System*
❑ Select source system type (from list of available source types in pop-up window)
❑ Enter a name and description for the source system

Create Application Component

An Application Component is used to organize InfoSources and InfoPackages, using a tree structure. The following steps are required to create it:

❑ Navigate to the *AWB*
❑ Select *Modeling*
❑ Select *InfoSources*
❑ Right-click on *InfoSources*
❑ Select *Create Application Component* (from choices displayed in pop-up window)
❑ Enter a name and description for the *Application Component*

Create InfoSource for characteristic data

Initially, in this step, an InfoSource is created. Subsequently, it is assigned a source (from where it will load its data) and transfer (mapping) rules are specified. The following is the typical sequence of steps to be followed:

❑ Navigate to the *AWB*
❑ Select *InfoSources*
❑ Right-click on *Application Component*
❑ Select *Create InfoSource*
❑ Select *InfoSource type* (master data/texts/hierarchies or transaction data)
❑ Create *InfoSource* (by entering InfoObject/InfoSource technical name and the Enter key, which assigns the *InfoSource* to the *Application Component*)
❑ Right-click on the *InfoSource* created in the previous step
❑ Select *Assign DataSource*
❑ Enter the source system (created earlier in the section titled *Create Source System*)
❑ Save assignment (DataSource to InfoSource assignment)
❑ Activate transfer rules (DataSource contains ETL/mapping information)

Create InfoPackage (to load characteristic data)

This step is used to specify how to select data and, also, when to transfer and load the selected data. The procedure includes the following steps:

❑ Navigate to the *AWB*
❑ Select *InfoSources*
❑ Select *Application Component*
❑ Right-click on *Application Component*
❑ Select *Create InfoPackage* (from pop-up window selections)
❑ Select *DataSource*
❑ Specify the *InfoPackage name*

❑ Select *External Data* tab
❑ Specify the file location (for external file to be loaded)
❑ Specify the load time options (on *Schedule* tab)

Create InfoSource for transaction data

In this step, in a procedure somewhat similar to creating an InfoSource for master data, which was described previously, an InfoSource is created for any transaction data that may need to be loaded.

Create InfoCube update rules

In this step, update rules are created, which specify how data in the InfoCube will be updated. The update rules are specified in the *AWB*. The following are the steps involved in creating update rules for an InfoCube:

❑ Select *Modeling*
❑ Select *Data Targets*
❑ Select the *InfoCube*
❑ Right-click and select *Create update rules*
❑ Select *InfoSource* option
❑ Enter the *InfoSource name*
❑ Specify the update rules (or accept default)
❑ Validate the update rules
❑ Activate the update rules

Create InfoPackage (to load transaction data)

In the final step, an *InfoPackage*, which specifies how and when data loading is to be performed, is created. The following are the steps included in this task:

❑ Select *Modeling*
❑ Select *InfoSources*
❑ Select *Application Component*
❑ Right-click on *Application Component*
❑ Select *Create InfoPackage*
❑ Select *DataSource*

This leads to the window where appropriate data loading options are selected and appropriate entries are made on various tabs (select data, external data, external data parameters, data targets, update parameters, schedule, etc.).

CHAPTER B13
DATA MIGRATION

NEED FOR DATA MIGRATION

The data to be analyzed in a BW system is imported from various systems and applications. The migration task is very complicated as the number, type, and quality of the sources feeding the BW can vary significantly. The migration effort requires considerable effort because the source data and processes need to be thoroughly analyzed before data is loaded. In conventional data warehouse implementations, 75% of the build time is spent on the following tasks:

❑ Extracting data from the sources
❑ Conditioning and transforming source data for meeting the data warehouse requirements (technical and business)
❑ Loading the data into the data warehouse

When BW is used, the ETL task is simplified as SAP has provided an embedded tool that enables data to be moved from the SAP R/3 transaction system to the BW data warehouse. When data for BW is required to be extracted from non-SAP sources, the data conversion and migration effort becomes more complex.

Data quality requirements

The quality of information provided to users is a critical BW success factor as it has the potential to directly impact the company's profitability. The BW is a gold mine that contains a company's strategic data, which can be used by decision makers at all hierarchy levels. If its data is inaccurate and unreliable, it will lose its credibility and, consequently, be ignored by the users. If inaccurate data is used for decision-making, the quality of decisions can be seriously compromised and severe consequences can be expected. Hence, BW data must be accurate, meet the highest quality standards, and have the following characteristics:

- ❑ Clean
- ❑ Consistent
- ❑ Accurate
- ❑ Complete
- ❑ Reliable
- ❑ Relevant and useful
- ❑ Understandable
- ❑ Current
- ❑ Timely

Concrete steps need to be taken to ensure data quality. The data cleanup process must start at the source data, which often requires complex cleaning. The data imported into BW, especially from non-SAP sources, must be checked and validated to ensure that it is properly structured, accurate, and complete. Failure to do so can have serious repercussions including project failure.

Problems with source data

Source data imported into a data warehouse is often dirty and inconsistent. For example, a vendor loaded into the data warehouse from three different sources may be referred to as IBM, International Business Machines, and IBM Global Services. Consequently, any summation or analysis performed on a BW system that contains these three variations will return inaccurate results.

The range of problems commonly encountered covers a wide spectrum. For example, field data does not match the field description, data files from various sources have different formats, name is spelled differently in various systems, address varies across sources, multiple names are located in the same field, name and address are in the same field, special characters are used inconsistently, addresses have missing zip codes, phone numbers have missing area codes, spacing is inconsistent, and data is truncated. Hence, an important task that needs to be performed at each BW project is to check and validate the data being imported.

DATA MIGRATION STEPS

Identifying data sources

The initial step in the data migration process is to identify the operational sources that will feed data into the Business Warehouse. Duplication is a common problem and many data elements can be found in multiple data sources. Therefore, the most appropriate source for feeding data into the BW must be identified in this task. Such a source and its data elements must be reliable and accurate. They must preferably be in the required format or need minimum transformation for import into the data warehouse. To perform the data identification task, considerable time and effort is usually required due to the differences and possible anomalies that can exist among the various source databases.

Data cleansing

Before source data is acquired and loaded into the target database, it is cleansed in order to remove errors that are commonly found in the source systems. This task can involve a number of steps such as identifying redundant data, rectifying erroneous values in fields, populating fields with missing values, standardizing the format, etc. There is a direct relationship between the amount of effort expended in data cleansing and the number of loading errors encountered when data is moved from the source to the target database. In general, greater the amount of data cleansing effort, lower is the number of expected errors.

Acquisition

After the data to be imported into a data warehouse has been identified, it is physically acquired from the source databases. In this step, called data acquisition, data is extracted from the source(s) and transported to the target database. However, before the data is transported and loaded into the target, it is subjected to some transformations that change its characteristics. The transformations can include restructuring the data, de-normalizing the tables, adding new fields and keys, etc. Before loading, the data can also be subjected to various operations such as consolidation (merging various data sets into a single master data set), standardization (of data types and fields), scrubbing (cleaning to remove inconsistencies or inaccuracies), summarization, etc.

In addition to BW's own ETL tool for performing this task, which is flexible and easy to use, a number of third-party tools can also be used for the transformation process. However, such tools are not preferred over the BW tool due to the additional time and effort required to customize them and make them work with the BW system.

Loading

The data from the various sources is initially fed into the BW in a massive upload. Subsequently, new data is introduced based on a frequency ranging from a few days to real-time, depending on the organization's requirements. Another type of upload is in the reverse direction. In such a case, the data warehouse data is fed back to its source—which can be a legacy system, another data warehouse (BW or non-BW), or a data mart.

DATA MIGRATION CHALLENGES

Legacy source data issues

The following challenging issues can be expected when BW is fed data from legacy systems:

❑ Accuracy: Typically, legacy systems' data quality is quite poor which, if not corrected, can translate into serious problems such as flawed analysis and, consequently, incorrect decisions

❑ Formatting: Files extracted from multiple sources for migration into BW will usually have data stored in different formats

❑ Field descriptions do not match the data values or follow business rules

❑ Data granularity in the source databases can vary considerably

❑ Mapping may not be simple or straightforward as the data structure and storage format can vary considerably across systems

❑ Difficult to match and relate entities, which can be a roadblock for a consolidated view (such as subsidiaries under a single organization); such data may need to be rebuilt

❑ Business entities may be represented in many ways, which makes matching and consolidation a complex task; hence, ensuring entity integrity becomes a requirement

Data preparation

The task of populating a data warehouse system with data from multiple sources is a very challenging task that requires a significant investment of time and resources. It has to be performed in an environment characterized by multiple data sources, varying data quality, inconsistent nomenclature and definitions, inconsistent data, data models that vary across the enterprise databases, consolidation requirements across non-standard aging legacy systems, lack of skilled legacy IT resources, etc.

These challenges and risks can be mitigated to some extent by the available state-of-the art tools for data transformation, cleansing, capture, and loading. In the case of BW systems, the problem is reduced considerably as most of them are fed by the SAP R/3 system, which has relatively clean data, and BW's embedded ETL tool can be used. However, when multiple non-SAP sources are used, the data preparation task can be quite challenging.

In the BW system, imported data can be checked in the PSA before it is loaded into its final destination—the InfoCube. If there are problems with the data, it can be rectified in the PSA. In cases where the issue is significant and requires considerable work, the data can be re-loaded after the source data has been fixed and made acceptable for loading into the InfoCube.

Automating data migration

The initial data load into a data warehouse is very large. Even though data marts (InfoCubes) are relatively smaller, their initial data load volumes can also be quite large. Subsequently, new data needs to be introduced, periodically, to refresh and update a data warehouse. For this purpose, pre-defined extraction, mapping, and loading routines are used to feed data from the source systems at pre-defined frequencies. As required, such routines can be automated to extract source data and move it to the BW system, while maintaining data integrity during the transfer, based on pre-defined business rules.

Selecting the tools

For migrating data from non-SAP systems to BW, a number of third-party software tools are available. Such products, which are quite versatile, can validate names and addresses when multiple sources are being consolidated, rectify errors in the data elements, create new data in the format required by the data warehouse, etc. The challenge is to select an appropriate tool that can meet the conflicting requirements of ease of use, data quality requirements, speed, scalability, cost, application requirements, and future usage

CHAPTER B14
BW FRONT-END TOOLS

DESIRED FEATURES OF FRONT-END TOOLS

A number of front-end tools are available for accessing and retrieving data from BW using queries, reports based on a selection of variables, which enable users to analyze business from various perspectives. A query is based on a single InfoProvider. It is typically configured using key figures (including calculated and restricted) and characteristics in a variety of combinations, along with filters.

The tool used to access BW, whether it is an SAP or non-SAP tool, needs to provide some basic capabilities as well as some advanced features. Some of the commonly desired features, which the BW front-end tool provides, include drilling, filtering, positioning/hiding totals, converting currencies, displaying results graphically, manipulating and/or formatting results, and sorting. Some of the important desired features, which are essential for analysis and professional presentations, are described in the following sections.

Slicing and dicing

The slicing and dicing technique, which refers to the re-arrangement of data so that it can be viewed from different perspectives (such as by period and cost center), is widely used for comprehensive data analysis. This technique enables the data returned by a query to be displayed in different ways by manipulating the initially displayed results. For example, the initial query results can display the total sales for each region. Using the slice and dice technique, the displayed results can be manipulated so that the sales for each state are displayed. Further slicing and dicing can lead to the display of sales by product line and by store.

Drill-down

The drill-down technique enables navigation from the summary results to the underlying detailed data. For example, a store manager can execute a report that, initially, displays the total store sales. Using drill-down, the sales for each product group can be displayed. If more comprehensive analysis is required, the manager can perform additional drill-down so that the sales for each product are displayed.

Drill-across

The drill-across technique is similar to drill-down with the difference being that the drilling is done horizontally, rather than vertically. For example, after initially displaying the annual sales results, drill-across can be used to display the sales for each month.

Conditions

Conditions are formulated with the objective of retrieving and analyzing data based upon restrictions that narrow query results. For example, a ranking list condition can be applied so that the query returns the results for the top ten customers (in terms of sales, orders, etc.) or the three best performing brands. Similarly, by specifying a value limit, the results can be restricted to key figures that fall above (or below) a certain value or within a range. Several conditions can be defined in a single query. Conditions can be modified, activated, or deactivated, as required. They can be specified using the BW Query Designer.

Exceptions

An exception defines a key figure value deviation from a pre-determined threshold value in order to highlight abnormal or critical results. Results that fall outside a set of pre-determined threshold values and intervals are displayed in different colors so that key figure variances are highlighted, thus providing an opportunity to take appropriate action. Exceptions, which are displayed as highlighted cells, can be prioritized (such as good or bad). They are defined in the BW Query Designer.

Summarization

This technique enables analysis to be performed against summarized data, rather than detailed data. Senior management and executives prefer to run queries against summarized data sets, rather than against detailed transaction data, because it provides a higher-level view that is more useful to them.

Swapping axes

This function enables the switching of rows with columns. For example, if the characteristics are displayed in the rows and key figures in the columns, executing the swap function will cause the characteristics to be displayed in the columns and the key figures in the rows.

Navigation

A query provides a view of data extracted from an InfoProvider, which can be modified using various navigation techniques. In BW, these new views are displayed in the results area of the query. The basic navigation functions are:

❑ Filter a characteristic by characteristic values or hierarchy nodes
❑ Drill-down by characteristic and then change the drill-down status
❑ Filter a characteristic and drill-down using a different characteristic
❑ Keep a filter value for retaining a characteristic that has been selected as a characteristic value or hierarchy node
❑ Hide and display key figures
❑ Distribute characteristics and key figures along the query's row and column axes
❑ Change sequence of characteristics and key figures on an axis
❑ Expand a hierarchy
❑ Switch active hierarchies on and off
❑ Revert to the initial view after some navigation steps have been executed

Presentation

The ability to provide results, which are aesthetically appealing and have a professional appearance, is a common reporting requirement. Some of the basic requirements include the ability to format reports by manipulating the font, size, colors, patterns, styles, alignment, graphics, etc.

Other common features

A number of other features are desired in front-end tools including sorting and exporting to other applications such as MS-Excel, where the results can be processed further or subjected to additional formatting. Other functions include filtering, scaling factors, displaying characteristics' properties, personalization through favorites (as in a browser bookmark), and variants (a query for which the variables values are pre-selected).

BUSINESS EXPLORER FUNCTIONAL AREAS

The Business Explorer is the BW component, which includes querying, reporting, and analysis capabilities for strategic analysis and decision support using OLAP functions. Its place in the BW architecture was depicted in Figure 13. Figure 110 shows the Business Explorer architecture.

Figure 110: Business Explorer architecture

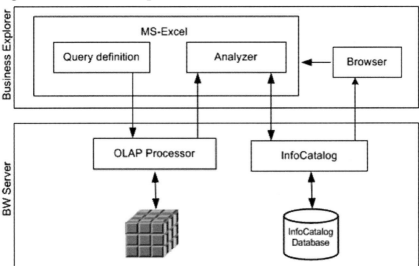

BW permits the use of third-party front-end OLAP tools. Some of the vendors whose data access tools are widely used with BW include Cognos, Business Objects, and Arcplan.

What the Business Explorer can do

The Business Explorer meets all the desired features of front-end tools, which were identified earlier. As a decision support tool, BEx meets the needs of strategic users (who want to analyze historical data) as well as operational users (who focus on current data). It supports analysis using either MS-Excel or the web. The following table lists the key functions and technical components of the Business Explorer:

Table 5: BEx Functional Areas and Key Capabilities				
Portal Integration, Collaboration and Deployment	Query, Reporting, and Analysis	Web Application Design	Formatted Reporting	Mobile Intelligence
Single point of entry	Query design via desktop or web	Web Application Designer	Pixel-oriented layouts	Online and offline scenarios
Role based information provision	Multi-dimensional (OLAP) analysis (Excel or Web-based)	Interactive analytic content over the web	Wizard-based layout definition	Support of WAP phones and PDAs
Personalization, collaboration, profiling, subscription	Geographical analysis	Information cockpits / dashboards	Static, form-based reports	Automatic device recognition
Integration of unstructured information	Ad hoc data exploration	Framework for building analytical applications	Pre-defined Crystal Reports within Business Content	Publishing via Web Application Designer
Drag and relate, unification	Alerting	Create iViews for the portal	Delivered over the Web	Alerts, charts, etc.
	iView publishing	Wizard-based visualization	Print options for comfortable printing	Integration into mobile portal
	Tight integration of Web- and Excel-based analysis	APIs for further web design		
Source: www.sap.com				

The Business Explorer has four functional areas, which are highlighted in Figure 111:

❏ Queries, reporting, and analysis
❏ Web Application Design
❏ Formatted reporting
❏ Mobile intelligence

Figure 111: Business Explorer functional areas

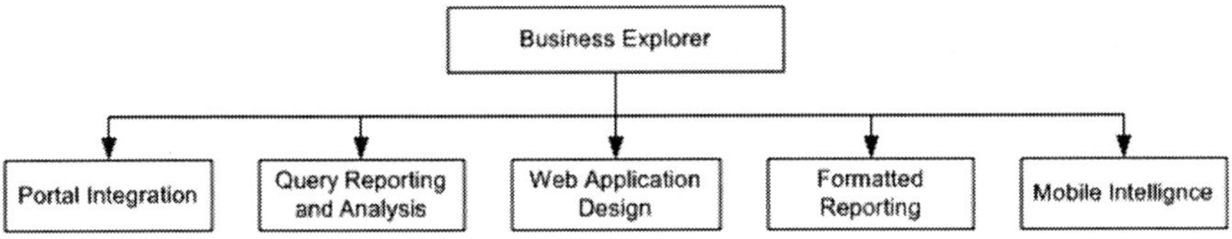

Queries, reporting, and analysis

The BEx Query Designer is the tool used to define queries that are to be run against the InfoProviders. Queries are designed by selecting and combining appropriate characteristics, key figures and, where available, reusable structures. Analysis can be performed in BEx Web Applications or the Excel-based BEx Analyzer, which are integrated. End users can switch seamlessly between Excel- and web-based analysis. A web browser can be used to view BEx Analyzer results, while a Web Application can be exported into Excel.

Web Application Design

Web Application Design permits BW users to use generic OLAP navigation in web applications as well as business intelligence cockpits for simple or customized scenarios. For this purpose, standard markup languages and web design APIs can be used. The BEx Web Application Designer is the desktop application for creating web applications, which can be saved as URLs and accessed via the Internet or mobile devices. The Web Application wizard is associated with the Web Application Designer. It can be used to create web applications in a step-by-step manner, which makes it a useful tool for those who do not design regularly or extensively.

Formatted reporting

Crystal Reports is a leading reporting tool that has been integrated with BW, which enables users to create formatted reports that can be designed with layouts that are pixel-precise.

Mobile Intelligence

Web applications created with the Web Application Designer can be retrieved using BEx Mobile Intelligence. A number of devices are supported including PDA's, WAP- and i-Mode-enabled mobile phones, as well as mobile devices with the EPOC32 operating system.

BUSINESS EXPLORER COMPONENTS

How BEx is organized

The Business Explorer, the top layer in the BW architecture, consists of the following components:

- ❑ BEx Analyzer: used to create and execute queries
- ❑ BEx Browser: used to retrieve and execute queries
- ❑ BEx Web: used to publish BEx Analyzer queries on the Internet or Intranet
- ❑ BEx Map: used to analyze geographically significant information on a map

BEx Analyzer

The Analyzer is the BW analytical tool where queries are defined, by selecting key figures and characteristics, primarily for multi-dimensional analysis. The query results are displayed in MS-Excel, where the results can be formatted, manipulated, and subjected to further analysis. Additional features of this interactive tool include the ability to:

- ❑ Analyze selected data by navigating through multi-dimensional data
- ❑ Add calculations, charts, graphics, and notes to a report
- ❑ Manipulate a report view as a document
- ❑ Combine various queries in a workbook
- ❑ Distribute reports via e-mail
- ❑ Provide navigation abilities that can provide different views of the data
- ❑ Drill-down or drill-across
- ❑ Filter, sort, cumulate, etc.
- ❑ Combine the benefits of OLAP with Excel's VBA (Visual Basic for Applications) development environment

BEx Toolbar functions

The BEx toolbar is an additional toolbar that is displayed when the Business Explorer is launched (Figure 112). It can be used for navigation and executing many powerful analytical functions. The toolbar leads to the:

❑ BEx Open dialog box, where existing queries can be opened
❑ BEx Query Designer, where new queries can be created or existing queries modified

Figure 112: BEx Toolbar

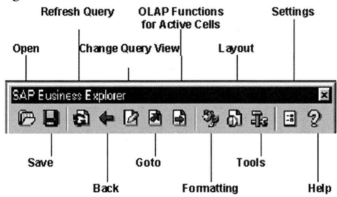

The BEx toolbar supports a number of functions including:

❑ Opening workbooks, queries, and saved query views
❑ Copying and deleting queries and workbooks; deleting results and detaching queries from the workbook, etc.
❑ Saving with various options including saving the workbook (as new or existing workbook) and saving the query view as a jump target or globally
❑ Refreshing queries after opening a workbook or when the query is filled with new variable values
❑ Routine navigation tasks (back, goto, etc.)
❑ OLAP functions
❑ Formatting (fonts, templates, borders, alignment, defining symbols, etc.)
❑ Modifying layouts for changing the query's appearance, attaching a diagram or map, displaying exceptions and conditions, etc.
❑ Launching the Query Designer

Query Designer

The BEx Query Designer is a powerful interactive tool used to navigate through and analyze BW data. It is used to define queries, which enable access to both multi-dimensional data providers (like InfoCubes) as well as non-dimensional data providers (like ODS objects and master data). The Query Designer provides the ability to combine key figures and characteristics into queries that can be executed against the selected InfoProvider, which may or may not be physically storing data. InfoProviders that physically store data include InfoCubes, ODS objects, and InfoObjects (characteristics with attributes or texts). Non-physical InfoProviders include RemoteCubes, MultiProviders, and InfoSets.

The Query Designer is a versatile tool with many features, some of which are indicated on the Query Designer Toolbar (Figure 113). It can perform various operations on queries (create/open/save/delete), define exceptions and conditions, identify objects where the query is used (where-used list), switch between OLAP and tabular reporting, etc. The Query Designer can be accessed from the BEx Analyzer, BEx Application Designer, Crystal Reports, and the Internet Explorer (using the menu path: Start>Programs>Business Explorer>Query Designer).

Figure 113: Query Designer Toolbar

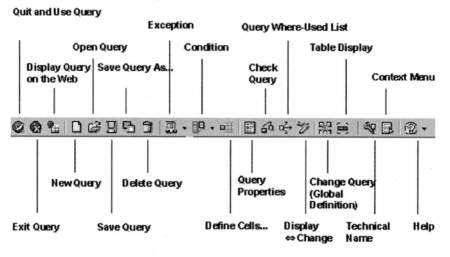

The Query Designer, Figure 114, is split into six windows:

❑ Content Tree, which displays the selected InfoProvider's available objects including structures, key figures, and dimensions in a tree structure that can be expanded or collapsed, as required.

❑ Rows, which are used to select the report's desired rows.

❑ Columns, which are used to select the report's desired columns.

❑ Free/drilldown characteristics, which are to be excluded in the initial query results to be displayed. Subsequently, they can be incorporated into the results by using interactive navigation functions. These characteristics can be used for selection by filter values.

❑ Filter, which is used to limit the data that is to be obtained from the InfoProvider.

❑ Preview, which provides a preview of the query results (based on the selections that are made in the other windows).

Figure 114: Query Designer: New query window

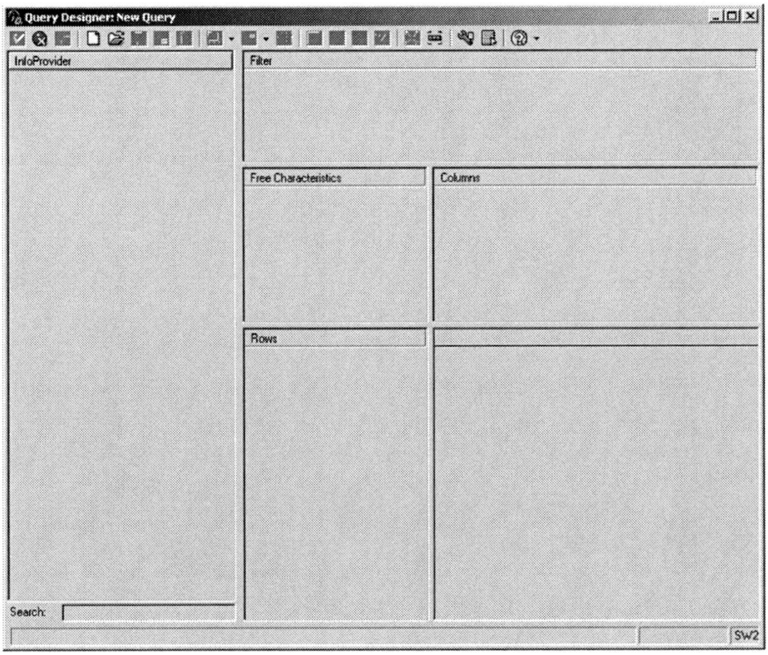

To create a query, a mouse is used to drag and drop structures, key figures and characteristics from the content tree into the other windows. A query can be executed using either the BEx Analyzer or the Web Browser. To execute a query on the web, the function *Display Query on the Web* is used, which displays it in the standard web template.

BEx Browser

The BEx Browser is a graphical interface that can organize BW reports and manage workbooks. It provides functionality similar to mySAP Workplace including a single point of access to the applications, services, and information needed by a user. Also, depending on a user's role, tasks can be integrated into functions, which are integrated into the roles.

The BEx Browser enables BW reports to be accessed through the web, eliminating the need to have the SAP client software installed on the desktop. It can create new objects and access R/3 transactions, reports, and URLs. It can store a user's favorite reports. The BEx Browser can work with many document types including BW workbooks, Business Document Service (BDS) documents (where files are stored), and BW web reports. It can copy documents and folders (from one role to another) and also create shortcuts to files on the PC.

BEx Web

BEx Web enables access to BW data using a web browser, such as Netscape or the Internet Explorer, without the need of any special software like the SAP GUI. It does not use ActiveX—only H™L with JavaScript. BEx Web enables queries, which have been defined in the BEx Analyzer, to be published on the Internet or the Intranet. Queries can be inserted and displayed on any H™L page. Web query data can be analyzed using various navigation techniques, such as drill-down and drill-across.

BEx Map

BEx Map is the Business Explorer's integrated Geographical Information System (GIS), which can graphically display geographically significant data on a map. The tool supports geographical drill-down, which enables geography-based evaluations to be conducted at different detail levels.

DESIGNING BEx WEB APPLICATIONS

BEx Web Application Designer

The Web Application Designer, whose architecture is shown in Figure 115, is a Business Explorer component used to create BW web applications and queries. This tool can create an HTML page, known as a web application, which can contain tables, charts, and maps. The web page is executed in a web browser. The tool can create complex and interactive web pages. The Web Application Designer can also create templates for the web application using a wizard, in a step-by-step manner, or through drag and drop actions using an integrated editor.

Figure 115: Web Application Designer architecture

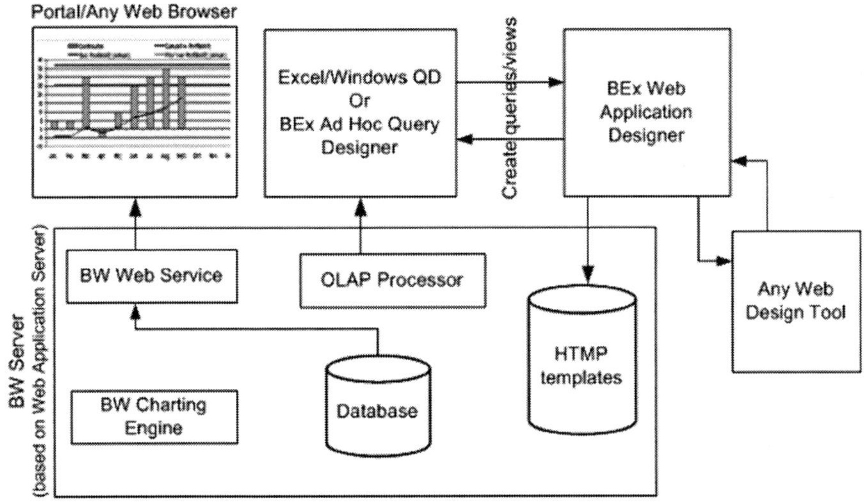

The Web Application Designer has three work areas:

❑ Web items: Includes all standard web items that can be used for creating a web query. Web items are objects that obtain data from data providers and make it available as HTML. They have attributes (such as height and width) and can create navigation links.

❑ Properties window: In this area, the properties of web templates and web items are defined.

❑ Templates window: Contains the web templates that are edited during design and form the basis of the web applications. A web template, which is an HTML document with BW-specific placeholders, is the foundation upon which a web application is defined. It is the starting point for creating a web application. It defines the web application structure and contains placeholders, which are placed by the Web Application Designer, for web items, data providers, and web addresses (URLs).

Although the Web Application Wizard can create web applications, it does not have all the functions available through the Web Application Designer.

Ad Hoc Query Designer

The Ad Hoc Query Designer is a tool used for creating queries, for all InfoProviders, just like the Query Designer. It can design ad hoc queries in a web environment. The capabilities of the Ad Hoc Query Designer include the ability to:

❑ Assign characteristics and key figures to columns and rows
❑ Define filters and free characteristics
❑ Restrict or filter key figures and characteristics
❑ Change conditions and exceptions
❑ Set or change query properties and key figure/characteristic properties

The Ad Hoc Query Designer is a useful tool but it has some limitations compared to the Query Designer. For example, it cannot use key figures or key figure structures in a filter. Also, it cannot create some types of objects like reusable structures as well as restricted and calculated key figures.

The Ad Hoc Query Designer Wizard can create queries in a web application in a step-by-step manner. However, the Wizard can only create queries, whose subsequent editing is performed in the Ad Hoc Query Designer.

Web Toolbar

The Web Toolbar, Figure 116, is a feature-rich and powerful tool that enables users to easily navigate though and analyze BW data and reports. It also enables access to the Ad Hoc Query Designer through the icon highlighted in Figure 116.

Figure 116: Web Toolbar

Copyright SAP AG.

Some of the functions accessible through the Web Toolbar include:

- Ability to create various types of charts
- Swap the query axes: rows (characteristics) with columns (key figures):
- Define, change, delete, and activate/deactivate exceptions and conditions
- Provide query information
- Launch the Ad Hoc Query Designer through which new queries can be defined and existing queries modified
- Export query data to MS-Excel or a comma separated value (CSV) file
- Support bookmarks, which are displayed in the browser's address line

Context Menu

The Context Menu is a very useful tool that enables navigation in many ways and, also, provides many additional functions. It can be accessed by clicking the left mouse button on a cell text in a web query, which pops up a menu of functions from which an appropriate selection can be made. The functions that are displayed, for selection, when the Context Menu is activated depend on the cell context, web item being used, and the settings of the web template in the Web Application Designer. Context Menu functions can be activated or deactivated for a web application. In the BEx Analyzer, the Context Menu can be activated by clicking the right mouse button.

There exist two Context Menu versions: Basic Menu and Enhanced Menu. The Basic Menu, with a limited number of functions, is a subset of the Enhanced Menu. Within the Context Menu, it is possible to toggle between the two menus (Enhanced Menu and Basic Menu).

The Context Menu contains many functions and features, ranging from basic to very advanced, including:

- Basic navigation techniques such as back, forward, back to start (for undoing navigation steps that have been executed), goto, etc.
- Keep filter value (for displaying only the data for a characteristic value, while the characteristic value itself is removed from the drill-down)

- ❑ Keep filter value on axis (for displaying the data for a characteristic value, if the characteristic value itself is to be displayed in the drill-down)
- ❑ Select filter value for filtering by values.
- ❑ Drilling across or down; remove drill-down
- ❑ Filter and drill-down according to: set a characteristic at a certain value (filter) and simultaneously drill-down using another characteristic on the same axis (row or column)
- ❑ Swap axes, which swaps query axes; if key figures are in columns and characteristics in rows, swapping causes characteristics to be displayed in columns and key figures in rows
- ❑ Swap a characteristic/structure with another characteristic/structure
- ❑ Expand hierarchy; expand or collapse hierarchy nodes
- ❑ Activate or deactivate hierarchies
- ❑ Sort in ascending or descending order
- ❑ Sort characteristic values or attributes for a drill-down characteristic
- ❑ Cumulate individual cells in an area.
- ❑ Currency translation
- ❑ Simple bookmark as well as bookmark with data.
- ❑ Export to Excel and CSV files
- ❑ Change different settings for the characteristic or key figure
- ❑ Change query properties

CHAPTER B15
CREATING QUERIES WITH BEx

DESIGNING A QUERY

Figure 117 is a graphic representation of the ultimate aim of a query—to create a customized view of the data that is being accessed in the storage area (InfoCubes, ODS, etc.). After a query has been designed, it can be analyzed from different dimensions, providing views that reflect the specific needs of its various users.

Figure 117: Creating a query view

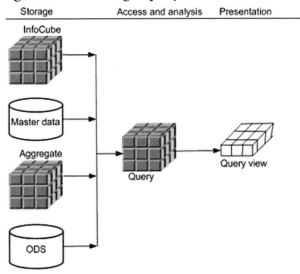

Accessing BEx and the Analyzer

The Business Explorer Analyzer is usually accessed through two methods. It can be launched through a BW launch pad or the Windows start menu (Start >

Programs > Business Explorer > Analyzer). Figure 118 shows the window that is initially displayed when BW is started through the launch pad.

Figure 118

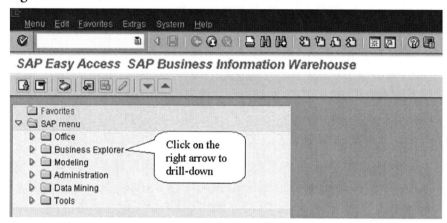

Copyright SAP AG.

To navigate to the BEx Analyzer:

❑   Drill-down on the arrow, as shown in Figure 118

This will lead you to the next window (Figure 119):

Figure 119

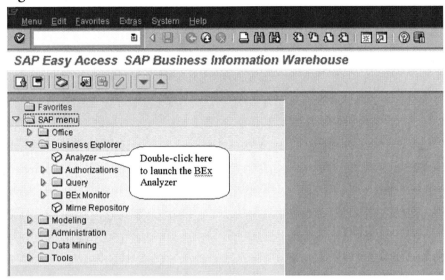

Copyright SAP AG.

To launch the BEx Analyzer:

❑ Double-click the *Analyzer* icon, which is highlighted in Figure 119

This will launch the BEx Analyzer, displayed in the next window (Figure 120), where the BEx Toolbar is located in the middle of the Excel spreadsheet screen.

Figure 120

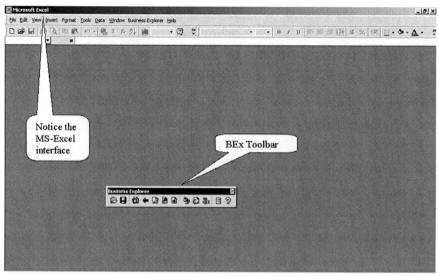

Copyright SAP AG.

Navigating to the design area

To access the query design area from the BEx Toolbar on the previous window (Figure 120):

❑ Click the BEx Toolbar's *Open* icon (as shown in Figure 121)

This action will cause a drop-down menu to appear, which is displayed in Figure 121:

Figure 121

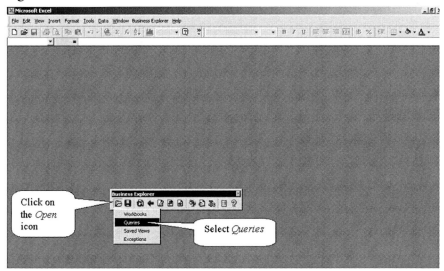

Copyright SAP AG.

From the drop-down menu in Figure 121:

❑   Select *Queries*

This will lead you to the next window, Figure 122, where a number of queries are listed—the ones which the user had previously executed. Note that the *History* button is highlighted.

Figure 122

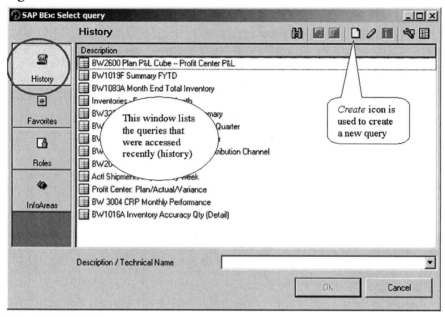

Copyright SAP AG.

A listed query can be executed by clicking on it. To create a new query, click on the *Create* icon, which is highlighted in Figure 122.

Selecting the InfoProvider

Before a query can be developed, its InfoProvider must be displayed and selected. To access the desired InfoProvider, we will first need to navigate to its InfoArea:

❑   Click the *InfoAreas* button, which will select and highlight it (as shown in Figure 123)

This action will cause all the currently available InfoAreas to be displayed, as shown in Figure 123:

Figure 123

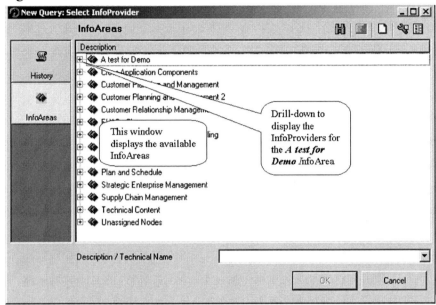

Copyright SAP AG.

From the displayed list, we will select the *A test for Demo* InfoArea, where the desired InfoProvider is located. To display the InfoProviders contained in the *A test for Demo* InfoArea:

❑ Drill-down, by clicking on the + sign located next to *A test for Demo*, as instructed in Figure 123

This will display the only InfoProvider, *Test InfoCube*, which is available for the *A test for Demo* InfoArea, on the next window (Figure 124):

Figure 124

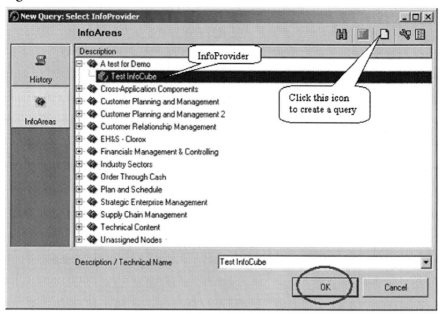

Copyright SAP AG.

❑   Click the *Test InfoCube* InfoProvider (to select it)
❑   Click the *Create* icon
❑   Click OK

This will lead you to the next window, Figure 125, where the query can be designed using the Query Designer.

Query windows

The Query Designer window is split into six distinct areas, which are highlighted in Figure 125:

Figure 125

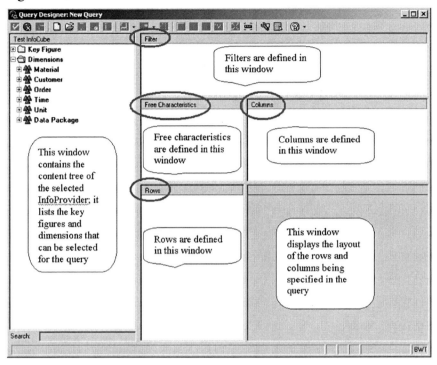

Copyright SAP AG.

To display lower level objects in the content tree, drill-down can be performed on key figures and dimensions. The next window, Figure 126, displays additional objects after drill-down was performed on the *Key Figure* and *Dimensions* folders (which were in collapsed mode in Figure 125).

Figure 126

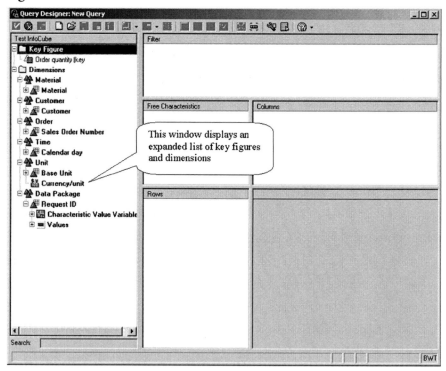

Copyright SAP AG.

Selecting query parameters

In the next step, the items (characteristics and key figures) that define the rows and columns, as well as any free characteristics and filters, are selected from the key figures and characteristics listed in the content tree window. Using the mouse to drag and drop, objects can be moved easily from one window to another. Key figures and characteristics can be placed either in rows or columns.

The next window, Figure 127, shows four items that were dragged and dropped from the left window into the four selection areas—windows on the right (columns, rows, filters, and free characteristics). Two of the items are highlighted (*Order Quantity* and *Material*).

Figure 127

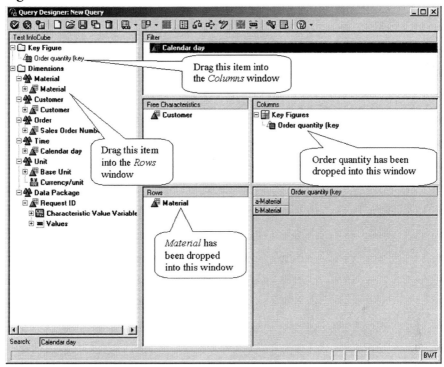

Copyright SAP AG.

Filtering data

On the previous window, Figure 127, the filter selected is *Calendar day*. To restrict the query results to a one-month period (June 1 through June 30):

❑ Right-click the *Calendar day* item, as shown in Figure 128

This will cause a menu to pop-up, which is also shown in Figure 128:

Figure 128

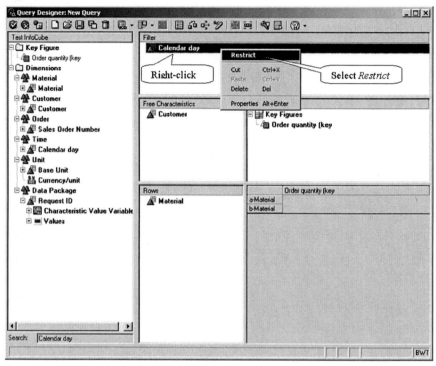

Copyright SAP AG.

❏ Select *Restrict* from the pop-up menu

This will lead you to the next window, Figure 129, which displays a calendar in the window on the left:

Figure 129

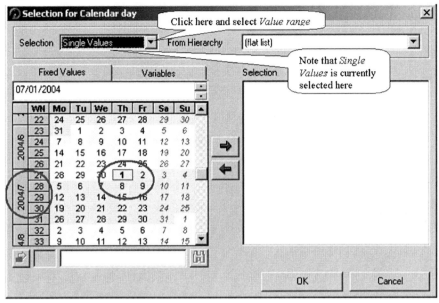

Copyright SAP AG.

To select a date range for the filter, use the appropriate drop-down arrows, as shown in Figure 130.

Figure 130

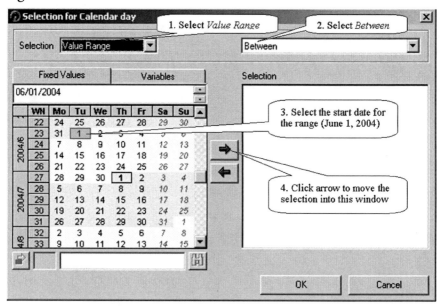

Copyright SAP AG.

- ❏ Select *Value Range* (step 1)
- ❏ Select *Between* (step 2)
- ❏ Select the start day for the range (June 1, 2004) by clicking on it (step 3)
- ❏ Click the right arrow (step 4)

This will lead you to the next window, Figure 131, which shows the single day selection (June 1, 2004):

Figure 131

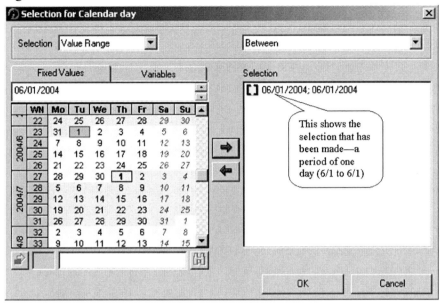

Copyright SAP AG.

As highlighted in Figure 131, the filter is now restricted to a start/end date of June 1, 2004. To select June 30, 2004, as the end date for the restriction (range), follow the steps listed in Figure 132:

Figure 132

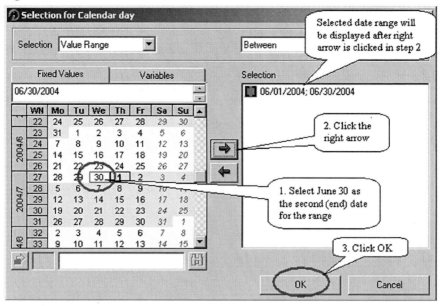

Copyright SAP AG.

❑ Highlight the appropriate date (June 30, 2004), by clicking on it (step 1)
❑ Click the right arrow (step 2)

This will complete the process and the upper end of the date range, June 30, 2004, will be placed in the right selection window, as shown in Figure 132.

❑ Click *OK* (step 3)

This will lead you back to the query design window, which is shown on the next screen (Figure 133):

Figure 133

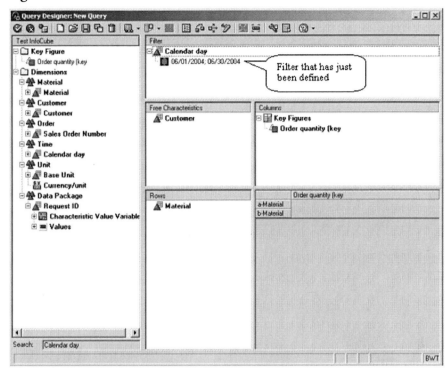

Saving the query

After the query has been designed, it needs to be saved. The *Save* icon, which is highlighted in Figure 134, is used to perform this function.

Figure 134

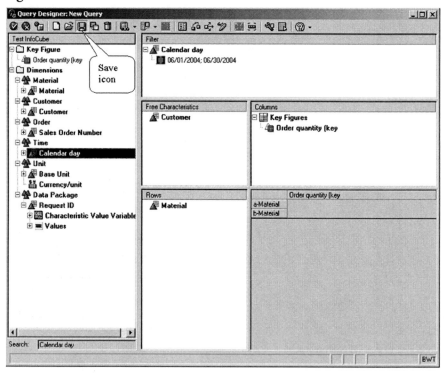

Copyright SAP AG.

To save the query:

❏   Click the *Save* icon

This will generate a system prompt, which will require the query name to be specified, as shown in Figure 135. You may also be provided with the option to save it in your favorites.

Figure 135

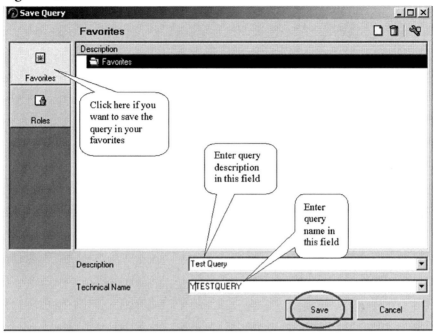

Copyright SAP AG.

In the appropriate fields, type in the:

❑ Technical name, YTESTQUERY, which is the query name
❑ Description (Query description)

In the final step:

❑ Click the *Save* button

This will save the query and a system message will be generated, which is highlighted on the next window (Figure 136):

Figure 136

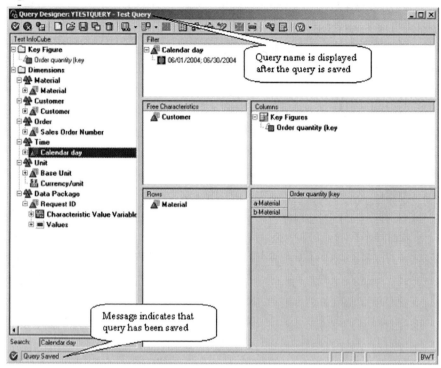

Copyright SAP AG.

EXCEPTIONS AND CONDITIONS

Defining an exception

Suppose we want to define an exception that indicates "*Good*" if the order quantity value lies between 500 and 1,000. To start defining the exception:

❑   Navigate to the Query Designer (Figure 137)

Figure 137

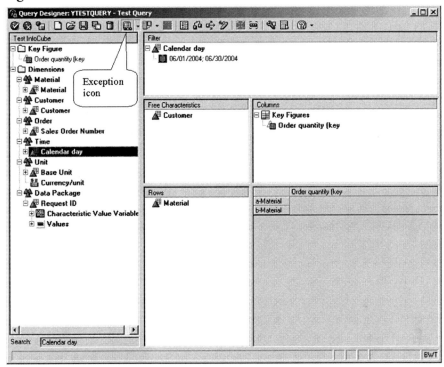

Copyright SAP AG.

❑ Click the *Exception* icon on the Query Designer Toolbar (Figure 137)

This will lead you to the next pop-up window, Figure 138, where the exception will be defined:

Figure 138

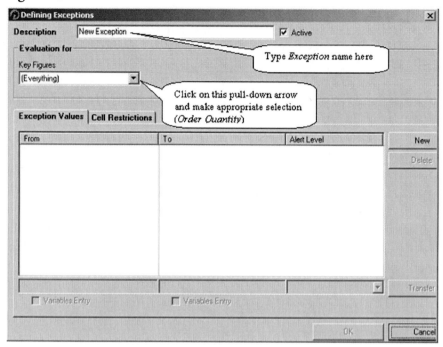

Copyright SAP AG.

In Figure 138:

- ❑ Type the *Exception* name (*New Exception #A*) in the *Description* field
- ❑ Click on the pull-down arrow (for *Key Figures*)
- ❑ Select the key figure *Order Quantity*

The next window, Figure 139, displays the results of these three actions:

Figure 139

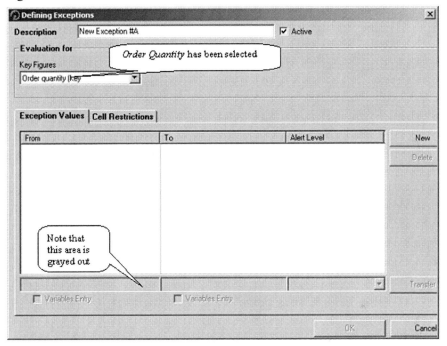

Copyright SAP AG.

❑ Click the *New* button (Figure 139)

This will lead you to the next window, Figure 140, where the area that was previously grayed out, in Figure 139, is now available for specifying the criteria for the exception:

Figure 140

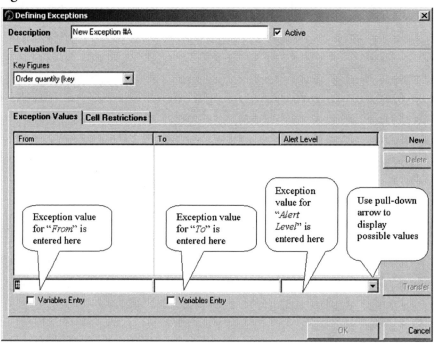

Copyright SAP AG.

Now enter the following exception values in the appropriate fields, as instructed in Figure 140:

❑ *From* = 500
❑ *To* = 1,000
❑ *Alert Level* = Good

The next window, Figure 141, displays the exception values after they have been entered. Note that the pull-down arrow for *Alert Level* was used to select *Good 1* (selection shown in Figure 141).

Figure 141

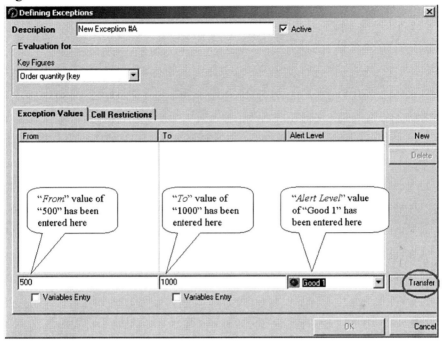

Copyright SAP AG.

❑ Click the *Transfer* button

This will lead you to the next window, Figure 142, where the exception parameters are displayed:

Figure 142

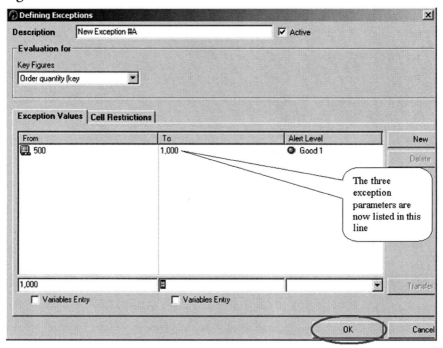

Copyright SAP AG.

❑ Click the *OK* button, which will save the exception

Defining a condition

Suppose we want to define a condition, which is triggered when the order quantity falls below 10. To start defining the condition:

❑ Navigate to the Query Designer (Figure 143)

Figure 143

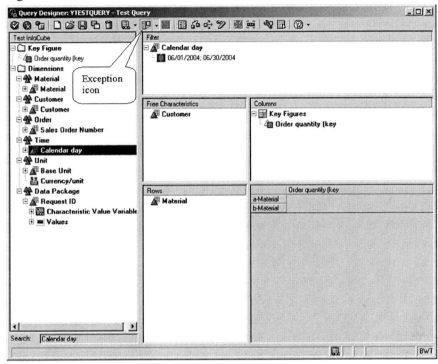

Copyright SAP AG.

❑ Click the *Condition* icon on the Query Designer Toolbar (Figure 143)

This will lead you to the next pop-up window, Figure 144, where the condition can be specified:

Figure 144

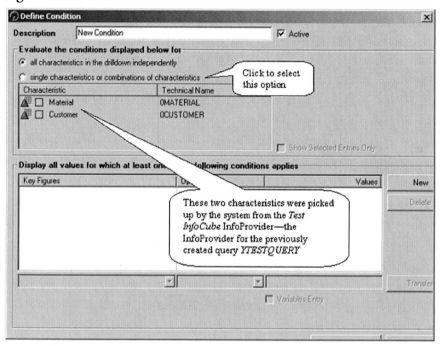

Copyright SAP AG.

❏ Type the *Condition* name (*New Condition #1*) in the description field
❏ Select the option *"Single characteristics or combination of characteristics"* by clicking on the appropriate radio button

After these two steps have been executed, the window display will be as shown in Figure 145:

Figure 145

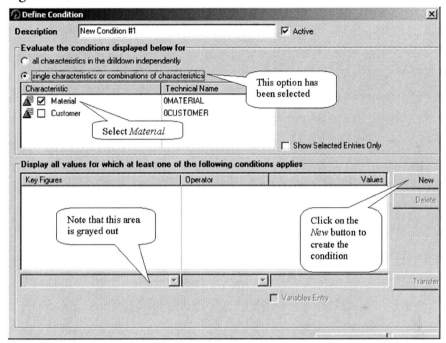

Copyright SAP AG.

❏ Select the *Material* characteristic (by placing a checkmark)
❏ Click the *New* button

This will lead you to the next window, Figure 146, where the area that was previously grayed out, in Figure 145, is now available for specifying the criteria for the condition:

Figure 146

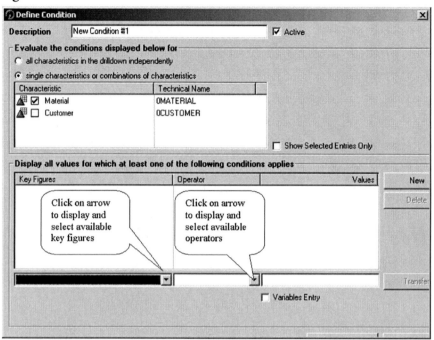

Copyright SAP AG.

Now enter the following condition values in the appropriate fields, as per the instructions in Figure 146:

- ❑ *Key Figures = Order Quantity*
- ❑ *Operator = Less than*
- ❑ *Values = 10*

The next window, Figure 147, displays the condition values after they have been entered.

Figure 147

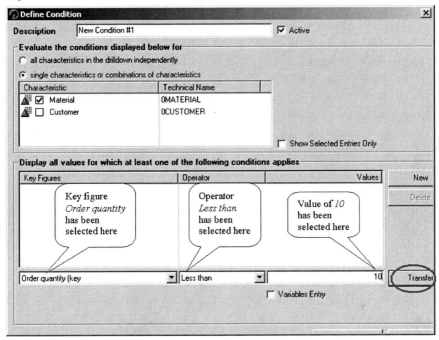

Copyright SAP AG.

After the desired condition values have been entered:

❑ Click the *Transfer* button

This will lead you to the next window, Figure 148, which displays the condition that has been defined:

Figure 148

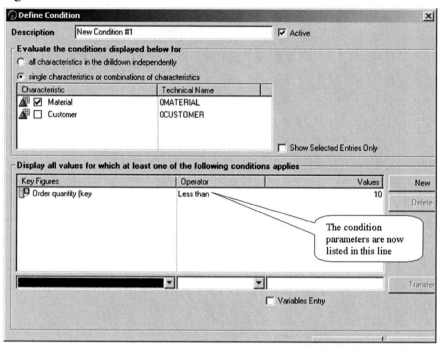

Chapter B16
Other Query Tools and
Navigation Techniques

USING THE AD HOC QUERY DESIGNER

Designing a query

In this section, a query will be designed using the Ad Hoc Query Designer. The following is a step-by-step procedure for creating a simple query:

❑ Launch the Web Toolbar (Figure 149)

Figure 149: Web Toolbar

Copyright SAP AG.

To launch the Ad Hoc Query Designer:

❑ Click the circled icon

The first step in creating a new query is to select an InfoProvider, upon which the query is to be based, which is done in the following dialog box (Figure 150):

Figure 150

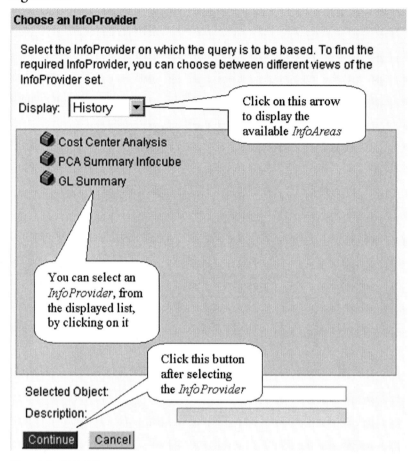

Copyright SAP AG.

You can choose an InfoProvider either from the history list that is displayed in Figure 150 or from the list of available InfoAreas. To list the available InfoAreas:

❑ Click on the pull-down arrow shown in Figure 150, which will lead you to the next window (Figure 151)

Figure 151

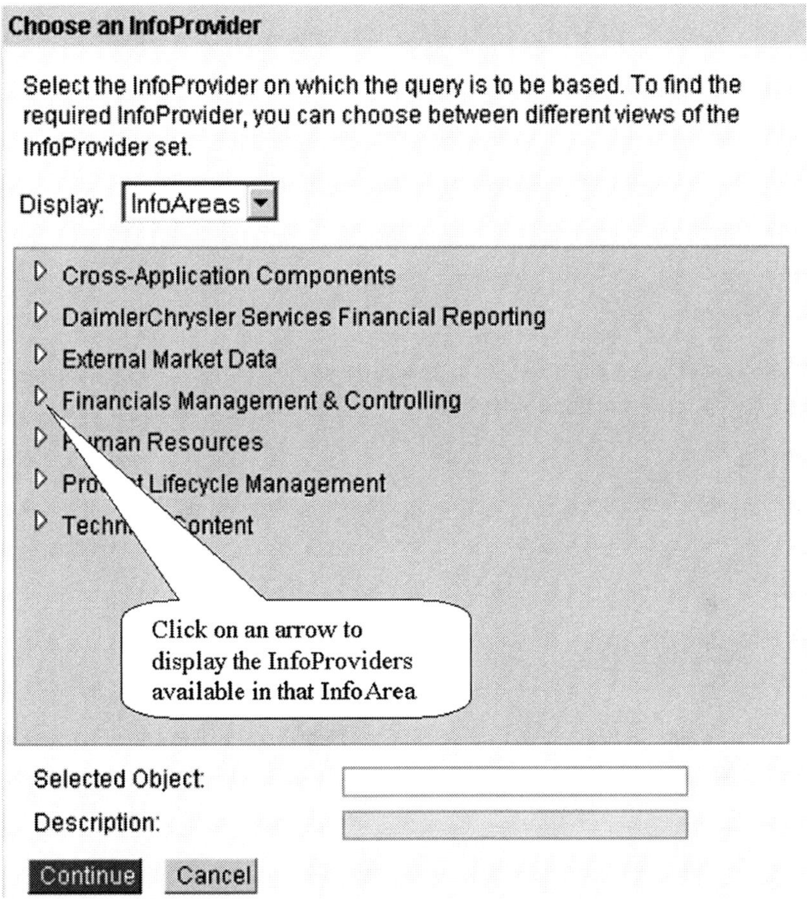

Choose an InfoProvider

Select the InfoProvider on which the query is to be based. To find the required InfoProvider, you can choose between different views of the InfoProvider set.

Display: InfoAreas ▾

▷ Cross-Application Components
▷ DaimlerChrysler Services Financial Reporting
▷ External Market Data
▷ Financials Management & Controlling
▷ Human Resources
▷ Product Lifecycle Management
▷ Technical Content

Click on an arrow to display the InfoProviders available in that InfoArea

Selected Object:
Description:

Continue   Cancel

Copyright SAP AG.

As instructed in Figure 151, drill-down by clicking on the arrow next to the InfoArea, which will display the InfoProviders contained in it (not shown here). After the InfoProviders are displayed:

❑   Click on the desired InfoProvider

This action will select it for the query that is to be designed. Clicking on the continue button, after the InfoProvider has been selected, will lead you to the next window where the query can be designed (Figure 152):

Figure 152

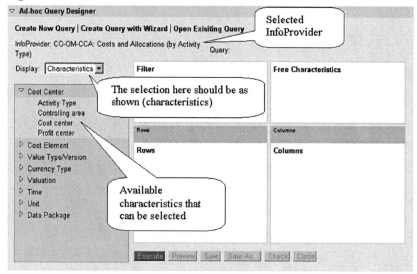

Copyright SAP AG.

The next step requires selecting the characteristics that are to be used in the query. As instructed in Figure 152:

❑ Choose *Characteristics* (in the highlighted *Display* drop-down box)

This will display the available characteristics from which the required characteristic(s) can be selected and moved into the desired window (such as the rows or columns window). To select and move a characteristic:

❑ Click the desired characteristic (such as *Cost Center*)
❑ Right-click the mouse

This will cause the *Context Menu* to pop-up. The *Context Menu* provides an option to move the selected characteristic into the desired window (row, column, free characteristic, or filter). Using the appropriate option from the *Context Menu*:

❑ Select the window into which the selected characteristic is to be moved
❑ Move the characteristic into the desired window

Follow this procedure for all the characteristics that are to be placed in the windows on the right. The circles in Figure 153 highlight the characteristics that were selected and moved into the three windows on the right.

Figure 153

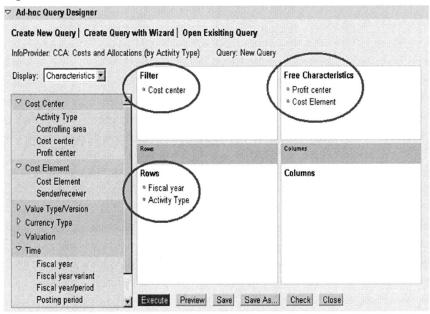

Copyright SAP AG.

The next step, after the characteristics have been selected, is to select the key figures required by the query. Figure 154 lists the steps required to define the key figures.

Figure 154

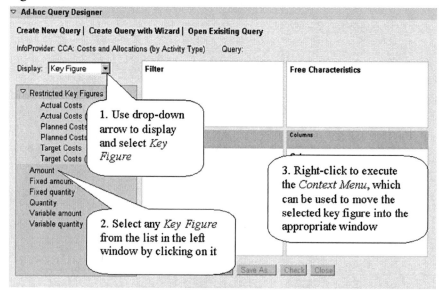

Copyright SAP AG.

□ Use the drop-down arrow to select *Key Figure* (step 1)
□ Click the key figure that you want to use, such as *Amount* (step 2)
□ Right-click to execute the *Context Menu* (step 3)

Using the *Context Menu*, which provides an option to move the selected key figure into the desired window:

□ Move the selected key figure into the desired window, as shown in Figure 155

Figure 155

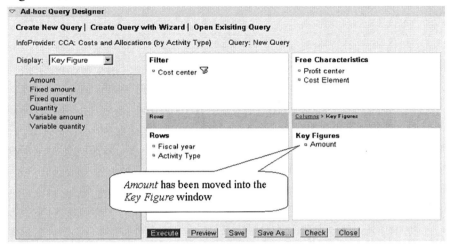

Copyright SAP AG.

The query is now ready to be saved or executed by:

❑ Clicking the appropriate button (*Save or Execute*)

Designing a query using the Query Wizard

The Query Wizard is a BW tool that can be used to create simple queries, using a procedure that is similar to the one described in the previous section. To create a query using the Wizard, the following steps need to be followed:

❑ Start the Ad Hoc Query Designer
❑ Select the menu option *Create Query with Wizard* (Figure 155)
❑ Choose an *InfoProvider* in the dialog box, which will pop-up
❑ Select the key figures, characteristics, free characteristics, and any desired filters

The next four windows show how the Query Wizard can be used to select or define key figures (Figure 156), characteristics (Figure 157), free characteristics (Figure 158), and filters (Figure 159).

Selecting a key figure

Figure 156

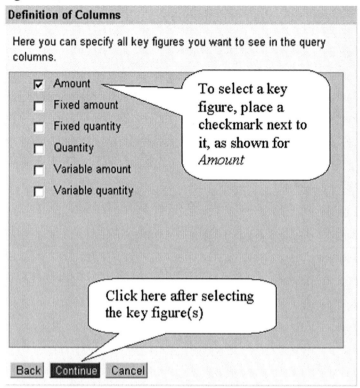

Copyright SAP AG.

To select a key figure in Figure 156:

❑ Place a checkmark next to the desired key figure (as shown for Amount)
❑ Click the *Continue* button

This will lead you to the next window which pops-up, Figure 157, where characteristics can be selected for the query rows:

Selecting characteristics

Figure 157

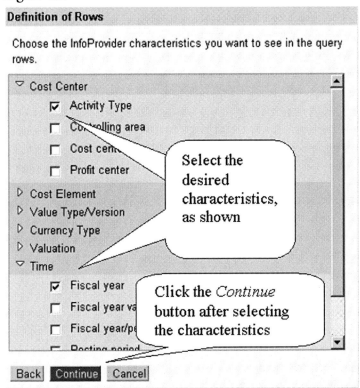

Copyright SAP AG.

To select the characteristics in Figure 157:

❑ Place appropriate checkmarks, next to the desired characteristics, as shown
❑ Click the *Continue* button

Defining free characteristics

The next window, Figure 158, demonstrates how free characteristics can be defined:

Figure 158

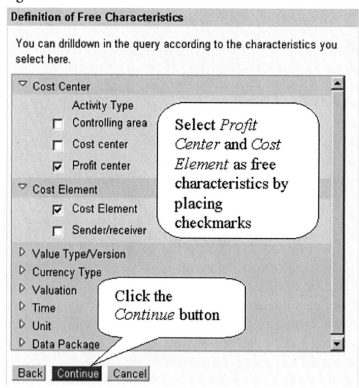

Copyright SAP AG.

❑ Place appropriate checkmarks next to the desired free characteristics (*Profit Center* and *Cost element*)
❑ Click the *Continue* button

Defining a filter

The next window, Figure 159, demonstrates how a filter can be defined:

Figure 159

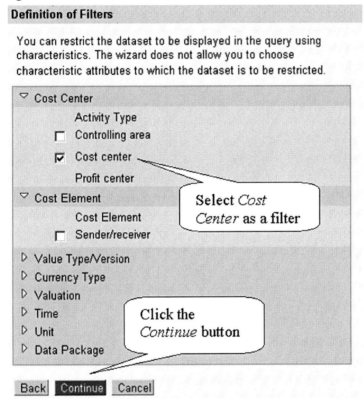

Copyright SAP AG.

☐ Place a checkmark next to the characteristic that is to be used for filtering the data (*Cost Center*)
☐ Click the *Continue* button

This will take you back to the query design window, Figure 160, where the query defined by the Wizard is displayed.

Figure 160

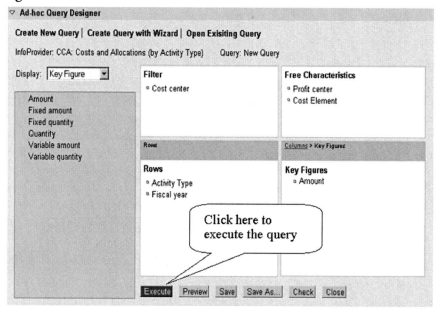

NAVIGATION TECHNIQUES
BW report elements

An SAP BW web report contains two distinct areas:

❑ Generic Navigation Block
❑ Results area

The Generic Navigation Block, which is displayed in the form of a table, presents the current navigational state of a report as shown in the next window (Figure 161). In addition to displaying characteristics and structures, it also displays any filters. The Generic Navigation Block permits rows and columns to be swapped, filters to be added or removed, and drill-down or drill-across functions to be executed. The query results are displayed in the Results Area.

Figure 161

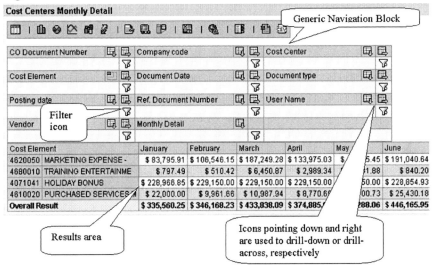

Copyright SAP AG.

Drill-down and drill-across

Two of the most commonly used functions in BW reporting are drill-down and drill-across, which permit analysis to be performed from different perspectives. The next window, Figure 162, shows the initial report results after a query is executed:

Figure 162

	North	South	East	West	Mexico	Total
Revenue	1,319,191,610	588,091,954	79,887,859	8,522,943	5,981,324	2,001,675,690
Depreciation	391,679,358	340,244,956	13,733,947	4,151,242		749,809,503
Interest Expense	453,771,531	125,522,811	32,776,247	2,980,856	457,755	615,509,200
Insurance	473,740,721	122,324,187	33,377,665	1,390,844	5,523,569	636,356,986
Legal Provisions	11,903,453	103,545,935		2,217,461		117,666,849
Credit Losses	107,434,903	23,158,570	-2,424,463	2,590,186	2,330,532	133,089,727
Operating Expenses	87,008,037	18,132,915	11,598,755	752,053	3,500,313	120,992,071
Division Contribution	267,394,329	-22,513,233	24,203,374	-4,168,855	-307,275	264,608,339

To obtain additional details, the drill-down technique can be used. The next window (Figure 163) shows the results after drill-down has been performed (by fiscal year/period):

Figure 163

	Fiscal year/period	North	South	East	West	Mexico	Total
Revenue	001/2004	447,824,619	200,272,691	26,866,047	3,070,346	2,008,674	680,042,377
	002/2004	424,553,765	194,189,606	25,168,010	2,795,677	1,938,954	648,646,012
	003/2004	446,813,226	193,629,656	27,853,802	2,666,920	2,033,696	672,987,301
	Overall Result	1,319,191,610	588,091,954	79,887,859	8,522,943	5,981,324	2,001,675,690
Depreciation	001/2004	128,470,453	113,723,534	4,686,057	1,507,112		248,387,156
	002/2004	130,604,572	113,480,958	4,594,712	1,399,580		250,079,821
	003/2004	132,604,333	113,040,464	4,453,178	1,244,550		251,342,526
	Overall Result	391,679,358	340,244,956	13,733,947	4,151,242		749,809,503
Interest Expense	001/2004	157,159,782	43,160,334	11,117,675	1,075,790	158,121	212,671,701
	002/2004	144,429,481	41,214,331	10,577,141	979,212	145,951	197,346,115
	003/2004	152,182,269	41,148,147	11,081,432	925,854	153,683	205,491,385
	Overall Result	453,771,531	125,522,811	32,776,247	2,980,856	457,755	615,509,200
Insurance	001/2004	162,194,385	43,388,823	11,062,315	487,443	1,850,553	218,983,520
	002/2004	149,519,712	39,494,318	9,996,157	416,885	1,793,003	201,220,076
	003/2004	162,026,623	39,441,046	12,319,192	486,516	1,800,013	216,153,390
	Overall Result	473,740,721	122,324,187	33,377,665	1,390,844	5,523,569	636,356,986

The next window, Figure 164, provides another view of the results after drill-across has been performed.

Figure 164

	North				South				East
Fiscal year/period	001/2004	002/2004	003/2004	Overall Result	001/2004	002/2004	003/2004	Overall Result	001/2004
Revenue	447,824,619	424,553,766	446,813,226	1,319,191,610	200,272,691	194,189,606	193,629,656	588,091,954	26,866,047
Depreciation	128,470,453	130,604,572	132,604,333	391,679,358	113,723,534	113,480,958	113,040,464	340,244,956	4,686,057
Interest Expense	157,159,782	144,429,481	152,182,269	453,771,531	43,160,334	41,214,331	41,148,147	125,522,811	11,117,675
Insurance	162,194,385	149,519,712	162,026,623	473,740,721	43,388,823	39,494,318	39,441,046	122,324,187	11,062,315
Legal Provision	5,577,022	2,443,236	3,883,195	11,903,453	26,816,111	45,775,156	30,954,668	103,545,935	

Jumping

A review of the results returned by a query may indicate that further in-depth analysis is required, which may require the execution of another report or navigation to the source data. For this purpose, BW provides a jump function that enables another report to be directly accessed and executed from the currently displayed report. By clicking on the left mouse button in the appropriate field, the jump feature is activated, which causes a pop-up menu to be displayed from where the desired secondary report can be executed.

CHAPTER B17
FAILURE CAUSES AND COMMON MISTAKES

A number of reasons have caused data warehouse projects to fail or fall short of expectations. While each data warehouse implementation is unique, that is defined by its own set of variables, a number of common factors and mistakes have been identified and associated with the failure of such projects, including BW projects, which are explained in the following sections.

PLANNING AND APPROACH

Not understanding DWH uniqueness

Data warehouse projects are unique, which is not realized at many implementations. A common mistake is to view them as database projects. The implementers do not realize that a data warehouse is a business rather than a technology project, which is unique due to a number of factors that make it more challenging. Failure to realize its uniqueness makes the project more risky, with greater probability of failure.

Lack of strategic planning

Many data warehouse projects are implemented without proper planning and consideration of its strategic importance to the organization. They are undertaken without the realization that a data warehouse project is different than an application development project that, consequently, leads to many unpleasant surprises. In many cases, data marts are designed and built without considering potential integration into an enterprise data warehouse architecture in the future.

Approach is over-ambitious

When an organization implements its first data warehouse or data mart, it typically does not have experienced data warehouse professionals on its staff. Therefore, the risk of making serious mistakes is fairly high. However, despite lack of experience, many companies have chosen to implement enterprise-wide data warehouse projects without first gaining experience through a pilot or data mart project. Such an ambitious and risky approach, without experienced staff to guide it, has often led to cost overruns, delays, and project failures.

Evaluation is lacking or flawed

A data warehouse system should not be implemented unless it is preceded by a thorough evaluation of the company's business, reporting and analytical requirements, as well as existing systems—transaction and reporting. The potential impact of the new system, and how it will integrate with or replace the organization's other applications, should be carefully studied before a decision is made to implement a data warehouse.

Focus is on technology

Some companies focus too much on technology because they are driven by the desire to be at the bleeding edge of hardware and software. Consequently, they focus on the technology—not the business and its requirements. This happens frequently when an IT department that pays too much attention to technology, rather than the business needs of the organization, drives the data warehouse project.

Approach is casual

Many data warehouse implementations are undertaken very casually on an ad hoc basis—without a formal project plan. A data warehouse should not be implemented without the structure of a project with specific tasks, schedules, and deliverables.

Implementation barriers are not identified

Many barriers can negatively impact the implementation of a data warehouse project. They include resistance from senior executives fearing loss of control, fallout resulting from lower level staff empowerment, functional process owners not being on board, hidden political agendas, departments having their own decision support systems, bad relationship with IT, inadequate funding, etc. The implementation barriers must be identified, at an early stage, in order to minimize the potential of their derailing the project. In many cases, this important task is not carried out and, consequently, project risk is increased.

Organization is not ready

An organization must be ready before it implements a data warehouse project. For such a project to succeed, it must have the support of three key groups: management, those affected by the implementation, as well as those implementing it. A data warehouse should not be implemented unless key personnel are behind the project and the organization is ready to accept change across the enterprise. In case the organization is not ready, it is advisable to delay the project until a higher level of support becomes available, which will increase the probability of success.

Deficient procedures

Procedural factors often play a part in the failure of data warehouse projects. They include poor or deficient implementation and deployment, lack of formal process for involving users, undefined process for upgrading pilot or small-scale data marts into an enterprise data warehouse, absence of scope control mechanism, and inadequate testing procedure.

Undefined scope

Many data warehouse projects are undertaken without clear goals or defined scope. In such cases, the implementation is disorganized, schedules and scope changes are the norm, developers and analysts work without direction, resources are pulled in and out, and the end result is failure.

One approach fits all

Even though some organizations may be similar, every organization is unique due to differences in company culture, hardware and software infrastructure, skill levels and technical expertise, budget constraints, business drivers, competition, objectives, management, etc. Hence, every implementation is unique even though there may exist some similarities with other projects. Therefore, every proposed data warehouse project should be approached, evaluated, and implemented based on studying its specific requirements. If an incorrect approach is selected, which does not suit a particular organization and implementation, failure is assured.

Do not use production support resources for projects

Some organizations use the same resources for fixing production problems on the BW system and an implementation (or enhancement) project. Since production problems can be unexpected and the time required to fix them can vary, staff assigned simultaneously to production support and projects have a difficult time remaining focused and completing their project deliverables on time. Also, typically, the mindset and attitude of those working on fixes differs from those who work on projects. Hence, whenever possible, different resources should be used for production support and projects.

Developer-based implementations

A very widespread approach for implementing BW is to assign a few developers with ABAP knowledge, typically those who can create BW objects such as InfoCubes and write extraction programs. Such resources are given a few months to come up with a BW system against which a few queries can be executed. Very little, if any requirements gathering is performed and typically, no enterprise architecture or roadmap is developed. Most of these projects fail to meet their objectives as they rarely meet the real requirements and needs of the users.

LEADERSHIP AND POLITICS

Wrong sponsorship

A senior functional executive who must have a vested interest in the project and its success should sponsor the data warehouse project. He should be powerful, respected, and decisive. The sponsor should be flexible, not be enamored by technology, and be user-oriented rather than technology-oriented. The sponsor should be able to obtain resources when required, encourage teamwork, motivate, and provide direction. A common mistake is to choose a sponsor who does not meet these basic characteristics.

Management is not on board

Many data warehouse projects, which demand a high level of commitment, have failed to meet expectations due to lack of management support, which is required at various stages of the project. When support is lacking or denied, the project can face serious problems due to funding issues, conflicts, failure to get adequate and appropriate resources, inability to resolve a wide range of issues requiring timely management intervention, etc.

Expectations are not well managed

In order to sell a data warehouse project, management expectations need to be raised. However, in some cases, such expectations are raised to unrealistically high levels, which can be a serious issue when they are not met. It is imperative that expectations be set very carefully, which can be a difficult task. If the expectations are not reasonably high, the project runs the risk of not being approved or its preferred resources may be allocated to a competing project. If expectations are too high, and they are not subsequently met, the project will be considered a failure.

Desire to control supersedes business needs

Data warehouse projects can be quite political as a number of organizations and departments, with different priorities and agendas, can be involved in its implementation. Many department heads fear loss of control and, therefore, are reluctant to let others encroach on their turfs or provide needed buy-in. Frequently, there is conflict between functional users and IT, which views it as a technology project and does not favor the empowerment of business users.

Wrong communications

A common justification for a data warehouse project is that it helps executive decision making at all levels within the organization. While this is true, it must be communicated with care or problems can surface. For example, justifying the project by naively saying that the data warehouse will help managers make better decisions, which implies that they are poor decision makers, can backfire and antagonize key executives.

Project is political

A number of factors make data warehouse projects very political. They cause organizational and departmental boundaries to be crossed, open access to previously restricted data, empower those who had been denied access to valuable information, sometimes reengineer processes, and impact how work is performed by many groups. Socio-technical factors, people and politics, which are relatively unimportant in conventional IT projects, are very important in data warehousing projects. In such projects, new rules exist and business users have more power. They need to be closely consulted during the design phase as well as the subsequent implementation phases.

Ownership lacking

Many data warehouse projects have failed due to lack of ownership, which can to lead to many problems such as lack of strategy, unclear objectives, weak project management, implementation issues, project funding, lack of appropriate resources, conflict between various groups and departments, poor coordination, scope control, etc.

DESIGN AND TECHNICAL FACTORS

Poor architecture

Many data warehouse projects fail because the system is built upon a poorly designed architecture. This can be manifested in a number of ways including deficiencies in schema, data access method, network architecture, client/server architecture, and metadata. Creating a data warehouse based on a flawed architecture is a very serious mistake because it is the most difficult, and costly, to rectify once it has been implemented. Hence, it is imperative that a top-notch data warehouse architect be used for designing the overall architecture.

Poor infrastructure planning

Inadequate infrastructure planning has led to many post-implementation issues such as performance, capacity, and scalability. It is common for well-designed and successful data warehouses to start having network overload and capacity problems shortly after becoming operational. The reason is that a successful data warehouse quickly draws more and more users, which can overwhelm it if the infrastructure is not designed to accommodate a quick and dramatic rise in usage. When demand soars, it affects both hardware and software requirements. This has caught many organizations by surprise and, consequently, forced them to make expensive unplanned hardware and software expenditures.

Database upgrade strategy is flawed

The introduction of a new database system in an organization has many risks associated with it and requires a careful and measured approach. The upgrade of the OLTP system from a legacy non-relational database to a relational database, which is a complex undertaking, should not coincide with the implementation of a data warehouse. The introduction of relational database technology, if required for both the OLTP and data warehouse systems, should be phased—not simultaneous. Many BW implementations are undertaken simultaneously with the SAP R/3 implementation. While there have been instances where such projects were completed successfully, they are inherently more risky. A method of reducing risk is to schedule the BW go-live 1-3 months after the SAP go-live, if both the R/3 and BW systems are to be implemented simultaneously.

Inadequate components and tools

The inadequacy of data warehouse components and tools can lead to serious problems and, in extreme cases, project failure. The selected components and tools can be inadequate or inappropriate for the particular project. There are many reasons for this problem including making decisions based on previously installed components or available tools, wrong selection criteria, accepting vendor claims at face value, inadequate testing, limited scalability, improper sizing, lack of network traffic analysis, incorrect data volume estimate, incompatibility between components and/or tools, etc.

Not differentiating between a database and a data warehouse

A fairly common and critical mistake made by those implementing their first data warehouse project is their flawed assumption that it is just like an OLTP database. Since they are unaware of the fundamental design difference between a traditional database and a data warehouse, normalization versus de-normalization, they incorrectly assume that a conventional database system has to be designed—a relatively simple task that can be performed by many experienced in-house IT personnel. However, they do not realize until it is too late that data warehousing is a process, encompassing many components and techniques, whose successful implementation requires knowledge of business as well as technology.

Consensus regarding data definitions is lacking

Users must have confidence in the data warehouse data that they access and analyze. If there are any inconsistent results, it can cause loss of confidence and, consequently, make the warehouse less likely to be used. A common problem causing inconsistencies is the delivery of data with definitions that are overlapping and confusing. For example, revenue can be defined as "total revenues minus returns" or simply "gross revenue." Unless such definitions are clear, queries will return results that are inconsistent and, consequently, lead to mistakes and unhappy users.

Inadequate or too much data

Importing insufficient data into the data warehouse can limit the analysis that can be performed. Since highly granular data allows maximum analytical versatility, import of transaction data should be maximized even though it significantly increases data volumes. In general, the usefulness and versatility of a data warehouse increases as the data stored in it increases. However, storing too much data, especially if it is irrelevant, can have a negative impact because it can require extra effort for the ETL and data validation tasks. Therefore, the amount and type of data to be selected for import should be limited to whatever is required to make the users effective and efficient.

Ignoring external data

It is a mistake to use summarized data as the foundation of a data warehouse because, in many cases, real value is to be found in the detailed transaction data. To maximize the benefits of a data warehouse, all potential external and internal data sources should be exploited. External data can be very useful and should not be ignored.

Integration challenge too much

The integration complexity involved in a data warehouse project can be extremely challenging. Integration of diverse systems can be required across various functions, departments, and regions. The importance and commitment accorded to the project, by those who can influence its success, can vary. The range of technical skills required for the integration effort are quite varied ranging from BW configuration, data modeling, ABAP programming, system administration, ETL, interfaces, legacy systems, query development, web development, etc. However, the inability of many companies and implementation teams to rise to the challenge has caused their projects to fail.

Data migration complexity

The data feeding into a data warehouse originates from many different types of sources. For a BW implementation, the sources can range from the SAP R/3 system, BW or non-BW data marts, legacy systems, flat files, other data warehouses, and external systems. Migrating data from these complex systems is a challenge that, if not well managed, can lead to data quality issues. In some cases, it can even cause the project to fail or be delayed.

Data quality

When data is imported into BW from an SAP system, it is usually of very good quality. However, the quality of data that is brought into data warehouses from non-SAP sources can vary significantly. In some cases, the quality can be very poor, especially when legacy systems provide the source data. In cases where the source data quality is acceptable, the loaded data can still be defective due to faulty ETL programs, issues with batch programs, incorrect dependencies, loading problems, etc. Hence, in all cases, the data must be checked before and after being brought into the data warehouse. Many implementations have faced problems, including very serious ones, when the data was not cleaned before import or checked after loading.

ETL task underestimated

The ETL task is the most difficult and labor intensive task in the data warehouse project. Often, it has been underestimated, leading to cost overruns and project delays. Some of the frequent reasons for underestimating this task include incorrect assumption about the quality of existing data, greater than expected programming effort, ETL tools unable to meet expectations, as well as complexity of extracting, transforming and loading files from numerous sources.

Poorly-designed star schema

Many data warehouses have failed or not met expectations due to poor design. The data model should be efficiently designed keeping in mind current needs as well as future growth. In many cases, inexperienced designers with little or no star schema design experience quickly develop a star schema design. In many major implementations, inferior designs were implemented due to the unavailability of data architects with superior architecture and modeling skills, which are in short supply even at this time.

IMPLEMENTATION AND DEPLOYMENT

Poor project planning and execution

As with any major IT project, poor project planning and execution of a data warehouse project can lead to failure. All implementations should follow a well-proven methodology, such as ASAP, and a well-defined project plan. Such as plan should be well managed and controlled. However, many implementations have failed to meet these basic requirements and, consequently, failed. In one implementation, which was executed without a formal project plan, over $800,000 were spent over a two year period with no meaningful results.

Project led by uninformed resources

Uninformed technical resources that did not even understand the fundamental differences between a database and a data warehouse have implemented many projects that have been delayed, overran budgets, or failed completely. In many such cases, they finally did appreciate the differences but, unfortunately, it was typically too late to make a difference and lead the project to a successful completion.

Project goals are not clear

If the project goals are unclear or inconsistent, it can spell trouble for the project. In the worst cases, where the deliverables are not specified and controls are lacking, the project can run into many serious problems due to ambiguous objectives, scope creep, disagreements over functionality, roles and responsibilities, implementation issues, etc.

Requirements unclear and/or changing

Once a project has started with defined requirements, scope, and deliverables, no changes must be entertained unless they are approved through a change control process. However, failure to follow this fundamental rule of projects, especially at implementations characterized by unclear or changing requirements, has led to numerous data warehouse failures.

Inadequate project plan and inaccurate estimates

A data warehouse project must always be implemented according to a realistic project plan. Without such a tool, a project cannot be monitored and controlled effectively. A project is doomed to failure if the costs for various systems, and the time required to implement various activities, are not accurately estimated. A project that is estimated inaccurately will invariably fail due to cost overruns and delays.

Scope creep

Scope creep is the bane of every IT project and frequently afflicts data warehouse projects. Scope must be controlled very tightly at every project stage. However, despite the best effort exerted by project management, scope does increase frequently. The key is to minimize scope creep if it cannot be eliminated completely. If scope is not carefully managed and controlled, risk will increase and the project will either exceed its budget or be delayed.

Inadequate testing and validation

Inadequate testing and validation can cause problems in two ways. First, the ETL effort will require additional work due to ETL failures, which can potentially impact the cost and schedule. Second, if the data being imported into the data warehouse is not cleansed and validated, it can lead to various issues associated with the lack of data integrity. For example, queries will generate incorrect results and, consequently, lead to loss of confidence among users who will be reluctant to use it.

Lack of adequate attention to deployment

The design and construction phases receive the maximum attention during a data warehouse implementation project. However, in some cases, the actual deployment does not get the attention it deserves even though it is an important and challenging task. When deployment problems arise, they can lead to the perception that the project is less than successful despite running very smoothly during the testing and user acceptance phases. In extreme cases, it can cause the data warehouse to be viewed very negatively by the users and, consequently, create an acceptance issue.

Operation issues are not addressed adequately

The operation issues that do not get the attention they deserve include managing users (who can number in the thousands), data ownership, scheduling of data updates, change management, process for approvals, warehouse usage measurement for billing and charge back, tuning required for optimal performance, monitoring processing times for queries, etc.

Shortage of skilled data warehouse resources

Data warehousing has evolved and matured in the past decade—from an unproven to an established mainstream technology. However, while the professionals required to implement data warehouse projects are available in large numbers at this time, it is still difficult to find key resources that really understand the overall data warehousing process. In particular, there is a shortage of data warehouse architects, or designers, who can translate an organization's business requirements into a technical architecture that can be implemented efficiently and optimally.

Inadequate resources planned for data cleanup and validation

A considerable amount of effort is required to clean source data before it is introduced into the data warehouse. If this task is neglected, it can create many data migration problems during the implementation phase. In many cases, failure to address this task adequately has caused serious operational problems, after the data warehouse went live, because queries based on incorrect data produced inconsistent and unreliable results.

Not realizing that data warehouse projects rarely end

The belief that issues will stop generating once a data warehouse project is up and running is misplaced. After a data warehouse goes live, users continue to ask for more data marts, enhancements, custom or additional reports, additional data (more fields and/or longer periods), etc. Operational problems can encompass issues such as performance degradation, security, disaster recovery, backups, software upgrades, adding new sources, modifying existing sources feeding the data warehouse, user management, and other support issues.

Extensive use of contractors

The use of consultants for data warehouse projects is required when in-house expertise is lacking. However, this has been counterproductive when, due to the unavailability of key employees and the requirement to rush a project, there has been excessive use of consultants. In such cases, limited knowledge transfer takes place and, consequently, there is prolonged dependency on consultants.

Inadequate funding

Many projects have failed because they were started without the structure of a formal approved project and budget. In many cases, projects did not have adequate budgets. In some cases, projects were initially funded for a specific period or phase with the expectation that additional funding would be forthcoming at a later stage. When such projects failed to get adequate or expected funding, they either failed or were scrapped.

REPORTING

Ad hoc reporting approach

A data warehouse project must be viewed as a strategic project that must be well planned and consider the organization's short-term as well as long-term reporting and analysis needs. In many cases, data warehouses have been developed without a roadmap in place. In such cases, the approach is to quickly rollout reports that the users need, without any long-term plan or consideration. The limitations of such an unplanned approach quickly become apparent.

Users cannot perform ad hoc reporting

The availability of powerful front-end access tools has been an important driver for the popularity of data warehousing. However, while power users have successfully mined data warehouses, end-users have not used the reporting tools to their full potential. Most of them limit their usage to executing starter pre-defined queries and reports provided to them. In a dynamic business environment, changes occur all the time. Therefore, when such users are unable to modify even simple reports, they are forced to seek IT help. However, creating or modifying simple reports is not the optimal use of highly skilled IT resources. Hence, a large pool of power users should be created so that the maximum benefit is gained from the system.

Decision support gets inadequate attention

When usage is primarily limited to ad hoc queries and simple reports, while decision support and analysis are neglected, it means that a very important data warehouse objective is being provided insufficient attention. It should be realized that the maximum benefit, the biggest bang for the buck, is typically obtained through strategic analysis of data warehouse data. Data mining, slicing and dicing, and in-depth analysis can produce results that can pay for the data warehouse many times over.

Wrong tools are selected

The selection of inappropriate tools can create many issues during implementation as well as ongoing operations. A company the author worked for bought a $600,000 ETL tool that was ultimately determined to be inadequate. Consequently, custom code had to be written to perform the required ETL tasks. Many tools, while adequate in some environments, are incompatible with other tools used on a particular project. Therefore, all tools and components should be selected very carefully.

Inappropriate data access tools

The choice of the front-end tool for accessing data warehouse data can have far reaching implications. The data warehouse will either fail or not achieve any measurable success if the users do not accept the front-end tool. Hence, the data access tool, which must be intuitive and user-friendly, must be selected carefully.

While a number of factors need to be considered such as cost, performance, and security, the most important factor is its ability to meet user needs. The BW has its own tool, the Business Explorer, which is user-friendly, has good analytical capabilities, and can meet the needs of most users. However, other third-party tools may be more appropriate in some cases requiring very specialized and sophisticated analysis.

Appendix A
Sample ASAP Project Plan

ID	Seq.	Title
BW project plan using ASAP methodology		
1	1	**Project preparation**
1.1	2	Initial project planning
1.1.1	3	Prepare project plan and environment
1.1.1.1	4	Identify project objectives and measurements
1.1.1.2	5	Create initial project plans
1.1.1.3	6	Review and confirm implementation plan
1.1.1.4	7	Assemble and approve project charter
1.1.1.5	8	Plan and setup environment
1.1.1.6	9	Define project organization and create teams
1.1.1.7	10	Conduct project team transition meeting
1.1.1.8	11	Plan and schedule project team training
1.1.1.9	12	Develop end user training and documentation recommendations
1.1.1.10	13	Conduct kickoff meeting
1.2	14	Project procedures
1.2.1	15	Define project management standards and procedures
1.2.1.1	16	Create project communication guidelines
1.2.1.2	17	Define project documentation
1.2.1.3	18	Create issue management plan
1.2.1.4	19	Create the organizational change management plan for BW
1.2.1.5	20	Create draft communication framework and plan for BW
1.2.1.6	21	Create scope management plan
1.2.1.7	22	Define project planning and monitoring standards
1.2.2	23	Define implementation standards and procedures
1.2.2.1	24	Define system configuration standards
1.2.2.2	25	Define testing strategies
1.2.2.3	26	Define post-implementation service and support strategy
1.2.2.4	27	Define system authorization standards for project team
1.2.2.5	28	Define system enhancement and modification approval process
1.2.2.6	29	Define performance optimization procedures
1.2.2.7	30	Define naming standards
1.2.2.8	31	Create implementation standards and procedures document
1.2.3	32	Define system landscape strategy
1.2.3.1	33	Determine required systems
1.2.3.2	34	Define transport strategy
1.2.3.3	35	Define interface strategy
1.3	36	Technical requirements planning
1.3.1	37	Identify technical requirements
1.3.1.1	38	Define technical infrastructure needs

1.3.2	39	Procure hardware
1.3.2.1	40	Size initial hardware
1.3.2.2	41	Review system sizing results
1.3.2.3	42	Approve sizing results
1.3.2.4	43	Order initial hardware and software
1.3.2.5	44	Order remote network connection
1.4	45	Quality management project preparation phase
1.4.1	46	Project preparation review
1.4.1.1	47	Conduct quality check
1.4.1.2	48	Conduct project preparation review
1.4.1.3	49	Sign-off project preparation phase
2	**50**	**Business Blueprint**
2.1	51	Project management business blueprint phase
2.1.1	52	Conduct project team status meetings
2.1.1.1	53	Conduct project team status meeting
2.1.2	54	Conduct steering committee meetings
2.1.2.1	55	Conduct steering committee meeting
2.2	56	Technical design planning
2.2.1	57	Create technical design
2.2.1.1	58	Document physical system(s) layout and distribution
2.2.1.2	59	Define front-end management strategy
2.2.1.3	60	Define and document printing infrastructure
2.2.1.4	61	Document interface topology
2.3	62	Establish development system environment
2.3.1	63	Setup development environment
2.3.1.1	64	Install hardware and verify the technical environment
2.3.1.2	65	Establish service level commitment
2.3.1.3	66	Install the SAP system software
2.3.1.4	67	Establish connection to source system
2.3.1.5	68	Configure and test the transport management system (TMS)
2.3.1.6	69	Install front-end software
2.3.1.7	70	Establish system security
2.3.1.8	71	Install and configure output devices
2.3.1.9	72	Configure and set up remote network connection to SAP
2.3.2	73	System administration procedures
2.3.2.1	74	Establish and verify backup and recovery strategy
2.3.2.2	75	Establish and verify system administration procedures
2.3.2.3	76	Establish transport procedures
2.3.2.4	77	Establish database administration procedures
2.4	78	Design training plans
2.4.1	79	Analyze end user training and documentation strategy
2.4.1.1	80	Attend project team training
2.4.1.2	81	Complete end user training needs assessment—W
2.4.1.3	82	Create end user training curriculum paths & documentation topics

2.4.1.4	83	Define SAP training environment requirements—W
2.4.1.5	84	Develop and conduct course developer'sworkshop
2.5	85	Business requirements analysis
2.5.1	86	Prepare for business requirements workshops
2.5.1.1	87	Schedule user requirements workshops
2.5.1.2	88	Develop agenda and approach for each workshop
2.5.2	89	Conduct user requirements workshops
2.5.2.1	90	Analyze roles and tasks
2.5.2.2	91	Review/refine business drivers and critical success factors
2.5.2.3	92	Determine information needs and key measurements
2.5.2.4	93	Analyze performance indicators
2.5.2.5	94	Determine and document reporting requirements
2.5.2.6	95	Determine data access requirements
2.5.2.7	96	Conduct IT workshop
2.5.2.8	97	Finalize documentation
2.6	98	Business Content check
2.6.1	99	Identify Business Content
2.6.1.1	100	Carry out Business Content check
2.6.1.2	101	Carry out Business Content check-bottom up
2.6.1.3	102	Determine fit
2.6.2	103	Identify business content enhancement requirements
2.6.2.1	104	Create data management requirements documents
2.6.2.2	105	Identify data modeling requirements
2.6.2.3	106	Identify data extraction & staging
2.6.2.4	107	Identify data presentation
2.6.3	108	Finalize the business requirements analysis
2.6.3.1	109	Create the business requirements analysis documents
2.6.3.2	110	Approve the business requirements analysis documents
2.7	111	Business information warehouse design
2.7.1	112	Determine and document BW design
2.7.1.1	113	Conduct BW design workshop
2.7.1.2	114	Check BW scope design against BW enterprise structures
2.7.1.3	115	Create BW design document
2.7.2	116	Document data extraction
2.7.2.1	117	Document SAP DataSources
2.7.2.2	118	Define non-SAP DataSources
2.7.2.3	119	Define remote InfoCube access environment
2.7.3	120	Document BW integration layer objects
2.7.3.1	121	Document BW master data structures & key figures (InfoObjects)
2.7.3.2	122	Document BW external hierarchies (InfoObjects)
2.7.3.3	123	Document transactional & master data InfoSources
2.7.3.4	124	Document ODS object integration structure
2.7.3.5	125	Document transfer rules for master & transaction data
2.7.3.6	126	Document data validation rules

2.7.4	127	Document scope specific BW reporting structures
2.7.4.1	128	Document multi-dimensional reporting structures (InfoCubes)
2.7.4.2	129	Document single record reporting structure. (ODS)
2.7.4.3	130	Document report to report scenarios
2.7.4.4	131	Define update rules
2.7.4.5	132	Define BW distributed scenarios
2.7.5	133	Document data flow procedures
2.7.5.1	134	Document load procedures
2.7.5.2	135	Document distribution procedures (BW distributed scenario)
2.7.6	136	Define BW performance and load aspects
2.7.6.1	137	Define initial aggregates
2.7.6.2	138	Define InfoCube/ODS-object load parameters
2.7.6.3	139	Develop sizing estimates
2.7.7	140	Define data access design
2.7.7.1	141	Define calculated key figures
2.7.7.2	142	Define queries templates
2.7.7.3	143	Define user exits
2.7.7.4	144	Define presentation and layout
2.7.7.5	145	Define data access design
2.7.8	146	Define authorization design
2.7.8.1	147	Define BW user roles and authorization concept
2.7.8.2	148	Define enterprise wide user role matrix (authorization list)
2.7.8.3	149	Define BW authorization templates
2.7.8.4	150	Define InfoObjects relevant to authorization
2.7.8.5	151	Define variables needed for authorizations
2.8	152	Quality management business blueprint phase
2.8.1	153	Business blueprint review
2.8.1.1	154	Conduct quality check
2.8.1.2	155	Conduct business blueprint review
2.8.1.3	156	Sign-off the business blueprint phase
3	157	**Realization**
3.1	158	Project management realization
3.1.1	159	Initial planning for production support and cutover
3.1.1.1	160	Determine production support plan
3.1.1.2	161	Determine cutover plan
3.2	162	Business information warehouse configuration
3.2.1	163	Configure data extraction
3.2.1.1	164	Configure SAP DataSources
3.2.1.2	165	Configure non-SAP DataSources
3.2.1.3	166	Configure remote cubes access environment
3.2.2	167	Configure BW integration layer objects
3.2.2.1	168	Configure BW master data structures & key figures (InfoObjects)
3.2.2.2	169	Configure BW external hierarchies (InfoObjects)
3.2.2.3	170	Configure transactional & master data InfoSources

3.2.2.4	171	Configure ODS-object integration structures
3.2.2.5	172	Configure transfer rules for master & transaction data
3.2.2.6	173	Configure data validation rules
3.2.3	174	Configure scope specific BW reporting structures
3.2.3.1	175	Configure multi-dimensional reporting structures (InfoCubes)
3.2.3.2	176	Configure single record reporting structures (ODS-objects)
3.2.3.3	177	Configure report to report scenarios
3.2.3.4	178	Configure update rules
3.2.3.5	179	Configure BW distributed scenarios
3.2.4	180	Configure data flow procedures
3.2.4.1	181	Configure load procedures
3.2.4.2	182	Configure distribution procedures (BW distributed scenario)
3.2.5	183	Configure BW performance and load aspects
3.2.5.1	184	Configure initial aggregates
3.2.5.2	185	Configure InfoCube/ODS-object load parameters
3.2.6	186	Configure data access environment
3.2.6.1	187	Create queries and workbooks
3.2.6.2	188	Define user exits
3.2.6.3	189	Configure business explorer browser
3.2.6.4	190	Configure BEx map
3.2.6.5	191	Publish report to the web
3.2.7	192	Implement authorization concept-development environment
3.2.7.1	193	Mark InfoObjects authorization relevant
3.2.7.2	194	Create reporting objects
3.2.7.3	195	Create roles
3.2.7.4	196	Create variables needed for authorizations
3.2.7.5	197	Create users
3.2.7.6	198	Assign authorization profiles to users
3.2.7.7	199	Validate authorization concept
3.2.7.8	200	Test user roles and authorization concept
3.2.7.9	201	Refine user roles and authorization design
3.2.7.10	202	Sign-off authorization design
3.3	203	Define BW test plans
3.3.1	204	Define data flow test plans
3.3.1.1	205	Define data extraction test plan
3.3.1.2	206	Define data distribution test plan
3.3.1.3	207	Define data retention test plan
3.3.2	208	Define data access test plans
3.3.2.1	209	Define query/workbooks test plan
3.3.2.2	210	Define assignment of workbook to roles test plan
3.3.3	211	Define authorizations test plan
3.3.3.1	212	Define authorization test plans
3.4	213	Create training materials
3.4.1	214	Develop end user training and documentation content

3.4.1.1	215	Develop end user training and documentation content
3.4.2	216	Prepare for end user training and documentation delivery
3.4.2.1	217	Develop training logistics plan
3.4.2.2	218	Conduct training systems test
3.4.2.3	219	Prepare and conduct train-the-trainer course
3.5	220	Develop system test plans
3.5.1	221	Develop technical test plans
3.5.1.1	222	Develop system administration test plan
3.5.1.2	223	Develop printing and faxing test plan
3.5.1.3	224	Develop failure scenarios test plan
3.5.1.4	225	Define disaster recovery procedures and test plan
3.5.2	226	Develop functional/performance test plans
3.5.2.1	227	Develop volume test plan
3.5.2.2	228	Develop stress test plan
3.6	229	Establish quality assurance environment
3.6.1	230	Setup quality assurance environment
3.6.1.1	231	Establish service level commitment
3.6.1.2	232	Install the SAP system software
3.6.1.3	233	Configure and test the transport management system (TMS)
3.6.1.4	234	Install front-end software
3.6.1.5	235	Establish system security
3.6.1.6	236	Install and configure output devices
3.6.2	237	System administration procedures
3.6.2.1	238	Establish and verify backup and recovery strategy
3.6.2.2	239	Establish and verify system administration procedures
3.6.2.3	240	Establish transport procedures
3.6.2.4	241	Establish database administration procedures
3.6.2.5	242	Develop InfoSource maintenance procedure
3.6.2.6	243	Create BW administration functions
3.7	244	BW quality assurance configuration
3.7.1	245	Configure quality assurance environment
3.7.1.1	246	Establish connection to source system
3.7.1.2	247	Transport development objects
3.7.1.3	248	Schedule data extraction/load processes
3.7.1.4	249	Check business explorer environment
3.7.1.5	250	Create aggregates
3.7.1.6	251	Configure BW web reporting (if required)
3.7.2	252	Implement authorization concept-quality assurance environment
3.7.2.1	253	Verify authorization object imports from BW development system
3.7.2.2	254	Create user master records
3.7.2.3	255	Assign roles to end users
3.7.2.4	256	Validate authorization concept
3.8	257	Execute BW test plans in quality environment
3.8.1	258	Load data in the quality environment

3.8.1.1	259	Execute load procedures
3.8.1.2	260	Review monitor
3.8.1.3	261	Rollup aggregates
3.8.1.4	262	Conduct data load performance tuning
3.8.2	263	Validate system technical test plans
3.8.2.1	264	Execute/validate the technical test plans
3.8.3	265	Execute data flow test plans
3.8.3.1	266	Execute data extraction test plan
3.8.3.2	267	Execute data distribution test plan
3.8.3.3	268	Execute data retention test plan
3.8.4	269	Execute data access test plan
3.8.4.1	270	Execute query/workbook test plan
3.8.4.2	271	Approve queries/workbooks test results
3.8.4.3	272	Conduct query performance tuning
3.8.4.4	273	Execute workbook assignment to roles test plan
3.9	274	Establish production environment
3.9.1	275	Define production system design
3.9.1.1	276	Verify workload and data storage quantity estimations
3.9.2	277	Setup production environment
3.9.2.1	278	Install hardware and verify the technical environment
3.9.2.2	279	Establish service level commitment
3.9.2.3	280	Install the SAP system software
3.9.2.4	281	Configure and test the transport management system (TMS)
3.9.2.5	282	Define BW system parameters
3.9.2.6	283	Install front-end software
3.9.2.7	284	Establish system security
3.9.2.8	285	Install and configure output devices
3.9.3	286	System administration procedures
3.9.3.1	287	Establish and verify backup and recovery strategy
3.9.3.2	288	Establish and verify system administration procedures
3.9.3.3	289	Establish transport procedures
3.9.3.4	290	Establish database administration procedures
3.9.3.5	291	Develop metadata object maintenance procedure
3.9.3.6	292	Develop workbook/query maintenance procedure
3.10	293	BW production configuration
3.10.1	294	Configure production environment
3.10.1.1	295	Check installed hardware and software
3.10.1.2	296	Establish connection to source system
3.10.1.3	297	Import QA tested development transport requests
3.10.1.4	298	Schedule load procedures
3.10.1.5	299	Check business explorer environment
3.10.1.6	300	Activate and turn-on BW statistics for InfoCubes
3.10.1.7	301	Create aggregates
3.10.1.8	302	Configure BW web reporting (if required)

3.10.2	303	Implement authorization concept-production environment
3.10.2.1	304	Verify authorization object imports from BW development system
3.10.2.2	305	Create user master records
3.10.2.3	306	Assign roles to production end users
3.11	307	Execute BW test plans in production environment
3.11.1	308	Load data in the production environment
3.11.1.1	309	Execute load procedures
3.11.1.2	310	Load historical data
3.11.1.3	311	Review monitor
3.11.1.4	312	Rollup aggregates
3.11.1.5	313	Conduct data load performance tuning
3.11.2	314	Execute data flow test plans
3.11.2.1	315	Execute data extraction test plan
3.11.2.2	316	Execute data distribution test plan
3.11.2.3	317	Execute data retention test plan
3.11.3	318	Execute authorizations test plan
3.11.3.1	319	Execute authorization production test plans
3.11.4	320	Execute data access test plans
3.11.4.1	321	Execute query/workbook test plan
3.11.4.2	322	Conduct query performance tuning
3.11.4.3	323	Execute workbook assignment to roles test plan
3.12	324	Final configuration and confirmation
3.12.1	325	Conduct configuration workshops (cycle 1-n)
3.12.1.1	326	Revise business blueprint documents (cycle 1-n)
3.13	327	Develop conversion programs
3.13.1	328	Create conversion procedures
3.13.1.1	329	Create conversion detailed definition
3.14	330	Develop application interface programs
3.14.1	331	Test and migrate interface programs
3.14.1.1	332	Define interface test procedures
3.15	333	Quality management realization phase
3.15.1	334	Realization review
3.15.1.1	335	Conduct quality check
3.15.1.2	336	Conduct realization review
3.15.1.3	337	Sign-off realization phase
4	**338**	**Final Preparation**
4.1	339	Project management final preparation phase
4.1.1	340	General project management
4.1.1.1	341	Continue organizational change management processes
4.2	342	Deliver end user training
4.2.1	343	Conduct pre-Go-Live end user training
4.2.1.1	344	Implement training logistics plan
4.2.1.2	345	Conduct end user training and evaluate course
4.3	346	System management

4.3.1	347	Establish systems operations support
4.3.1.1	348	Finalize procedures for systems operations
4.3.1.2	349	Train system administration staff
4.4	350	Conduct system tests
4.4.1	351	Conduct technical tests
4.4.1.1	352	Conduct system administration tests
4.4.1.2	353	Conduct backup and restore procedure test
4.4.1.3	354	Conduct failure scenarios test
4.4.1.4	355	Conduct disaster recovery test
4.4.1.5	356	Conduct Going-Live check
4.5	357	Detailed project planning
4.5.1	358	Refine cutover
4.5.1.1	359	Create checklist
4.5.1.2	360	Determine production readiness and approve cutover
4.5.2	361	Refine production support plan
4.5.2.1	362	Establish help desk
4.5.2.2	363	Reorganize team for production support
4.5.2.3	364	Define long-term production support strategy
4.6	365	Cutover
4.6.1	366	Perform cutover to production system
4.6.1.1	367	Transport to production environment
4.6.1.2	368	Perform conversions
4.6.2	369	Final approval for going live
4.6.2.1	370	Confirm production readiness
4.6.2.2	371	Verify users are ready
4.7	372	Quality management final preparation phase
4.7.1	373	Final preparation review
4.7.1.1	374	Conduct quality check
4.7.1.2	375	Conduct final preparation review
4.7.1.3	376	Sign off final preparation phase
5	377	**Go-Live and Support**
5.1	378	Project end
5.1.1	379	Project closing
5.1.1.1	380	Conduct end user training and complete knowledge transfer
5.1.1.2	381	Manage and resolve issues and problems
5.1.1.3	382	Review business benefits
5.1.1.4	383	Close open issues and sign off go-live and support phase
5.1.1.5	384	SAP BW strategy creation for rollout

Appendix B
SAP Purchasing InfoCube

The following table lists the key figures and characteristics that are contained in the pre-configured InfoCube 0PUR_C01 (Purchasing Data).

Key Figures (InfoObjects)	Description
0DELIVERIES	Number of deliveries
0DEL_DT_VR1	Delivery date variance 1
0DEL_DT_VR2	Delivery date variance 2
0DEL_DT_VR3	Delivery date variance 3
0DEL_DT_VR4	Delivery date variance 4
0DEL_DT_VR5	Delivery date variance 5
0QTY_DEV_1	Delivery quantity variance 1
0QTY_DEV_2	Delivery quantity variance 2
0QTY_DEV_3	Delivery quantity variance 3
0QTY_DEV_4	Delivery quantity variance 4
0QTY_DEV_5	Delivery quantity variance 5
0IR_VAL_RE	Invoice amount: Returns
0WTDDELTIME	Weighted total delivery time
0EFF_VAL_RET	Effective order value of returns
0GR_VAL	Value of goods received in local currency
0GR_VAL_PD	Goods receipt value as at posting date
0INV_RC_QTY	Invoice Receipt Quantity as at Posting Date
0INV_RC_VAL	Invoice Amount as at Posting Date
0GR_QTY	Actual goods receipt quantity
0GR_QTY_RET	Goods receipt quantity of returns
0GR_QTY_WDT	Goods receipt qty in base unit (calculate wtd.delivery time)
0GR_VAL_R_P	GR value: Returns as at posting date
0INVCD_AMNT	Invoiced amount
0IR_QTY_RET	Invoice receipt quantity of returns
0IR_QTY_R_P	IR quantity: Returns as at posting date
0IR_VAL_R_P	IR value: Returns as at posting date
0IV_REC_QTY	Invoice receipt quantity
0ORDER_VAL	Effective purchase order value
0TAR_DL_QTY	Target delivery quantity
0PO_QTY_RET	Order quantity (returns)
0CONTR_ITEM	Number of contract items
0DEL_SCHEDS	Number of scheduling agreement schedule lines
0PO_ITEMLNS	Number of purchase order schedule lines
0PO_ITEMS	Number of purchase order items
0PO_QTY	Order quantity
0QUOT_ITEMS	Number of quotation items
0RFQ_ITEMS	Number of request for quotation items
0SCH_AGR_IT	Number of scheduling agreement items
0TOTDELTIME	Total delivery time in days

Characteristics (InfoObjects)	Description
0COUNTRY	Country Key
0MATERIAL	Material
0MATL_GROUP	Material Group
0PURCH_ORG	Purchasing Organization
0REVERSEDOC	Indicator: Data to Be Canceled
0VENDOR	Vendor
0VERSION	Version
0VTYPE	Value Type for Reporting
0PLANT	Plant
0INFO_REC	Number of purchasing info record
0INFO_TYPE	Purchasing info record category
0CT_FLAG	Flag for Contracts

Time Characteristics (InfoObjects)	Description
0CALDAY	Calendar Day
0CALMONTH	Calendar Year / Month
0CALWEEK	Calendar Year / Week
0FISCPER	Fiscal year / period
0FISCVARNT	Fiscal year variant

Some of the queries delivered with the SAP Purchasing DemoCube include:

❑ Average delivery time—Vendor
❑ Fulfllment rate—Deliveries
❑ Purchasing order—Quantities

APPENDIX C
SAP SALES INFOCUBE

The following table lists the key figures and characteristics that are contained in the pre-configured accounts receivable, line items, InfoCube 0FIAR_C03.

Key Figures (InfoObjects)	Description
0DEB_CRE_DC	Amount in foreign currency
0DEB_CRE_LC	Amount in local currency
0NETTERMS	Terms for net condition
0CREDIT_DC	Credit amount in foreign currency
0CREDIT_LC	Credit amount in local currency
0DSCT_PCT1	Cash discount percentage 1
0DSCT_DAYS1	Cash discount days 1
0DSCT_PCT2	Cash discount percentage 2
0DSCT_DAYS2	Cash discount days 2
0DSC_AMT_DC	Cash discount amount
0DSC_AMT_LC	Cash discount amount
0DISC_BASE	Cash discount base
0DEBIT_DC	Debit amount in foreign currency
0DEBIT_LC	Debit amount in local currency
0NETTAKEN	Net period used
0INT_CALC_1	Interest Calculation Numerator Days 1 (Agreed)
0INT_CALC_2	Interest calculation numerator days 2 (agreed)
0INT_CALC_N	Interest Calculation Numerator Net (Agreed)
0INT_CALCT1	Interest Calculation Numerator Days 1 (Realized)
0INT_CALCT2	Interest Calculation Numerator Days 2 (Realized)
0INT_CALCTN	Interest Calculation Numerator Net (Realized)

Characteristics (InfoObjects)	Description
0CLEAR_DATE	Clearing date
0AC_DOC_TYP	Document type
0DOC_DATE	Document date in document
0POST_KEY	Posting key
0COMP_CODE	Company Code
0GL_ACCOUNT	G/L Account
0C_CTR_AREA	Credit Control Area
0DUNN_AREA	Dunning area
0LAST_DUNN	Date of last dunning notice
0DUNN_BLOCK	Dunning block
0DUNN_LEVEL	Dunning level
0DUNN_KEY	Dunning key
0NETDUEDATE	Due date for net payment
0REASON_CDE	Reason code for payments
0DSCT_DATE1	Due date for cash discount 1
0DSCT_DATE2	Due date for cash discount 2
0SP_GL_IND	Special G/L indicator
0BLINE_DATE	Baseline date for due date calculation
0PYMT_METH	Payment method
0PMNT_BLOCK	Payment block key
0PMNTTRMS	Terms of payment key
0CHRT_ACCTS	Chart of accounts
0ACCT_TYPE	Account type

0COUNTRY	Country key
0DEBITOR	Customer number
0FI_DOCSTAT	Item Status
0FI_SUBSID	Account Number of the Branch
0PSTNG_DATE	Posting date in the document

Time Characteristics (InfoObjects)	Description
0FISCPER	Fiscal year / period
0FISCVANRT	Fiscal year variant

Some of the queries delivered with the SAP Sales DemoCube include:

❑ Returns per customer and month
❑ Incoming orders
❑ Credit memos
❑ Deliveries
❑ Fulfillment rates
❑ Orders and sales values
❑ Order, delivery, and sales quantities

Index